D1228750

Medieval Parliaments

A Comparative Study

Medieval Parliaments
A Comparative Study

ANTONIO MARONGIU
Professor of the History of Law in the University of Rome

Translated and adapted by
S. J. WOOLF
Reader in Italian History in the University of Reading

With a Foreword by
HELEN M. CAM, LITT.D., F.B.A.
Professor Emerita, Harvard University

Studies presented to the International Commission for the History of Representative and Parliamentary Institutions

XXXII

Etudes présentées à la Commission Internationale pour l'Histoire des Assemblées d'états

---

EYRE & SPOTTISWOODE · LONDON

First published in Great Britain 1968 by
Eyre & Spottiswoode (Publishers) Ltd
11 New Fetter Lane, E.C.4
Originally published as Il Parlamento in Italia
nel medio evo e nell' età moderna (*1949*)
Revised 1962. *All rights reserved*
English translation © *1968 Eyre & Spottiswoode (Publishers) Ltd*
Printed in Great Britain by
Billing & Sons Limited, Guildford and London

328.4
M354

DISTRIBUTED IN THE UNITED STATES OF AMERICA
BY BARNES & NOBLE INC.

Contents

9-11-69 Barnes 11.25

Appendix to Part IV. Italian parliaments of the 17th and 18th centuries

Part V. The characteristics of parliamentary assemblies

Appendices

The map on pages 152 and 153 of Western and Central Europe at the end of the 15th century, showing some of the main assemblies, was drawn by John Flower

Foreword

BY HELEN M. CAM, LITT.D., F.B.A.

L'istituto parlamentare in Italia was first published in 1949, under the auspices of the Senate of the Italian Republic, in connection with the celebration of the centenary of the Italian parliament. The title hardly indicated the scope of the book. To explain the growth of the Italian parliament Professor Marongiu examined the rise and development of parliamentary institutions also in Spain, England, France and Germany. Ever since it appeared I have been hoping that the book might be translated into English. The revised version – the author will not allow it to be called a second edition – came out in 1962, and at last a translator appeared. Dr S. J. Woolf agrees with me that this is a work that ought to be available to English students of the history of parliament, who are only too apt to ignore the European setting of the institution, and fail to recognise the widespread character of the transition from feudal to representative government which took such a variety of forms in the different countries of the continent.

Some of this insularity may be attributed to the very wealth of material, both original and secondary, for the study of the English parliament. Professor Marongiu comments on the thoroughness with which its history has been investigated. The unbroken continuity of the institution in this island has led not only to the preservation of official documents, but also to the concern for its history both of active politicians and of scholars from the 16th century onwards. The fading out of representative institutions on the continent after the end of the Middle Ages accounts both for the disappearance of much source material and for the comparative absence of historical studies on the subject. But in this century, interest has revived and there has been much research in this field.

In 1936, owing to the initiative of a group of Belgian, French and Italian scholars under the auspices of the International Committee of Historical Sciences, there was founded the *International Commission for the study of Assemblies of Estates*. This last was a generic term for the diverse representative assemblies of medieval Europe (local and national), some of which survived down to the end of the *ancien régime*. The terminology is not familiar here, though we speak of the "estates of the realm" and of the "three estates" of parliament. From the first the Commission had English members, and at its first reunion after the war, in 1950, its designation was changed to the *International Commission for the History of Representative and Parliamentary Institutions*. Professor Marongiu's 1949 volume was the ninth of the *Studies* presented to the Commission, and its revised version of 1962, the basis of this translation, was the twenty-fifth. The present volume will be the thirty-second *Study*. The Commission, which now includes members of thirty nationalities, stands for the comparative study of representative institutions, and there could be no better introduction to such an exercise than the present volume.

Antonio Marongiu, formerly a professor in the University of Pisa and now a professor in the University of Rome, and Vice President of the Commission, has devoted his researches more particularly to the history of the parliaments of the Spanish peninsula, with their important influence on the development of the parliaments of Sicily and Sardinia. But his familiarity with the work of English, French and German scholars has made possible this learned and admirable survey of the development of representative institutions all over western Europe.

The story is a fascinating one, if far from simple. To the wide diversity of the political, social and economic circumstances in which the assemblies established (or failed to establish) themselves must be added the lack of documentary evidence which Professor Marongiu so frequently has occasion to lament. Many questions are, as yet, unanswered, and we have to guard against too hasty generalisations. Professor Marongiu constantly warns the student against reading history backwards – against interpreting earlier phenomena in the light of conceptions formed after the lines of development have been clearly drawn. "Pre-parliamentary" assemblies must be distinguished from fully-fledged parliaments; we must not settle how institutions "ought to" have developed and then base our account on such a pattern of growth. Nor are the political theorists given undue weight: the famous maxim "what touches all should be approved by all" is relegated to a minor role in the story. The various terms – *curia, colloquium*, the word *parlamentum* itself – are used so freely and diversely in the sources that it is impossible for the author to find a cut-and-dried formula for development. His emphasis on practical problems and special contingencies as influencing the growth of the institution, by contrast with conscious purpose or logical theory, will be not uncongenial to English students, accustomed as they are to recognise growth by trial and error, and more familiar with the pragmatic habits of mind of writers on the English constitution than with the more formally logical processes of thought of those trained in the school of Roman law. What we are studying is, in Maitland's words, "not an ideal result of ethical or political analysis; it is the actual result of facts of human nature and history".

But Professor Marongiu has his own criterion of what makes a parliament, and refuses to accept as such the earlier occasional or experimental assemblies that seem to anticipate the fully formed institution. It is not the use of any specific term, but the fact of common consciousness and common action, above all in a political sense, that marks the appearance of the parliament, as distinct from the "pre-parliamentary" assembly.

For Spain, England, France and Germany the story is taken no further than the end of the 14th century, but the history of the parliaments of Italy – of Sardinia, Sicily, Naples, Friuli, Savoy and the States of the Church – is carried down to the end of the 18th century, with an analysis of their structure and working that will be of the greatest value to students of Italian history, for whom such an account has not hitherto been available in English.

It only remains for me to express once more my pleasure in seeing this book, the work of a fellow-historian and friend of many years standing, made accessible to English readers, and my gratification at being allowed to introduce it to them.

June 1967 HELEN M. CAM

Author's Preface

I am delighted and proud that my history of medieval parliaments is being published in English. I can think of no language more suitable; for it is the tongue of so many great historians of parliament.

I should like to express my gratitude to the publishers and to my distinguished colleague and friend Helen M. Cam who has done me the honour of writing the introduction. I should like to thank Dr S. J. Woolf for undertaking so successfully the arduous task of abridging and translating the Italian version.

I have taken the opportunity of this English edition to make a few minor revisions and to bring the bibliography up to date.

ANTONIO MARONGIU

Translator's Note

The abridgement of the present volume has been made bearing in mind the interests and requirements of English-speaking readers of university level.

The text has been reduced in its entirety, so as to offer a shorter and handier volume to English readers. Two major changes from the original edition have been made: the detailed chapters on Italian parliaments have been reduced severely, and nearly all the notes have been eliminated. An appendix to the original edition on the Sicilian parliament of 1848 has also been omitted, as it seemed out of context in this abridged version.

The volume which is offered to English readers is thus concerned with a comparative study of medieval parliaments in Western Europe, accompanied by a detailed study of Italian medieval parliaments and a summary of parliamentary developments in the early modern period. To assist further reading, a bibliography is included.

S. J. WOOLF

PART I

The precedents and origins of parliamentary institutions

I

The medieval state and its great assemblies

The year 887 saw the end of the Frankish empire. It marked the collapse of the old ambitions of a unified Christian Europe and the emergence of the first national states which, with their territorial basis, differed in concept and structure from the previous tribal or dynastic organisations.

These states were monarchies, characterised above all by the limited nature of the powers of the sovereign, both within his state and in his relations with the emperor and pope. In religious and ecclesiastical matters, indeed, internal and external affairs could not be separated, given the extreme deference of the kings towards the Church and its organisation, and their recognition of the legitimacy of a so-called divine right, based on the religious and moral precepts of the Old and New Testament. The religiosity of the society was such that the sovereign himself appeared as virtually an intermediary between his subjects and God, occupying a position which contained elements of both the sacred and the profane.

The medieval state was not just a political and legal institution. It was an ethical state, whose authority and activities were at the service of the divine law, and of religious principles and precepts. It was almost the "secular arm" of the Church. Society, the community was Christian. The State was Christian. The king – its head and symbol – proclaimed himself Christian on all possible occasions. He was obliged to live and act as a Christian and, even more, to ensure that his subjects followed his example. He had to defend, honour and enforce respect for the Church, its commandments, its hierarchy, its privileges, its possessions. This was so inherent a part of his duties that, in a sense, he considered himself – and wished to be considered – as little less than a priest. In fact, ecclesiastical councils addressed the king more or less as they addressed the bishops and other members of the hierarchy – to enlighten and (in their own way) protect them.

Ecclesiastical authorities and councils laid down advice, regulations and sanctions for the king, not as the holder of temporal power, but rather as a particularly distinguished child of the Church.

It is easy to point to examples of this relationship. Charlemagne's deposed elder son and heir, Louis the Pious, refused to resume his imperial authority after the defeat of his enemies until the Church had absolved him from its previous condemnation and had reconsecrated and blessed him. In 836 the council of Aix-la-Chapelle dedicated to him a series of dicta and regulations about good behaviour, including St Isidore's well-known maxim that only he who governs and acts well is a true king. The council then elaborated upon this, laying down that the sovereign must govern and administer his Christian people with fairness, according to justice; that he must ensure peace and concord; defend the churches, the servants of God, widows, orphans and the poor; act as judge of the judges; teach both nobles and people the due respect owing to priests; observe and ensure the observance of feastdays; enable and ensure that the religious carry out their duties; restore to the Church the possessions it had been despoiled of.

In such a society it was not surprising that the authority of the pope and bishops was not purely spiritual, and that the ecclesiastical hierarchy should often intervene decisively in the choice of new sovereigns, at least where a regular pattern of succession was not as yet generally accepted.

Alongside the bishops, the nobles and great lay lords were also influential in matters of state. For the monarchy of the post-Carolingian era was built around the collaboration of the feudal vassals of the sovereign and, in their turn, of the vassals' liegemen. Feudalism was not just a complex network of personal relationships; it was a political system, a body of principles and attitudes underlying the power of the sovereign. Nor was the sovereign's power authoritarian, in the sense of an unqualified duty of obedience. For feudalism expressed a relationship of mutual trust and agreement, a readiness to collaborate and assist each other reciprocally. These feudatories had been transformed from subjects of the king into his boon companions, his army commanders, councillors, ministers, public administrators, and lived with the king – in Lot and Ganshof's apposite phrase – in symbiosis. They were the expression, the backbone of the system, providing the personnel for the civil, military and ecclesiastical powers of the state, especially after the bishops, abbots and ecclesiastical dignitaries had been accepted as forming part of the feudal class in the later 10th century. In moments of rivalry and civil strife they were inevitably attracted to one or another faction. But apart from such exceptional occasions, they remained the *fideles*, the faithful followers of the sovereign, the most important element in his state. They were no longer ordinary subjects, but possessed economic and legal privileges, granted or accepted by the sovereign. They were only impugnable – and then by carefully regulated procedures – for grave excesses. They were considered outside the "general subordination" of subjects by custom and by the very terms of their investiture. They owed fealty, counsel and aid, but in return were exempt from all other obligations and impositions. They represented and personified both the population of their territories in their relations with the sovereign, and public authority within their territories.

Because of the spread of the feudal system, the head of the state was, in a sense, not a territorial sovereign but rather the head of a personal hierarchy, perhaps the sole expression of the unity of the different parts of the whole, the guarantor of justice and peace, the defender of the common good. He stood out because of his sacerdotal attributes; because he was the first of the great vassals; because he was recognised as head of the state by the pope, the emperor and other foreign powers; because he continued to administer directly large areas within the boundaries of the state, and was in possession of his own force of armed men; because he was the supreme representative of judicial authority, as guarantor of justice and peace, and because fiefs without heirs reverted to him.

Nevertheless, the king was anything but omnipotent. He had particular duties towards privileged subjects, as towards the Church, widows, and the poor and needy.

This is not to say that the royal curia or court represented a sort of executive "arm" of the feudal forces. But it consisted of barons and lords with important positions in the feudal hierarchy, and it could not ignore the opinions and interests of the feudatories. The most able sovereigns were gradually successful in introducing experts on public matters into the curia from the ranks of the "ordinary" people, and in thus creating a small but efficient bureaucracy. But basically this changed neither the legal position nor mental attitudes. For a radical change could only emerge under unusually energetic and authoritarian sovereigns, who were also convinced of the need to break away from the pressures exerted by feudal and ecclesiastical circles. Even when sovereigns managed temporarily to reduce such pressures, they still did not refute the philosophy which lay at the foundations not only of the exercise of monarchical power, but of the very ideological and legal concept and doctrine of sovereignty.

Thus in the 10th and 11th centuries, the stuff of politics was not the "kingdom" or "empire" of a single ruler, but rather the circle of great feudal lords. The internal structure of the kingdom was conditioned, if not dominated, by the great ecclesiastical and lay domains. Political power was, to some extent, broken up and divided between the king and great dignitaries. The prerogatives of supreme authority lay entangled in a web of reciprocal rights and duties, according to the spirit and practice of the feudal order. These relationships were neatly expressed by Matthew Paris, the English chronicler of the mid-13th century: "as subjects are bound to their lord, so the lord is bound to his subjects".[1] In practice, the vassals needed the support and favour of the sovereign, while the sovereign was equally dependent – in peace as well as in war – on the devotion and collaboration of those he regarded as personifying the "people" or the "kingdom".

[1] *Sicut subditus domino, ita dominus subdito tenetur*: Matthew Paris, *Chronica majora*, ed. H. R. Luard, a. 1240, vol IV (1877), p. 59. The same assertion can, of course, be found in many other medieval writers. Thus H. de Bracton (*De legibus et consuetudinibus Anglie*, f. 78 b, ed. G. E. Woodbine, New Haven, vol. II (1922), p. 228) states that "the act of homage creates so strong a bond between lord and tenant, that the lord owes the tenant as much as the tenant owes the lord, with the sole exception of paying reverence". A Spanish text only slightly later (Gil of Zamora, *Liber de preconiis civitatis Numantine*, a. 1282, vol. VI, 3, quoted in J. Beneyto Pérez, *Textos politicos españoles de la baja edad media*, Madrid, 1944, n. 320) explains the reciprocal nature of the relationship: "One can state that the lord owes the same, indeed greater, faith to his subject, as the subject to the lord. For if a subject seizes his lord, or does him harm, he can only be considered a traitor; but if a lord seizes his subject unjustly, or unjustly exacts something from him, then he commits the crime of treachery. Thus, since fealty is doubled by an act of homage, lords commit a greater crime of treason if, after an act of homage, they harm those vassals whom they are bound to defend and favour." At about the same date Philippe de Beaumanoir (*Coutumes de Beauvaisis*, ed. A. Salmon, Paris, vol. II (1900), p. 383) also underlined the reciprocity created by the act of homage: "As a man owes his lord fealty and loyalty because of his homage, so lords owe the same duties to their men."

Political writings of the period are full of exhortations to sovereigns to seek the counsel and collaboration of their subjects. The French annalist Flodoard (884–966) stated that to govern without or against the consent of the greater number (*plurimorum*) was not only incorrect, because presumptuous, but also dangerous. But this advice was obviously given for practical reasons.

One of the *Breton* chansons or *lais*, which go under the name of the poetess Marie de France (a. 1170 circa), offers an interesting example of this state of mind when it portrays the energetic protests of the courtiers and councillors of a certain lord who refuses to legitimise a love-affair by marriage:

Jamés pur seinur nel tendrunt
Ne volonters nel servirunt,
Si il ne fait lur volenté.[2]

This counsel and collaboration were asked for and given in the *concilia, conventus, curiae, tractatus,* etc. These assemblies or reunions were attended not only by the king's ministers and courtiers, his *consiliarii* and *aulici*, who shared with him the responsibility for the day to day administration, but by the ruling classes of the country, the *proceres, praelati, magnates, barones*. It was this larger group which chose and elected or recognised the new sovereign, which witnessed great dynastic events, or the signing of treaties with sovereigns of other countries. On every great or solemn occasion the sovereign was surrounded by them. Through their attendance the *curia* became *solennis* or *generalis,* for it implied the presence of the king in all his majesty and authority, surrounded by the most important personages of the kingdom. The lords came to pay homage, to present their sons to him, to assist in the judgement of the most important criminal or civil cases, to consult him, offer their counsel and, if requested, their financial and military aid. Because the royal court travelled continually, these reunions took place in the major cities or local centres of the kingdom, obliging the lords to travel to the most varied places to meet their sovereign.

Many of these reunions were not merely a formality, but were used consciously as a means to settle immediate problems. They were called frequently and everywhere accepted as normal, as they offered

[2] Marie de France, *Lais* (ed. A. Ewert), Oxford, 1944, p. 43.

an occasion when those responsible for public affairs could renew contacts and exchange opinions. In this sense, their function was not different from that of assemblies of earlier periods – or indeed of modern party congresses. Ecclesiastical chronicles and archives offer a wealth of information about the series of assemblies which dealt with matters relating to religious discipline or church life. But frequently we know little or nothing about assemblies which dealt with civil matters. Probably no assembly was purely secular in its composition, for ecclesiastical dignitaries played a leading part both at court and in the government, and consequently also in the great national assemblies. Quite frequently an initial meeting of sovereign and ecclesiastical leaders, held to discuss and settle matters of their exclusive competence, was followed immediately afterwards by another session held together with the great lay lords to discuss and make proposals about political, administrative or legal matters. These reunions were described as councils, synodal diets or the like, thus confusing the two meetings, or – in ecclesiastic records – ignoring the secular session.

In England alone some 116 synods, *conventus* or *witanegemots* were held between the Danish and Norman invasions (851–1066). They were restricted assemblies of local lords, ecclesiastical dignitaries and other royal officials (thegns, ealdormen, etc.) or of important men convoked for specific reasons. The meetings were not called periodically, nor held in any fixed place; they possessed no formal legal character or regulations on which to base a claim to continuity or justify their importance; they did not represent an institution or deliberative body. The sovereigns convoked them because it seemed natural and useful to listen to the suggestions of those who attended.

The meetings usually coincided with the great religious festivals, such as Easter or Whitsun, which the sovereign habitually spent together with his followers. There were always reasons for holding the meetings: the king might want to hear further opinions, or involve those present in the responsibility for a decision, or prepare his subjects for a particularly important resolution. The discussions were likely to range over a wide field, from political and legislative to judicial and financial matters. At one such assembly, King Alfred who, according to the chroniclers, displayed particular concern for the advice of his *witan*, apparently asked for its counsel about the succession to the throne in the event of his death. Similar assemblies were summoned by his successors.

William the Conqueror continued this tradition: he was declared king by acclamation in one of these assemblies,[3] and held three more in the first year of his reign. The meetings were transformed into assemblies of great feudal vassals, in whose presence the new sovereigns swore to observe the laws of God and respect and protect the Church and clergy. For the first time attendance was explicitly regarded as obligatory.[4] These courts (curia) or *concilia* settled pleas, controversies or matters exceeding the competence of the administrative organs. But because they lacked any institutional basis, they did not possess ultimate authority. Their composition and size varied on each occasion as, in summoning participants, the king probably bore in mind the questions to be discussed and where the meeting was held. But by Henry I's reign these assemblies had acquired a permanent nucleus, consisting of members of the royal court or council. Perhaps this is why such solemn, enlarged, special sessions of the royal court are described as *curiae* or *consilia*.

Despite innovations the courts were thus definitely related to the *witanegemots*. As they became more frequent and larger, their effectiveness in the life of the country grew and new terms began to be used – *colloquium, tractatus, magnum concilium* and finally *parlamentum*. William the Conqueror asked the opinion of a court about his proposed reform of the episcopal laws. Henry I, at the moment of his accession, swore solemnly to take counsel of the archbishop of Canterbury and all others who possessed a similar duty to give counsel. Henry II stated in 1177 that he wished to offer justice and follow custom, taking counsel with his earls and barons.

The importance of the curias derived from the continuous, unavoidable ties between king and barons, from his military and financial dependence on them (whatever his despotic tendencies) for all initiatives. But the barons were equally unable to act alone or in

[3] At this, as at so many other assemblies, the participants acclaimed the king without any pretence of constitutional rights or powers. It was no more than a multiple oath of homage and obedience, not unlike similar manifestations in the Byzantine empire.

[4] The first known example of sanctions being applied for failure to attend is that of Robert Mowbray, who was placed outside the royal peace for his refusal to attend the assembly of Easter 1095: *The Anglo-Saxon Chronicle* (ed. B. Thorpe), a. 1095. London, 1861.

secret. Henry II successfully resisted the revolt led by his son in 1173–74 because he was supported by the majority of the barons.

The similar development in Germany is explicable in terms of the weakness of the emperor. He was elected king of Germany by its princes and named emperor by the pope. He maintained himself in Italy through the approval of the great feudal lords and ecclesiastical dignitaries. The very fact of his election implied the possibility of his deposition. The famous imperial expeditions to Italy were dependent on the voluntary support of his vassals, not on any obligatory military service.[5]

Within the empire national assemblies – *Hoftage* or court diets – were held. They were attended by the major dignitaries of the empire and its kingdoms, by bishops, abbots and the heads of the various branches of the administration. But besides this customary nucleus, other particularly important subjects attended from time to time. In a writ of summons to a colloquium of 1084 Henry IV spoke of "all the faithful princes of our kingdom" and of those whose presence could prove of use, and then went on to state that he would not start a projected expedition "until what was to be done had been considered in common council". The documents call these assemblies *colloquia, consilia, curiae generales, conventus,* and indicate that attendance was obligatory. In the brief period when the emperor was Italian, the Italian diets also assumed a certain importance, although it seems doubtful whether they had the right of electing the sovereign.

Among the official documents which bear witness to the importance of the decisions or opinions expressed in the imperial diet, there are two particularly significant declarations. The first is a statement by Emperor Henry V in 1119, in the course of negotiations with Pope Calixtus over the investiture question, that so important a problem could not be decided by the emperor without convoking

[5] Only Frederick Barbarossa was able to conciliate the creation of principates with the interests of the monarchy, for the crown had maintained sufficiently independent powers to hold the princes in check. In contrast, Frederick II's absence from Germany had the effect of weakening the personal ties between sovereign and lay and ecclesiastical princes, and hence the traditional duties of aid and service. Even when acting as mediators between the pope and Frederick II in 1230, the German princes acted in an independent manner to favour their own interests. The situation worsened notably between the death of Frederick (1250) and the accession of Rudolf of Habsburg (1272).

a general colloquium of the princes of the empire. The second is a similar statement by Frederick Barbarossa in 1159: even this authoritarian ruler believed that the "princes and wise men" had to be consulted about the most serious matters.

These declarations undoubtedly corresponded to the practice of the times. Various emperors of the 11th and 12th centuries held diets at Roncaglia. It was here that Lothar III promulgated the constitution *De feudorum distractione* in 1136, "following the exhortation and counsel of the archbishops, bishops, dukes, marquises, counts palatine and all others present, nobles, and city magistrates"; this may have been the first occasion on which communal representatives entered the great state assemblies. It was at Roncaglia that Frederick Barbarossa held a series of diets, which were attended by the heads or representatives of the Italian cities. One of these diets (November–December 1154) was described by the annalist Otto Morena by the still unusual word *parlamentum*. Obviously these curias were wholly different from parliaments as we understand them, and the communal representatives were summoned not only to explain their point of view, so much as to justify their alleged omissions before the emperor, his dignitaries and legal experts and to listen to his judgement. The chronicler Landolfo described the session of 1136 as a curia held by the emperor in an authoritarian manner, where he laid down the laws.

The most famous of these diets was that held at Roncaglia by Barbarossa in 1158 to decide the difficult question of the limits of imperial power and of the autonomy of the communes. The plenary session (*concio*) was preceded by four days of discussions between the emperor, his most immediate collaborators and councillors and Italian ecclesiastics and lay princes, who stated their opinions, requests and even protests. There is no evidence that the envoys of the cities took part in this first stage. Finally the emperor spoke to the participants in a plenary session. He opened the discussion, and was followed in order of precedence – "according to Italian custom" – by the bishops, great lay lords and then the consuls and representatives of the individual communes. The renowned "four doctors" (Bulgarus, Martinus, Jacobus and Hugo), disciples of Irnerius, took part as legal experts for the court. In the following days the assembly assumed its definitive character of a court of justice, and decided the various disputed points more or less according to imperial wishes. Finally, all those present unanimously accepted and subscribed to the decisions. Thus, the diet had acted as a "grand council", a parliament and a court of justice.

Representatives of the communes continued to attend imperial curias with reasonable regularity. Naturally, when Barbarossa was at war with many Italian cities, the assemblies changed their nature and composition.

Among the Italian assemblies of the 12th century, those of the Kingdom of Sicily are fairly important. In 1130 an assembly of "ecclesiastics, princes, earls, barons and worthy men" was called at Palermo, probably at Roger II's instigation, to acclaim his accession, and was followed by another assembly of the people of Palermo for the same purpose. In contrast to these ceremonial meetings, the assembly of Ariano of 1140 offered an example of a dialogue and collaboration between the sovereign and the leaders of the country. In this court of magnates and bishops the king discussed "many questions" (in the words of the chronicler Falco da Benevento), and apparently promulgated his celebrated *Assise*.

On various other occasions assemblies were called for political purposes, sometimes with irregular procedure. They were summoned to solemnise great dynastic events, such as the marriage of William II to Joan, daughter of Henry II of England, or the disputed accession to the throne of the last Normans or the Swabian Henry VI; or else to encourage acceptance of the doubtfully legal condemnation of political opponents. But naturally even irregular assemblies could assume practical importance: Tancred, William III, Henry VI and, half a century later, Manfred legitimised their claims to power by means of such assemblies.

In post-Carolingian France the king governed and administered the part of the kingdom he still controlled with the aid of his great vassals. Some lived with him in his palace and followed him on his travels. Others remained in centres more important for him or for themselves, but joined him more or less periodically when he summoned the customary great assemblies (*concilia*, *placita*, general or plenary curias).

These assemblies acted as government councils, courts of justice, administrative and financial bodies and even organs of administrative justice: for this enlarged version of the royal court exercised control over the activities of public officials and agents. The king continued to convoke most of his lay and ecclesiastical vassals at fairly regular intervals to ask for their collaboration, counsel and help. In the course of the 13th century the writs of summons were occasionally extended from the traditional group of vassals – who were obliged to give their lords *consilium et auxilium* by feudal practice – to include the *bonnes villes,* communes with the status of feudal vassals. But it was only under Philip the Fair, at the beginning of the 14th century, that communal representatives were treated as the equals of the prelates and barons.

The early Capetian kings (from the late 10th century) were obliged to convoke the assemblies fairly frequently, because of their financial needs and because their immediate councillors were incapable of administering and defending the country. It was making a virtue of necessity that inspired Lothaire's advice to his son Louis V to govern in agreement (*consilio et dispositione*) with the great lords.[6] For similar reasons Abbo of Fleury advised the early Capetians to remember to gain the consent of the bishops and leading men of the kingdom in order to stamp out injustice. When Hugh Capet was invited to attend the council of Monzon in 995, he replied that he could not do so without the participation of those whose counsel he required for all decisions. The frequency, solemnity and selective nature of the courts (*curiae*, *conventus* or *concilia*) depended on the contingency and the character of the sovereign. For example, the Paris assembly of 1059 was attended not only by the leading ecclesiastics and nobles, but also (though perhaps not at its outset) by numerous knights and "greater and lesser people". The suffragan bishops and many *mediocres viri* from all over France and Aquitaine took part in another assembly of 1137. According to a contemporary account, a third assembly of 1173, described as a *magnum concilium,* was attended by the leading lay and ecclesiastical lords and also by the "clergy and people of the kingdom of France". But all three

[6] These assemblies possessed neither particular legal recognition nor deliberative powers. Only the most important dignitaries could speak. The others acclaimed. When the king was unsure how the participants would accept his declarations, he convoked smaller, more trustworthy assemblies.

meetings were held for special ceremonial reasons, such as a coronation or the witnessing of an alliance.

In other assemblies, however, the principle of counsel, collaboration and even consent was practised. Following feudal custom, the king was not obliged to request the opinion or consent of his vassals. But whatever the legal position, there remained practical reasons of political, military or financial expediency. The kings of France counted for little before Philip Augustus. In the 11th century they were wholly bound by the feudal society in which they were born, and were obliged to observe customs and traditions which not only seemed legitimate, but which formed the basis of their own power and royal functions. From these traditions a new principle of public law emerged, achieving maturity by the 13th century.

In Spain the frequent councils of the 10th and 11th centuries were sometimes purely ecclesiastical synods. Often, however, they were also political, judicial or general assemblies, mixed in composition and in the subject-matter of their discussions, examinations, counsels or proposals. These assemblies were more than simple meetings between a feudal lord and his vassals. They represented an encounter between the king and the nation, or the community of his subjects, arranged in its secular and ecclesiastical hierarchies.

Christian Spain possessed no political or institutional unity, nor even the concept of such a unity. The kingdom of the Asturias, which became the kingdom of León, preserved strong traces of its Germanic ancestry, placing the assembly of freeman alongside the king and insisting on the Christian precept of *rex a recte agendo* ("king insofar as he rules well"). The king was merely an official in charge of the government of the community. He possessed the title of *dominus,* but was no absolute lord. Indeed the documents state that he was king *in* (not king *of*) this or that territory (*in Obieto, in Legione,* etc.). He possessed no rights over the kingdom, least of all that of leaving it to his heirs. But in practice the sovereign tended to be elected from the same family by members of the royal curia (princes and leading dignitaries) in the presence of the people.

A wholly different concept characterised the political structure of some of the Pyrenean counties and the other post-Carolingian states. In Catalonia the counts of Barcelona possessed prerogatives which clearly derived from Roman traditions. Succession was hereditary not elective and was accompanied by far reaching rights and the claim to direct authority over the whole state. Similar concepts gradually spread over all the territories of the Carolingian *marca hispanica* – for example to the kings of León, the counts and kings of Castile.

But political considerations, the spread of feudal concessions and respect for ancient traditions contributed to preserve frequent contacts between subjects and sovereigns in great assemblies. The nobles and higher clergy – and later the city leaders – expected to be consulted and take part in important decisions. It was in the sovereign's interest to satisfy them and obtain not only their counsel but also – through their consent – the aid of the wealthier subjects and communes. For although such aid was obligatory in certain cases specified by feudal agreements, in many other instances it was purely voluntary.

The initiative for convoking these great assemblies did not even always come from the sovereign, but often took the form of a request for a council from the higher clergy. These councils were then frequently transformed into political assemblies with all the characteristics (composition, procedure, matters discussed, agreements) of "pre-parliaments".[7] Such, for example, were the "councils" of Leon in 1020, Coyanza in 1050 or 1055, Vich in 1068, Santiago de Compostela in 1124 or 1125, Palencia in 1129. But between the 11th and 12th centuries, perhaps in connection with the Gregorian ecclesiastical reform, this confusion tended to disappear. Councils remained councils and dealt with religious problems of ecclesiastical discipline and the like. Questions touching the state were dealt with separately in distinct assemblies, *curiae* or *cortes, corts,* identical with the *curiae, colloquia, tractatus* or even *parlamenta* of other countries. At this point, according to some Spanish legal historians, a new important organ of the central administration of the state had come into being – the *curia plena* or normal royal court, large in its composition and competence. I have serious reservations about such a development, not only because of the inadequate documentation, but because there is no positive evidence that these assemblies – however powerful politically when faced by weak or irresolute

[7] See below, p. 48 ff.

sovereigns – possessed any legal powers, constitutional authority, or capacity to deliberate on matters specified as within their competence. They were *de facto,* not true *cortes.*

One exception – almost an historical anticipation – can be found to this general pattern: the curia of León of 1188. Here for the first time in medieval European history the sovereign recognised and accepted that power be shared directly and fully with the bishops, nobles and "good men" of the cities. According to the document describing the assembly, Alfonso IX's concession to this assembly of lay and ecclesiastical lords and communal representatives was spontaneous. But there is, in fact, no proof of such spontaneity nor that the new constitutional regime ever worked. Nevertheless, a certain collaboration between king and *cortes* did continue.[8] And at all events the assembly of León is valuable as a precedent, pre-dating King John's Magna Carta of 1215.

What characterised the Middle Ages was not the monopoly of power and law by the sovereign, nor the assertion of the principle that "what pleases the prince, has the force of law" (*quidquid principi placuit, legis habet vigorem*), but rather the priority of law and justice, with the king as guarantor of all rights. Law was created, in the words of the edict of Pitres of 864, "by the consent of the people and royal decree", by the will of the community, whose rights the king had sworn to respect when he ascended the throne. The king could issue particular laws, but could not arbitrarily change the legal basis of society. He held office not as the creator, but as the conservator of law and justice. To change the laws – which included regulations sanctioned by custom – was considered an exceptional measure, tantamount almost to the alienation of a valuable possession, of a sacred inheritance passed down through the wisdom of ancestors, to be maintained intact from generation to generation.

These limits conditioned the king in his relations with the lords and dignitaries of the kingdom, and indeed with all his subjects, as he was responsible for guaranteeing them justice and a quiet life. He could not act arbitrarily as a tyrant or despot. He had to exercise his power according to the prevailing traditions and concepts. For example, he alone was permitted to mint coinage and regulate the

[8] King Alfonso held further general assemblies at León in 1190 and 1194.

exchange rate. It was within his powers, with due discretion, to alter its weight or alloy. But before he could enact monetary reforms of any significance, he was obliged to consult with his subjects,[9] although in this case not necessarily with the great lords but with economic experts. Directly or indirectly, he needed the consent of his subjects. He needed to confirm the principle of popular participation in the administration, which in local administrative or judicial matters was a reality. In general the great assemblies discussed here consisted of feudal lords and their equals. But this was a result of the mechanism and structure of the assemblies rather than of their essence. The feudal system was not itself a cause of the rise of parliaments. But where parliaments were born and developed, it influenced their composition and structure and became one of their component parts and co-ordinates.

2

Quod omnes tangit

As we have seen, theory and practice influenced each other in turn. The medieval sovereign was bound to his ruling classes by ideological and legal ties, as well as by the fact that they represented the basis of his power and strength. Because of feudal custom and agreements he was obliged to exercise his authority within reasonable limits, to persuade and exhort rather than command. He was forced to maintain constant contacts with the feudatories, not just in moments of political crisis. He was a leader, not a master. However great his influence and personal ascendancy, he relied on the conscious and willing collaboration of his subjects as the most effective and easiest instrument of success.

[9] There was no legal obligation to consult the subjects, but practical reasons – to avoid protests and disorders – served the same purpose. A legal obligation only emerged quite late. In fact, in France (especially in the 14th century) the kings obtained aids and subsidies by threatening to alter the exchange rate or alloy.

Thus the doctrine of collaboration and consent emerged because it was the result of experience and not of theory. At a certain point it began to be conceived of as a legal principle. It was relatively easy to express in a formula which dated back to Roman law. It was then adopted by canon law and spread from ecclesiastical circles to the imperial and papal curias, Edward I's court and the Italian communes, meanwhile permeating an important body of politico–legal writings.

The actual wording of the formula – *Quod omnes tangit* ("What concerns all") – was subject to certain variants. The Justinian prototype stated *ut quod omnes tangit ad omnibus comprobetur* ("as it concerns all, it should be approved by all"); but one finds *quod omnes tangit ab omnibus debet comprobari* ("what concerns all, ought to be approved by all"), or in Matthew Paris *quod omnes tangit ab omnibus tractari et approbari debet* ("what concerns all, ought to be treated and approved by all"), besides various alternatives. In the version still current in canon law (*Corp. Iur. Can.* c. 101, 1, n. 2) – *Quod omnes, uti singulos, tangit, ab omnibus probari debet* ("what concerns all, as individuals, should be approved by all") – the specification "as individuals" substantially modifies the extent of its applicability. Later, the addition *in ardua causa, ob ardua negocia* ("for difficult matters") tended to be added, as if it were necessary to distinguish the need for consultation and consent for serious matters from ordinary questions of administration.[10]

The two parts of *Quod omnes tangit* are first to be found in the constitution of the Emperor Justinian of 531, drawn up after the first edition of his code. If a tutelage is entrusted to more than one guardian, the text says, it should be exercised by them jointly, as what concerns all should be approved by all (*q.o.t. ob omnibus comprobetur*). The formulation is new, but the rule is not. For already in the Digest Paulus had stated that the judgement of law suits should take place with the participation of all concerned; and Ulpian had similarly pointed to the need for all interested parties to agree about a concession of rights of water. In the so-called "dark ages" at least one statement exists expressing the same concept in a message of Pope Nicholas I to Michael, emperor of the east. With the revival

[10] This development can already be found in Honorius III's writ of summons to the colloquium of Verona of April 1222 (*in tanto negotio*) and in Frederick II's writ of 1244 (*in tam solemni et arduo . . . negotio*).

of a school of jurisprudence and the renewed study of Roman law, the formula re-emerged and was then extended in scope with the development of canon law. By the late 12th century it had become a general principle of ecclesiastical and public law. It is to be found in the *Summa* "*Reverentia sacrorum canonum*" of the Bolognese law school (1183–92); it was regarded as well known in Bernard of Pavia's *Summa decretalium* (c. 1198); it was confirmed by Innocent III for a small sector of ecclesiastical organisation relating to rural deans. It was almost certainly borne in mind in canon 19 of the third Lateran council of 1179 about the taxation of the clergy, and was undoubtedly noted in the fourth Lateran council. Finally, the maxim was explicitly used by Honorius III to explain the convocation of ecclesiastical or secular assemblies. On 25 April 1222 the pope sent out an invitation to Christian sovereigns and princes, great ecclesiastical dignitaries and many other "faithful" to attend a great assembly (*celebre colloquium*) at Verona, in the presence of both the pope and emperor, in order to deliberate on an expedition to the Holy Land: "so that the prosecution of the said business, which concerns all Christians together, be settled by discussion – as is necessary for so great a matter – and each and everyone be the more inspired to further it".[11]

From then on many references can be found, as the expression was regarded as a principle and practice of ecclesiastical organisation. Indeed the canonists began to refine the concept, only recognising its validity when individuals acted for themselves and not as members of an organised community. But by now it was used as the premise and justification of summons to the great secular assemblies; it was an obligation on princes, a right of their subjects, virtually a condition for the validity of deliberations over the general interests of the country.

A striking example of the importance of the principle is to be found in the writ of summons to an assembly at Verona in 1244. Frederick II invited all the lay and ecclesiastical princes of the empire to discuss what conditions were necessary to re-establish good relations with the Church, "as what concerns all should be approved by all . . . as

[11] This last consideration – that one is more inclined to accept and carry out what one has agreed to – anticipates Marsiglio of Padua's similar observation (*Defensor pacis*, I, 12, 6–7).

we wish to avail ourselves of the counsel and assent of the princes in so solemn and serious a matter". The summons to the imperial curia of Nuremberg of 1274 called by Rudolf of Habsburg stated even more explicitly that as the burden of ruling was excessive for a single sovereign, it was necessary to have the assistance of the princes, meeting in a general curia, "where what is recognised as concerning individuals, should be approved by individuals".

In England Stubbs pointed to the writs of summons for ecclesiastics to the so-called Model Parliament of November 1295 as transforming the expression "from a mere legal maxim into a great and constitutional principle".[12] But Stubbs was mistaken in believing that the principle emerged first in England. He ignored the imperial and papal precedents of 1222, 1244 and 1274, and even Edward I's own precedents of 26 June and 1 November 1294, when his request for aid and counsel from his vassals against the French in Gascony was justified on the grounds that "the fact concerned the community". In 1295 Edward was merely using a widely accepted principle, which he repeated in 1300 in a reply to Boniface VIII over the invasion of Scotland. Indeed, he used against Boniface the pope's own confirmation of the principle in his decretals of 1298.

In the Italian communes the principle was also accepted. In Florence in 1284 the council of the heads of the major guilds and the *savi* declared that a decision over war or peace with Pisa could only be reached in agreement with the magnates, even though the latter had been excluded from the government, as "what concerns all, should be approved by all". In Bologna in 1315, adoption of the principle resulted in the appointment of fifty *sapientes* from the various quarters of the city.

In the first half of the 14th century the disputes over the ultimate authority of pope or council strengthened the diffusion of the same concept. By 1385 it was clearly to be seen in Portugal. The three estates of the *cortes* protested to the new King John I at Coimbra in their petition of grievances (*capitulos de agravamento*) that the former King Ferdinand had surrounded himself with evil counsellors and had not listened to popular complaints. He had decided the extremely important questions of war and monetary reforms without discussing

[12] W. Stubbs, *The Constitutional history of England in its origin and development*, 3rd ed., Oxford, 1887, vol. 2, p. 133.

them in the *cortes*. To avoid a recurrence of such evils, the Portuguese assembly reaffirmed the validity of the principle of collaboration between sovereign and assembly, and also stated that matters that related to all should be decided or judged by all. It was on this affirmation that it based its demands that the new king hold a parliamentary session every year and seek the consent of the assembly.

3

The representative principle in the organisation of religious orders

G. de Lagarde, the well-known author of *La naissance de l'esprit laïque au déclin du moyen âge,* sees a clear connection between ecclesiastical organisations and representative institutions. He makes two general points about the terminology of certain parliamentary institutions in medieval society. In the first place, he notes the crystallisation of society into *états*, each with its own individuality, its own statutes and its own representation for relations with authority. In the second place, he points to the development of a coherent pattern of relations between members of the same "estate" and then between the various "estates", which culminates in the *jours*, diets, parliaments and "estates general" which claim to "represent" the entire country. This individuality and constitution of "estates", according to Lagarde, derived its terminology from the Church, which was particularly concerned about the various *status* and orders of society, especially the ecclesiastical order (*ecclesiastici corporis compaginem*). It is not only an imitation of, but a reaction against the ecclesiastical order within the *ordo laicorum*, of nobles, communes, etc. He sees a clear and conclusive example of this in Hungary, where the first of the "estates" to find its identity and claim a special legal position was that of the clergy, which was then imitated by the others. He sees this as a valid example, for a similar evolution is not to be found in the neighbouring countries which had no experience of canonical institutions. This example he would extend to all Christian Europe.

De Lagarde then continues that it is difficult to follow the historical evolution of the doctrine of representation in medieval society without taking into account the evolution of the same doctrine within the Church. The idea of representation would appear to have developed more easily in the Church because of the character of its complex organisation, more clearly defined and coherent than medieval secular society.[13] It is not difficult to accept that the concept of a common life, fundamental to the Church and religious communities, carries with it the idea of representation and collective deliberation. But this is different from demonstrating that such a development had any decisive influence on secular society. For the Church differed fundamentally from secular society in the supreme emphasis it placed on hierarchy, on the absolute authority of a superior *veritas* to be upheld and respected by all, independent of the will of the faithful.

It has also been argued that the conciliar theories of the early 14th century influenced parliamentary institutions. According to Marsiglio, Dietrich of Niem and William of Ockham the council was the representative assembly of the Church. But it can be argued against this that by the time of the councils of Constance and Basel parliamentary institutions were already a concrete reality. Conrad of Gelnhausen in fact refers explicitly to the general curia of the empire as corresponding to the church council.

Yet a third way in which ecclesiastical assemblies may have influenced parliamentary institutions is through the example of the great assemblies convoked to decide about ecclesiastical taxation. The second and third Lateran councils of 1179 and 1215 had passed extremely restrictive measures, only permitting such taxation by the secular authorities with the consent of the bishops and clergy (canons 19 and 46 of the respective councils). In consequence, the clergy taxed itself when necessary. Among the laity this must have created a desire for analogous treatment. Indeed it bore fruit within the

[13] G. de Lagarde, "Les théories représentatives du XIV–XVe siècle et l'Eglise", *Xe Congrès international des sciences historiques*, Rome, 1955 (*Études*, XVIII), Louvain, 1958.

Church itself, with the clergy insisting on the principle of *quod omnes tangit* against the papacy, as for example in 1225, 1226, 1234 and 1281.

But it is in the ecclesiastical organisation of the religious orders, particularly the Cistercian and mendicant orders, that the most significant influence can be traced. The monastic law *par excellence*, the Benedictine Rule, stated at least the principle of consultation, if not of consent. In Cluniac practice such consultation had given way to authoritarian tendencies, and was in fact one of the reasons for the breakaway of the Cistercian order.

According to Ernest Barker, certain of the new orders, and in particular the Dominicans, had introduced the practice of representation in the 13th century before it was accepted by the state (at least in England).[14] The friars of each convent elected their prior; the chapter of priors and two members of each community elected the provincial head; the general chapter was composed of the provincial fathers and two friars for each provincial chapter. In this way the order was organised according to a form of representative democracy and its decisions resulted from collegial deliberation. This legislative and representative structure had been laid down by the first general chapter of the Dominican order at Bologna in 1220. The Dominicans settled at Oxford in 1221, and five years later, in 1226, their protector Stephen Langton, archbishop of Canterbury, applied an analogous representative and deliberative procedure to the convocation of the clergy. In 1273, when for the first time a Dominican, Robert Kilwardby, became archbishop of Canterbury, he applied the same principle, calling proctors of ecclesiastical communities with regular mandates to the great assembly of the clergy. The adoption of a similar system by the state was, according to Barker, a logical and easy development.

This thesis has often been criticised. On the one hand, it seems curious, if the Dominicans managed to put their principles into practice only five years after their entry into England, that they should have had to wait a half century for further recognition of the same kind. On the other hand, in 1213, before the statutes of the order had even been drawn up, King John had convoked (though perhaps never held) a great assembly, or great council, of the barons

[14] E. Barker, *The dominican order and convocation. A study of the growth of representation in the Church during the thirteenth century*, Oxford 1913.

and four knights for each county. Clearly the English parliament was no simple imitation of the ecclesiastical assemblies. Indeed in this period, neither the knights of the counties nor the borough representatives thought of claiming the right to be convoked and to deliberate like the ecclesiastics. Nor were the ecclesiastical convocations an absolute novelty. Nevertheless, all Barker's critics are ready to admit that the ecclesiastical example may have exercised some influence on the secular world. Maude Clarke[15] finds a "typical coincidence" in the revival of the great ecclesiastical councils and the development of national representative assemblies and regards the example of the secular clergy as fundamental in extending the representative method to the financial system.

The weakness of these arguments is that they are limited and episodic. The phenomenon within the religious world was far wider than the arguments so far brought forward. It is true that from the first (at the beginning of the 12th century), the monks of the Grandmontines order adopted a rule not unlike that later adopted by the Dominicans. It is also true that, still earlier, the Premonstratensians may have adopted a discipline and organisation diverging from that of the rigidly centralised discipline of the Cluniac order. But the origins of this new general phenomenon can be found in the definitive regulation of the Cistercian order in 1152. This was a truly original combination of traditional collegial with new representative practices and even incorporated elements of the principle of the division of powers. It was a new approach towards a democratic form of government.

The most original and typical innovation was the general chapter, which was imitated by a series of religious orders, not just by the Dominicans, Franciscans, regular canons, Benedictines and so on, but by military orders, and finally by the Cluniac order itself. The fourth Lateran council ordered the metropolitans to call an annual assembly of their suffragans and the bishops and clergy of their dioceses in order to correct abuses (canon 6). It further decreed the triennial convocation of abbots and priors of religious communities (canon 12). The provincial councils were to be preceded by thorough enquiries, the bishop's synods were to publicise their decisions. The

[15] M. V. Clarke, *Medieval representation and consent. A study of early parliaments in England and Ireland*, London, 1936, pp. 294, 304 f., 308.

general chapters, which had authority over a kingdom or "province", were to follow the procedure of the corresponding general chapters of the Cistercian order. Decisions were to be adopted unanimously, or by a qualified majority, which was to include the two abbots who presided and two counsellors with deliberative powers. The analogies with parliamentary assemblies are so close that one can point to the same weaknesses of absenteeism, partisanship or slowness through the excessive number of representatives. But these chapters formed legislative assemblies, regularly constituted, and superior to the executive organs.

By the 13th century the organisation of the ecclesiastical orders contained a series of elements of modern constitutional practice: the electors of the religious houses could revoke the mandate of their representatives to the chapter assemblies; executive and legislative powers were clearly delimited; deliberative techniques were fully developed. By then the Dominicans had been followed by the Franciscans, Carthusians and various Benedictine congregations.

One cannot be too specific about the degree of influence of ecclesiastical representative principles on similar developments in the lay world. It is difficult to separate the lay or civil element from the religious in the organisation of medieval communal life. The law of the Church was one of the laws of society, *utrumque ius*; ecclesiastical hierarchies were social and, directly or indirectly, political hierarchies. Ecclesiastical and civil society were not mutually antagonistic, but closely bound together by identity of opinions, ultimate objectives and personnel. One should beware of asserting that parliamentary institutions, or even the parliament of a single country, arose as a counterfeit of ecclesiastical assemblies. Civil society obviously could not remain unaware of the advanced pattern of representative organisation which was beginning to spread in the Church. In return, this aspect of the Church's life could not but absorb the effects of the movement towards greater democratisation, towards the participation of individuals in the decision of matters which concerned all. These changes affected not only the growth of parliament but invaded all levels of political association.

PART II

From the great medieval assemblies to parliamentary institutions

I

Forerunners of parliament and true parliaments

As we have seen, solemn reunions of secular and ecclesiastical dignitaries were summoned by sovereigns whenever it seemed opportune to ask their counsel or opinion. They were also used to publicise among the king's subjects special events, such as new legislative or judicial measures, international treaties, or dynastic marriages. These assemblies were nearly always events of great importance in the history of their countries. But our information about them is extremely fragmentary, making it difficult to delineate their character and traits with any precision. According to some historians, however, it is possible to differentiate and distinguish two separate types of meetings.

The assemblies were widespread. They varied in importance and at some stage acquired a definite role as an institution related to the practice of government in the different countries. Some of the members of these assemblies – because of what they represented in the country – possessed an exceptional position and function which cannot be ignored. At a certain point, varying from country to country, these great assemblies ceased to represent purely isolated moments in the history of the country. They developed with increasing clarity, authority and awareness into institutions distinctly related to each other by something more than mere chronological succession or the arbitrary caprice of sovereigns. At this point a new type or category of assembly had emerged which superseded and substituted, without abolishing, the old type of assembly.

In practice, the earlier assemblies were political manifestations, called to give solemnity to dynastic events, such as the accession of a new sovereign, the promulgation of laws or the solemn publication of treaties. But alongside these, other more frequent assemblies were convoked by sovereigns to obtain the counsel of particularly qualified or authoritative subjects and to ask them for assistance.

They were consultative assemblies, but when unanimous they could accept or grant like deliberative bodies. Then, as if by natural evolution, most of the members of the earlier assemblies seemed to disappear, and the assemblies acquired a new logical form, a new spirit, dimension and political significance. Their external formal structure remained similar to that of the preceding consultative and executive assemblies. Indeed, the division and organisation of these assemblies or parliaments into "chambers", "houses", *bracci*, *stati* or *stamenti* came quite late and was dependent on a formal institutional grouping of the three main social categories. It was a purely structural phenomenon which, once fully established, gave many of the medieval and post-medieval representative institutions the appearance and name of "assemblies of estates", or simply "estates", *stati, stamenti, Stände*, etc. But the true novelty, the new unitary, psychological, teleological dimension, is to be found in the self-consciousness of the approach towards public affairs of those most concerned – the sovereign, members of the assembly and the country itself. This development is to be found before any formal changes.

These assemblies embodied a new institutional, representative situation and became a power in the state. Their members acted in a legally coherent and politically responsible manner, as constitutive elements expressing the will of a greater common body – the community. The self-conscious awareness of this new thing was an essential moment of the transformation. The assemblies developed from the earlier ones and did not contradict the system of consultations with the most important subjects. But it was no automatic or logical development.

Once the new institution had arisen, it tended to act as an institutional link between the king and his subjects, while its members acted as personal links between all the subjects and the general representative body. By now this assembly or parliamentary institution was an important element in the organisation of the state. Its convocation and sessions assumed an entirely different value from those of the old assemblies: it signified the recognition and exercise of the principle of representation, combined with those of collaboration and consent.

This seems to me the manner in which the older great assemblies evolved into a new pattern, containing genuine elements of the medieval parliament. Despite the fragmentary nature of the evidence, it seems possible to distinguish three distinct categories: (*a*) "public relations" assemblies, called to give solemnity to certain events; (*b*) great consultative assemblies, which often expressed consent by votes or acclamation, but which – lacking any collegial unity – possessed no deliberative powers; (*c*) a more complex and complete version of the latter, which as a body was juridically representative of the will of the country (or at least of the social groups organised within the country), and which through its deliberative powers acted, and was recognised, as a fundamental element in the structure of the state.

There seem to have been two distinct phases, each with its own concepts and structures. We should describe these as forerunners of parliament or pre-parliaments, and parliaments. The distinction is not original. For a long time historians have regarded the *cortes* of León of 1188 as different in character from the traditional great assemblies of the same period and even of the following period. What had appeared to be a normal meeting of ecclesiastical and lay dignitaries, called arbitrarily by the king for his own purposes, in order that its members might listen and acclaim and perhaps express personal opinions and points of view binding only on themselves, had been transformed into a new political and legal entity, reflecting a new order of social relations, political and administrative activities, etc.

But historians now seem more ready to move from this isolated case and accept the distinction as a valid criterion for comparative and analytical purposes. In England, Plucknett has differentiated between prototypes of parliaments and true parliaments. Spanish historians have distinguished *de facto cortes* from *de jure cortes*, limited curias (*curia reducida*) from the *curia plena*. Even French historians have expressed doubts about what character to attribute to the first great national assemblies – traditionally considered "estates general" – held under Philip the Fair and his immediate successors.[1]

[1] T. F. T. Plucknett, "Parliament", in J. F. Willard and W. A. Morris, *The English government at work, 1327–1336*, Cambridge, Mass., vol. I, 1940; J. Coroleu and J. Pella, *Las cortes catalanas*, Barcelona, 1876; S. Bove, *Institutions de Catalunya: Las Cortes, la Diputacio, la Concell de Cent, los Gremis y 'l Consolat de Mar*, Barcelona, 1895; M. Danvila y Collado, *Estudios criticos acerca de los origines è vicisitudes de la legislacìon escrita del antiguo reino de Valencia*, Madrid, 1905; F. Olivier-Martin, *Histoire du droit français des origines à la Révolution*, Paris, 1951; F. Lot and R. Fawtier, *Histoire des institutions française au Moyen Age*, vol. II, *Institutions royales*, Paris, 1958.

2

Pre-parliamentary and parliamentary assemblies

The new term "parliament" (*parlamentum*, *parlement*, etc.) was used as a synonym of *colloquium*. From this concept of a "conversation" or "discourse" between two or more persons it became synonymous with *conventus*, *curia*, *concio*, etc. In French the term was already to be found in the *Chanson de Roland* in the late 11th and early 12th century.[2] In Latin it is first found in a papal document of Urban II of 1089, and then in the *Annali genovesi* of the chronicler Caffaro for 1101.[3] In another papal document of 1107–10 it is to be found in a list of the feudal obligations of the inhabitants of Ninfa, where it is understood as a review of the feudal or citizen military contingents.[4] Soon after, the chronicler Otto Morena used it to describe one of the diets of Roncaglia held by Frederick Barbarossa. It was frequently employed to describe similar events in France and England as well. In Italy it was a common term to describe the popular assemblies of the communes (*parlamento, concione, colloquio*).

These communal popular assemblies fall outside the scope of our study. For we have restricted ourselves to representative and deliberative assemblies of large territorial areas such as states or provinces, as only these exemplify the concept we have given the term: the exclusion of any direct and immediate participation by the inhabitants in the government because of the size of the territory, and hence the need of forms of representation. We have consequently excluded all the communal popular assemblies, as well as the city councils (of Florence, Venice, etc.), even though these latter are similar to our representative institutions.

[2] Verse 2836. Cf. H. G. Richardson, "The origins of parliament", *TRHS*, 4th ser., vol. XI, 1928.

[3] J. v. Pflugk-Harttung, *Acta pontificum romanorum inedita*, Stuttgart, vol. 2, 1884, p. 145, n. 178; *Annali genovesi di Caffaro e de' suoi continuatori dal MXCIX al MCCXCIII*, (ed. L. T. Belgrano), Rome, 1890, p. 9.

[4] L. Muratori, *Antiquitates italicae medii aevi*, Milan, vol. 2, 1739, p. 12.

The term "parliament" is undoubtedly ambiguous, as it described such diverse assemblies and changed in significance in different periods. Indeed, many writers prefer to speak of the history of "estates", of *assemblées d'états*, rather than of the history of parliaments. In fact, in continental Europe since the 15th century (in France, the Netherlands, Germany, Scandinavia, and even Savoy, Piedmont, Navarre and Sardinia) representative institutions were spoken of as *états*, *stati*, *stamenti*. Nevertheless, the term parliament seems more correct, as assemblies of "estates" were only a species of the genus parliament, defined according to their internal structure. It is clearly important to know whether a parliamentary institution consisted of one, two or three chambers – because of the effect this had on its procedure and activities. But all parliamentary institutions possessed basically similar functions. Moreover, the presence of "estates" – differentiated elements of society, true social bodies which developed common personalities and public functions of great importance from the 14th century onwards – seems to be neither original nor general (and consequently not essential) to parliaments. In France, Spain, Sicily, Flanders and elsewhere the division into estates within the great parliamentary assemblies arose later than the first assemblies. At first the participants spoke and acted purely as individual members of a single assembly. Only subsequently did they begin to speak and vote as members, not of parliament but of their respective *stato* or *braccio*.[5] In Friuli the idea, name and organisation of the estates or *membri* came quite late and never managed to destroy the corporate character of the old *colloquio della Patria*. In this sense, the idea and concept of parliament and parliamentary institutions is both a larger and earlier phenomenon than that of estates, although the latter term was already used as early as 1769 to describe the parliamentary institutions of the *ancien régime*.[6] J. J. Moser, a lawyer and councillor of the *Land* of Württemberg, described the *Landstände* as a body of subjects which, because of local liberties and customs, was entitled to be summoned by the sovereign on specific occasions to give counsel or approval, or to

[5] The Flemish "parliaments" of the 14th century were assemblies of representatives of certain cities (Ghent, Bruges, Ypres), and ultimately of a rural district (the *Franc* of Bruges). The estates only appeared in 1384.

[6] Cf. J. J. Moser, *Von der teutschen Reichs Stände Landen, deren Landständen, Unterthanen, Landesfreyheiten Beschwerder, Schulden und Zusammenkünften*, Frankfurt–Leipzig, 1769.

direct or organise matters concerned with the good of the country. The negative side of these *Landstände* was brought out by later German scholars, such as G. von Below, who pointed to the class character of the "estates", their lack of truly representative qualities, the limitations they placed on the power of the sovereign by their legal right to be summoned.

From the large body of literature on the definition of parliaments it is worth our while to pause and examine the contributions of Cadier, Lord and Lousse.[7] Cadier concentrated on the differences between the earlier irregular great assemblies, when the sovereign summoned his vassals to witness an important act, and later *assemblées d'états* in which the three orders had achieved their participation in the government and administration of the country. He was concerned with "provincial estates", but his observations can be applied to "estates general". He placed much emphasis on the regularity of the meetings. Undoubtedly the timing, customary nature and regularity of convocations are important elements to distinguish parliamentary institutions with a continuous life and functions of their own from sporadic, casual reunions, however solemn, which remained extraneous to the organisation of the state. Nevertheless, the regularity of reunions, while important, is merely indicative of the institutional nature of the assemblies, and is not an essential element. Indeed Cadier failed to take into account the representative character of these institutions and the functions and general implications of representation.

Lord also emphasised the regularity of meetings and the fixed forms of representation, but for him the decisive step in the transformation of the old feudal assemblies into something which could be considered representative of the entire population was the participation of the "third estate". This participation was undoubtedly important and reflected the development and growing influence of the cities and towns. But it was not, as Lord supposed, sufficient by itself to transform state or provincial assemblies from *de facto* bodies into institutions, from consultative into deliberative assemblies, or

[7] L. Cadier, *Les états de Béarn depuis leurs origines jusqu'au commencement du XVIe siècle*, Paris, 1888; H. Lord, "The parliaments of the Middle Ages and the early modern period", *Catholic Hist. Rev.*, vol. XVI, 1930; E. Lousse, "Parlamentarisme ou corporatisme? Les origines des assemblées d'états", *RHDFE*, 4th ser., vol. XIV, 1935.

to give them a unity and personality, a common will, new and precisely defined attributes.

Lousse's definition remains the most persuasive. The *assemblée d'états* was "a political assembly composed of the representatives of the politically privileged order or orders of a country, who act in the name of these orders and of all the country, on the one hand to watch over the maintenance of the privileges of the orders, groups and individuals and the conservation of the fundamental rights of the country, and on the other hand to offer the prince the counterpart of the rights and privileges recognised and conceded by him". With this definition Lousse underlines the close relationship between the assemblies, the corporative organisation of medieval society and the representative and deliberative functions of the assembly. By defining the assembly as political, he agrees that the organ cannot be purely consultative. He denies that the number of orders is a determinant element, and emphasises that the parliament was representative not merely of this or that group, but of the community.

The weakness of his definition is its excessively comprehensive character. It is too broad to distinguish between the type of assembly he is interested in and the earlier medieval assemblies. His definition applies equally to assemblies of estates which met occasionally, sporadically, without continuity, and to those which possessed a legal continuity by virtue of their permanent insertion in the state structure as an intermediate organ between government and governed. Moreover, Lousse's definition would seem to be based on the idea of representation chosen "from below" (rather than nominated "from above") and in consequence over-emphasises the position and right of subjects in relation to their sovereigns.

What conclusions can we draw? The fundamental criterion for differentiating the varying types of *colloquia, tractatus, parlamenta, curiae, concilia,* etc., in the 12th century and later is, according to us, whether or not they were institutional bodies of political and legal importance and constitutional character. The way to ascertain this is to study whether they were of occasional or permanent character, the degree of their autonomy, their legal status, and the extent of their attributes and powers. Once these have been established, the nature of the assemblies – pre-parliaments or parliaments – can be determined.

3

The transformation of the early assemblies into parliaments

The transformation of traditional medieval assemblies into parliaments did not occur everywhere, nor was it complete and definitive, nor did it occur at any specific moment. Above all, it meant a change of attitudes, a transformation of the will and determination of the members of the old assemblies. Hence it was frequently determined or facilitated by contingent factors, and often achieved only temporary results. In short, the transformation was slow, by no means always continuous, nor complete.

At the risk of over-simplification, we would suggest that this process occurred in one of the following ways:

1. The pre-parliamentary assembly of great feudal nobles (whatever its official title) became aware of itself as an organic whole, with a capacity and power of initiating and decision-making. As it acquired self-confidence, it developed and surpassed the limits originally placed on the activities and prerogatives of its members, and increasingly usurped power and initiatives without any previous agreement with the sovereign.

2. Through incapacity, weakness or even broadmindedness, or through inability to achieve a given end on his own, at a certain moment the king decided to consider the members of the assembly as embodying the community of which they were leaders. He decided to ask them for aid not as individuals, but also on behalf of those magnates who were absent, and indeed on behalf of the whole community. In this way he implicitly recognised in, or attributed to, the assembly the functions and powers of representation and decision.

3. Political groups in the country organised in leagues or unions, swore to act together and showed their strength in informal gatherings. They rose in arms and forced the sovereign not only to grant their petitions and complaints, but to accept that an assembly which represented either them or the "estates" of the country should

participate in deciding major political questions as a matter of course. What the victors considered a triumph was, in purely legal terms, merely a concession. But once it had been achieved it formed a precedent, and by its continuation and repetition became obligatory and normal.

4. A parliamentary institution was created by imitation of analogous institutions in other countries, or as the specific result of international agreements. In fact, even if one leaves aside examples of territorial conquests or changes of dynasties (such as the hispanisation of the Sicilian parliament following the accession of King Martin of Aragon), one must take account of the reciprocal influences and similarities of institutional developments in neighbouring countries or at analogous levels of civilisation or community life. In western Europe state boundaries never created an effective barrier against the spread of doctrines, of moral, legal, social or political beliefs.

Once these parliaments or "estates" were born and recognised as exercising their own distinct activities and powers within the structure of the state, they had reached the half-way mark of their evolution. They possessed and exercised representative functions for the most part as the result of an explicit legal decision and not through popular election. This was reflected in the nature of their relations with the sovereign and in the normally antithetical (but not hostile) position they assumed towards the organs of government. The consequences were a long and varied series of contractual agreements between the "realm" (or the people), personified by the assembly, and the king, holder of supreme power. These agreements normally included a grant of money by parliament, binding not only on its own members but on the whole country, in return for the sovereign's pledge to sanction and observe regulations and measures which possessed the force of law or statutes. The laws were thus irrevocable and could only be modified by a new agreement between the contracting parties.

The assemblies represented and deliberated. Within the limits imposed by the authority of sovereign and government, they expressed the participation of the "people" or "country" in the direction of public affairs, either by taking the initiative or by subsequent control. What an assembly stated or approved seemed to have been approved by all the people through the collaboration of the whole community. In this sense it could be said that the people had found the method and instrument of making their contribution to the government of public affairs.

This development could be seen not only when the parliament consisted of a single assembly, but when it was formed of "chambers", "estates", *stamenti, bracci, membri* or the like. In this latter case, the transformation of a *de facto* organisation into a new body expressing and realising a collective will took place at a double or multiple level. The various estates of each multiple parliament expressed themselves not as separate single parliaments, but as groups, each of which underwent the same process of unification we have considered in relation to the overall parliamentary body. This phenomenon of the consolidation and realisation of a collective will by the estates, the clergy, the higher and lower nobility, etc., merits further research, because it ran parallel, and was frequently related to the rise and early consolidation of parliamentary institutions themselves: sometimes indeed it was identical to them. For the most part one can explain this pattern of organisation in terms of the communal spirit of the medieval world. Wherever it occurred, the sovereign found himself confronted not by individuals, but by groups and bodies. In consequence, the structure of the new parliaments frequently emerged in the form of assemblies of "estates".

4

The initial repercussions of parliamentary action

The new parliamentary institutions were without any solid doctrinal basis. They had arisen out of practical attempts to enlarge on the area of consent and collaboration in the government of public affairs of political and social forces. Hence it was never a question of achieving the best possible organisation of government and state, but rather of searching for immediate results which would gain most approval from those interested in their realisation and who were, in fact, obliged to bear the cost.

The path had been prepared by the tradition of fairly regular convocations of great assemblies, which made possible a dialogue between sovereign and people. But ultimately it had also been prepared by the Germanic concept of the king as head and leader of his people, and the medieval ideal of a king who did not commit, but who avoided abuses. The assemblies were an inherent part and consequence of the feudal order, for the king needed the counsel and aid of his vassals. Thus where parliaments were born they consisted of feudatories. The most suitable place for royal requests of counsel and aid was the parliamentary assembly. Moreover, parliament presented distinct advantages as an instrument of government, especially at difficult moments. By the meeting of assemblies, the sovereigns and their governments were able to keep in contact with the main currents of public opinion. They could seek to direct them towards their own objectives and bring to their notice certain facts (or the official version of such facts) and so influence them and encourage sentiments of loyalty among widespread social groups throughout their territories. At the same time, because parliament possessed representative responsibilities, it could be asked to supply soldiers and financial means. For until the later 15th or 16th century, the king had as little power to impose military service or arbitrary taxation on his subjects – and especially on his vassals – as the vassals had over their own dependants.

Thus parliamentary institutions were no more created out of a void than were fiefs and the feudal system. The conditions which gave birth to them could have lasted without change much longer, if human actions had not overcome the deadweight of inertia. No conscious choice was made to create either feudalism or parliamentary institutions. They developed out of the actions of inevitably only a small number of people. For the dialogue could only take place between the sovereign and subjects with a legal, economic or social status of such importance that the sovereign could not ignore them. In fact, the sovereigns sought for their loyalty, friendship and collaboration. Sovereigns had a right to ask counsel and aid of their vassals. But it was the king who chose his vassals and gave them their place in the feudal order.

In the corporative and feudal society of the Middle Ages, everyone was subject to precise limitations: royal vassals could not mobilise their dependants until they had shown that such an act corresponded to their own "privileges" and did not harm those of others. But what no individual vassal could do, parliament was able to, through the fiction that it represented the entire country including those who were not represented in or summoned to the assembly. In a sense, the new institutions filled a gap and gave reality to the terms "country", "land", "patria", "people", "kingdom", "the community of the subjects", which hitherto had existed as mere abstractions or figures of speech. Through parliament these abstractions came to life, and by their vote gave royal decisions unlimited authority and the moral support of "consent".

But parliament represented even more. The community felt itself united in the recognition of its general and common interests, and in the formation and co-ordination of the interests of its separate parts, each of which had acquired an individuality through its parliamentary functions. This parliament–assembly of estates created a new solidarity between the members of all the various categories and groups, attributing to them a common responsibility. Moreover, its members also possessed certain rights, besides such obligations as attendance and concession of grants: the right to adjudicate and limit government requests and make their own demands.

At a later stage various limitations and obstacles to the general utility of parliamentary assemblies emerged. But in the early period, from the 12th to the 14th centuries, the novelty was generally welcomed and parliament represented a useful intermediary body between the sovereigns and the most important leaders of the country.

Naturally parliamentary action was subject to various limitations which conditioned its efficacy and even its existence. Above all, parliament was convoked by the sovereign's act of will which, although not arbitrary, remained within his discretion. In consequence, periodic convocations only occurred in so far as they appeared of use to the sovereign. Even if a certain regularity of meetings existed, it was not automatic but remained dependent on the king's will. If he failed to respect the legal or customary interval, his subjects could only protest respectfully; they could not oblige him to issue a writ of summons. The most effective influence on the king's decision was his evaluation of the reciprocal concessions or *octrois* between king and parliament, between government and estates. But the choice was his.

A further limitation was that at a certain point this representative organ of the subjects found itself bound and constrained by a regime of almost unlimited dependence of subjects on their monarchs. Nevertheless, even after the medieval ideology of consent had been abandoned, parliaments continued to exist. They undoubtedly appeared as instruments of conservation, and unquestionably they frequently lost the sense of their representative functions. But they did not only act in defence of particularist interests, they also attempted to resist the increasing tendency of governments to escape from any check or control of their subjects.

PART III

The great medieval assemblies of the 13th and 14th centuries

I

Spain

a. León and Castile

It is in Spain – with the great assembly of León of 1188 – that we find the first clear signs of the evolution of the old *concilios* into true parliamentary institutions.

As a kingdom León is older than Castile, which originally formed part of León. The history of the two territories, however, is so closely interwoven that it cannot be separated: indeed, between 1037 and 1065 the king of León was also count of Castile.

The great assemblies convoked by the king were attended by the most important ecclesiastical and secular lords without distinction or separation of orders. The composition of these assemblies remained basically the same, whether their members discussed the Church and ecclesiastical matters or political questions relating to internal or foreign affairs. The clergy were willing to discuss their own problems in the presence of the king as, if necessary, he could confirm their decisions by his own assent and authority. When dealing with more specific questions of government business the king was, as always, surrounded by his dignitaries and officials: the ecclesiastics were among his most important counsellors and collaborators. When the great assemblies were attended not only by ecclesiastics, but by the lay lords from the whole country, it is difficult to decide whether they should be described as councils – meetings of an ecclesiastical nature – or rather as political assemblies. They have commonly been called *cortes* (for example, the assemblies of Palencia in 1192, and of Burgos in 1135); some historians, however, have merely called them councils (*verdaderos concilios al estilo wisigodo*). The assemblies of Nàjera of 1137 (or 1138) have even been called *cortes* because they were so described in an official document written two hundred years later. The great assembly held at Burgos in 1169 has also been called a *cortes* for no other reason than the desire to date the origins of the parliamentary institution as early as possible. This uncritical tendency was particularly widespread at the time of the liberal revolutions of the first half of the 19th century, when the exaltation of the great past of the old *cortes* acquired a definite political value for Spanish patriots.[1]

As has been mentioned, the new elements in these assemblies is visible only in the meeting of León in 1188. It was not simply the participation of representatives of the towns in the discussions and decisions: for the "people" (as a public, not as chosen representatives) had taken part in other solemn assemblies.

This assembly, held by Alfonso IX in the first year of his reign, is important because of the decisions taken there. After petitions had poured in from all sides, the king had summoned to his capital the archbishops, bishops, magnates and "chosen" of the cities. In all probability the protests were neither altruistic nor unco-ordinated. It is extremely likely that the mature citizens were responsible for some of them. The presence of the "elected citizens" of the individual cities in these assemblies is wholly exceptional for the period. These facts, the new name of *curia* given to the assembly, and the extent of the concessions made by the king to the representatives of the country, support the hypothesis that the king did not act spontaneously (as even recent official historiography has asserted in the absence of reliable chronicles), but was forced to take and guarantee these decisions by a virtual coalition between the aristocracy and the cities.

There can be no doubt that the decisions taken in this *curia* were intended to create a new political constitution for the country; they were equivalent, in the modern sense of the word, to a constitutional charter, a *pacto político civil*. This is demonstrated clearly by two of the decisions:

(1) the undertaking given by the king to follow the counsels of his bishops, nobles and wise men in all circumstances in matters of peace and war;

[1] An outstanding example of this school of liberal historians is F. Martínez Marina's *Teoría de las Cortes ó grandes juntas nacionales de los reinos de León y Castilla*, Madrid, 1813. During Joseph Bonaparte's occupation of Spain, the defence *junta* of Seville summoned an independent *cortes* at Cadiz, in order to take the necessary measures for the public good and the happiness of the community ("cosas que sabemos hacer los Españoles, y que las hemos hecho con otros pueblos sin necesidad que vengan los Franceses a enseñarnoslas"). It was stated that the meeting was summoned in accordance with the tradition of the old *cortes*. Similarly, the Constitution of Cadiz of 1812 affirmed its close link with "the ancient fundamental laws of the Spanish monarchy".

(2) the promise of the bishops (for ecclesiastics had been forbidden to take oaths by numerous councils since the 8th century) and the oath taken by the others (that is, the knights and citizens) to counsel the king faithfully for purposes of justice and peace.

Thus the necessary premises exist for us to assign this assembly to a higher level, legally and politically, than the preceding assemblies we have discussed, whether Spanish or of other countries.

Unfortunately, information on the successive assemblies is not sufficiently detailed to prove whether or not this constitutional transformation became effective. For example, we know little or nothing about the assembly held by Alfonso IX at Benavente in 1202 and attended by the bishops, vassals and numerous citizens from various cities of the kingdom in the presence of Queen Berenguela and their son Don Ferdinand. It was a *plena curia*, and must have been, as its heterogeneous composition suggests, one of the many exceptional assemblies which I should describe as "parliaments in a purely formal sense".[2]

By 1208, when the *cortes* were again called at Benavente, this mixed gathering would seem to have been reduced to its normal terms. Besides the members of the two aristocratic orders, many citizens participated, but as representatives, not by chance. Unfortunately, in the absence of fuller information, it is impossible to be more precise.

Equally little is known about the Castilian assemblies before the union of the two kingdoms. The *curias* were quite frequent and large and were held at court, wherever the court happened to be; sometimes, so-called "full", or "solemn" or "general" curias met alongside, or in place of, the ordinary curia. The extremely solemn meeting of Carrión of 1188 merits special mention: besides the ecclesiastical and lay lords, forty-eight governors of cities (*maiores*) met together to swear acceptance of the marriage contract arranged

[2] The composition of such assemblies was wholly different from that of real parliaments, and the participants merely listened and approved, playing no active part. They were summoned on the occasion of unusually important dynastic or political events, and frequently ended the meeting with oaths of fealty or similar promises, which were usually written down. They lacked any formal or regular constitution, possessed no legal recognition, and had neither the power nor the possibility of discussing or deliberating. Those who took part acted in an individual capacity, and not as members of an assembly. Meetings of this kind were held in Saragossa in 1164, Huesca in 1188, Barbastro in 1192, Tortosa in 1225, etc.

between Conrad of Swabia, son of Barbarossa, and the Infanta Berenguela. The importance of the clauses of this contract justified the holding of this remarkable assembly, because one clause arranged for the final devolution of the kingdom to the princess, her husband and their successors. The *cortes* of Seville of 1250 – the first after the union of the two kingdoms – have been judged even more important: like the preceding León assemblies, but for the first time in the history of the Castilian assemblies, the representatives of the cities also took part.

Little detailed information is available for the assemblies of the immediately following period. However, the accounts which have survived, though only of a summary nature and concerned for the most part to document the decreeing or promulgation of legislative measures, enable us to deduce certain important developments. In the first place, the group of town representatives assume major importance in these *cortes*; the ecclesiastical group become insignificant and are frequently absent; the tense relations existing between the king and the aristocracy result in a strengthening of the citizen element. The nobles under Alfonso X and the citizen representatives at the *cortes* of Palencia in 1281 presented long lists of grievances or protests against abuses in the administration, and forced the king to hold several public sessions to answer their complaints. In the *cortes* of Valladolid of 1293 the practice was adopted of compiling and presenting to the sovereign for his approval a comprehensive document containing a large series of petitions or requests of various kinds (complaints and proposals for general or special measures). The king carried out a detailed examination and replied point by point, either accepting, modifying the petitions, or reserving his reply, which in practice meant a refusal of the request. After this, the accounts of parliamentary deliberations take the form of a series of questions and replies.

The struggles over the succession to the throne after the death of Alfonso and then that of his son Sancho which marked the difficult reign of Ferdinand IV, Sancho's son, left the cities, which had united in leagues – and hence the *cortes* – more or less as arbiters of the country, and (especially during the minority of the new king) as direct participants in the administration of public affairs. Royal prerogatives seemed more than ever limited. The agreements between the cities, between the *ricos hombres* and the other lords, even between the ecclesiastics, diminished the power of the king; instead of impugning these agreements, he was forced to admit and recognise them. This can be seen clearly, for example, in the *cortes* of Valladolid of 1307, whose deliberations have been defined by one historian as a solemn pact between king and people.[3]

b. Catalonia, Aragon and Valencia

In contrast to the assemblies of León and Castile, we possess considerable information about the Aragonese and Catalan assemblies of the 13th century. Their history is of particular interest, not only for the light it throws on the problem of the common elements of early parliamentary institutions in western Europe, but also because the Aragonese and Catalan parliaments formed the model of both the Sardinian parliament and the Sicilian parliament in the period following the Vespers.

One may conveniently begin with the Catalan assemblies, because of their antiquity, and because of the relatively abundant documentation. If one were to accept as parliaments the famous assemblies of Jaca of 1063 and of Barcelona of 1164, when the celebrated customs (*Usatici, Usatges*) of Barcelona were published, they would be among the earliest in Europe. The documents, however, do not support such a thesis. Our information on the assembly of Jaca is far too fragmentary, while the documents relating to the assembly of Barcelona only date from the 13th century. The most trustworthy of these documents, which includes the text of the *Usatici*, states that these customs were approved by the consensus and acclamation of the lords. The famous 14th-century chronicle of the Prepyrenean monastery–sanctuary of San Juan de la Peña states that the pontifical legate, bishops, prelates and nobles (and no one else) participated in

[3] M. Colmeiro, *Cortes de los antiguos reinos de León y Castilla, Introducción,* Madrid, 1883, I, 207. The assembly was attended by the procurators of the city councils. Following the precedent of the assembly of Medina del Campo of 1305 (and possibly earlier precedents), these representatives sat alongside the nobles and high ecclesiastical dignitaries, whereas previously they had sent representatives and requests, but had sat separately. At this Valladolid assembly, the king declared that there had been so many petitions – in fact, thirty-six – that he could not concede them all. The cities protested and complained about the bad administration and abuses of all kinds; they requested the king to be accurate in explaining his financial needs, and then to refrain from demanding payments and services besides those due. The sovereign promised that from then on he would not exact taxes which had not been granted.

this "general council". A third document – one of the various manuscripts containing this important text of the customary law of Barcelona – states that besides the bishops, clergy and magnates, "a great number of good Christians" also took part in the assembly. But one should be extremely cautious about considering the reunions of this period as parliamentary assemblies, when they only published laws, or swore fealty to the sovereign or the observance of treaties, and when the "people" or a multitude of unqualified persons took part. The participants did not discuss or propose: they merely acclaimed, giving solemnity and publicity to some expression of the sovereign's will.[4] They seem, in fact, to lack the element of self-consciousness and desire to represent which I believe to be the distinction between the great assemblies of the feudal states and the parliamentary assemblies.

On more than one occasion, the counts of Barcelona (who were also kings of Aragon from the middle of the 12th century) convoked the bishops, abbots and magnates in council before their court or curia, "to treat of matters of common utility for the country". The documents state that they "treated" or "deliberated". These councils (in 1131, perhaps in 1143, in 1173, perhaps in 1177, in 1188, etc.) dealt with matters of foreign or internal policy, such as the signing of a peace or a truce, or decisions capable of arousing grave political repercussions. Such assemblies – probably far more numerous than those we know about – have been variously described. They are often called "general curias", but this is anachronistic as the name is not to be found in the original accounts, but only in later chronicles. One such assembly, held in 1192, probably at Barcelona, was attended not only by the prelates and "other clerics" and all the "magnates and knights" (that is, the higher and lower nobility), but also by the "good men" and populace of both the cities and minor centres (*ceteri tam civitatum quam villarum probi homines et populus*). Two archbishops, eight lay lords and numerous ecclesiastics and lay persons took part in an assembly held at Corvera in 1202. King James I the Conqueror stated that he had taken counsel in the reunion of Lérida of 1214 with the bishops and

[4] The Icelandic assembly of Thingvellir of 930, which has been described as "the most ancient legislative assembly of Europe", was a typical example of this type of meeting: the members assembled in the open, on a plain, listened to the proposals of the wise man, Ulfljøt, and acclaimed them.

prelates of both Aragon and Catalonia, and with other "prudent men".

Explicit mention of the participation of representatives of the cities and towns only occurred with the assembly of Barcelona of 1228, which was attended by various bishops and abbots, the greater lords and "many other knights and citizens and good men of the towns of Catalonia". They all swore on the Bible to observe and enforce the observance of the "perpetual peaces and truces" published at this assembly by King James, and promised their aid for the Majorca campaign. This oath and the plenary nature of the reunion bring to mind what we have stated previously about analogous manifestations: they may possess the formal aspect and even official denomination (*cortes*, *cortes generales*) of parliaments, but they differ in nature and substance. This would seem to be confirmed by the fact that, contemporaneously with this assembly, the king presided over a "solemn curia", attended by prelates and lords, but not by honest men and citizens. On the other hand, the concession of a subsidy suggests discussions and deliberations, typical of a true parliamentary assembly; the same would seem to apply to the *cortes* of Monzón of 1236. These two assemblies, in fact, listened to and approved the sovereign's plans, giving him the means to carry out the Majorca and Valencia campaigns.

Participation in the general curias, which was normal for the greater members of the ecclesiastical hierarchy and the more important lords, was, at least in this early period, only occasional for all others: at Barcelona in 1251, the members of the first two groups were listed name by name; all other participants in the assembly were lumped together, as if they were spectators rather than actors, as "many other knights and honest men of Barcelona".

The "general curia" of Barcelona in 1283, presided over by King Peter III the Great, the so-called liberator of Sicily, marked an innovation. The list of participants was long and complete. Bishops, prelates, clerics, barons, knights and "the citizens and men of the towns of Catalonia" were divided into three groups; the list of citizen envoys shows that while every major city sent four or five, the *ville* sent only two each; the list, however, may not be complete, as it states that, besides the representatives indicated by name, other citizens from these cities and *ville*, as well as from other localities, also took part. The *cortes* have been convoked to treat of the good state and order of the country (*del bon stament e reformatio de la terra*).

"On bended knees", as the parliamentary vote states, but with the self-consciousness and explicit assumption of their quality of representatives of the entire Catalan people (*nomine suo et tocius universitatis Catalonie*), the participants laid before the king "a petition and request" that he confirm and guarantee all the liberties and privileges of his subjects. The king, in his preamble, enunciated the formula – so common in analogous circumstances – of the duty of sovereigns to watch over the good of their subjects and to reward them for their fealty, and expressed his gratitude for the sacrifices they had made; he then formally accepted the parliamentary votes. He promulgated a whole series of legislative decrees to guarantee both the rights of his subjects and an upright administration, especially in matters of taxation and justice. There were specific decrees – such as those which forbade taking legal cases involving Catalan subjects outside Catalonia, or prohibited arrest for debt, etc. – and more general ones, like the abolition or reduction of some of the heaviest taxes, recognition of ecclesiastical immunities and of the urban and rustic communities' rights of common, various reforms of aspects of private and procedural law and so on. The underlying motive for this remarkable innovation was the government's financial weakness, because of its need to wage war against the Angevins following the conquest of Sicily.

What is of particular interest for the purpose of our study is that on this occasion the king also made a double promise and declaration, which was regarded as possessing the authority of a legislative measure. On the one hand, he promised that henceforth sovereigns would not issue general constitutions or statutes in Catalonia without the previous deliberation and consent of the prelates, barons, knights and citizens, or of the majority (*major et sanior pars*) of the members of appropriate assemblies. On the other hand, he declared that, unless legitimately hindered, the king would hold a general curia of the Catalans once a year on a date and location to be determined each time. It is interesting to note that the Catalan text of the constitution was traditionally called by the Catalan word for once a year: *una vegada lo any*. The purpose of the meeting, to be attended by the clergy, aristocracy and men of the *ville*, was to treat of the good state of kingdom and all necessary reforms (*de bene statu et reformacione terre*).[5]

There can be no doubt that this legislative act constituted the basis, indeed the birth certificate, of the Catalan parliament. Even Catalan writers who are most concerned to uphold the traditions of their country, and the real or supposed priority of its parliament, agree that the first true parliamentary assembly was this one, and that until then there had only been *cortes de facto* or pre-parliamentary assemblies. The new element, as we have seen, consisted in the agreement between king and country to establish a new constitutional order for the state.

Grave circumstances prevented the sovereign from convoking a new assembly the following year, as he should have done. But the *cortes* (in Catalan, the *corts*) of Barcelona of 1291 fitted perfectly into the new system, confirming all the liberties, franchises and immunities of the subjects and formulating 41 new requests. The prelates, religious, clerics, *ricos hombres*,[6] knights, citizens and men of the *ville* and of the kingdom of Majorca are mentioned. But perhaps there was no real meeting: the king may have just received the representatives of these groups and deliberated with them in an informal manner. At all events, he thanked the parliamentary envoys for swearing fealty and homage to him (and probably giving him some subsidy) and assured them that the failure to convoke the assembly would not serve as a precedent; in fact he promised to convoke a general Catalan curia before Christmas day of the same year.

But, as exceptional circumstances continued, the Catalan *corts* could not be convoked until February 1299 at Barcelona. On this occasion, in agreement with its members, the king decreed numerous measures of the utmost importance. Among these was one which declared that, although the clergy had abstained from taking part in the deliberations because of disagreements with the noble and citizen groups, all acts and other measures passed by these orders in the assembly were to be regarded as valid in this and all similar circumstances. The king also completed the existing arrangements

[5] The words *reforma, reformacio* were a commonplace of requests of representatives and promises of sovereigns throughout the Middle Ages in Western Europe.

[6] The *ricos hombres* or *ric omens* were members of the highest nobility, more important even than the *hijosdalgos* or descendants of the oldest noble families.

by decreeing that the annual sessions of the *corts* be held alternately at Barcelona and Lérida on the first Sunday of Lent or, if this proved impossible, within one month of the return of normal conditions. But these regulations, although confirmed by the royal constitution *Nos è los successors nostres*, were also of short duration. In 1301, under James II, the practice of triennial convocations was introduced, with the proviso that extraordinary assemblies might be convoked at the request of the permanent parliamentary commission (the *Generalitat*).

The quantity and reliability of our information about the Catalan *corts* offers a startling contrast to our ignorance of the history of Aragonese *cortes* in both their initial period and successive phases.[7]

The kingdom of Aragon became separate after the death of Sancho III, king of Navarre in 1045, but it only obtained full independence a century and a half later on the occasion of its union with Catalonia. Naturally Aragon also had its councils from an early date, religious assemblies which were easily transformable into politico-administrative assemblies by the mechanism we have already observed (for example at Jaca in 1060 and 1063). In other words, it possessed pre-parliamentary assemblies, dominated by the *ricos hombres* who had taken part in the liberation and who in consequence could claim to share in the sovereignty of the kingdom. The assemblies common to both Aragon and Catalonia, or to Aragon and Navarre – of Huarte (1090), Borja, Monzón, Pamplona (1134) and Huesca (1162) – merit particular mention because of the discussion they have aroused among historians.

There is nothing on the first of these assemblies in the 16th century *Annals* of Jeronimo Zurita, our major source of information for this period; what little we know derives from a document published in the last century by a Navarre historian.[8] It is a brief account of a reunion of the "princes" of Pamplona and of "a great multitude of people, both men and women" held before King Sancho Ramirez to complain of misgovernment, which ended in a pact sworn by all present guaranteeing protection against the repetition of such abuses. Clearly such a "plebiscitary" reunion

[7] We know even less about the early *cortes* of the kingdom of Navarre, a state which periodically asserted its independence of the kings of Aragon.

[8] J. Moret, *Anales del reino de Navarra*, Tolosa, vol. III (1890), 94 ff.

possessed different characteristics from a parliamentary assembly: it is enough to note the presence of a crowd of both sexes, as well as the oath, which is an element wholly outside normal parliamentary practice.

The assemblies of 1134 were separate reunions – held close at hand, but hostile to each other – of the subjects of Navarre and Aragon who were struggling for the success of their respective candidates for the throne of Alfonso the Warrior. There can be little doubt that on both sides the cities played a great part on this occasion. It used to be believed that once Ramiro the Monk had been proclaimed king of Aragon, he declared his particular gratitude to the city of Jaca by granting a special privilege to commemorate the fact that they had elected him king; but this tradition has rightly been challenged, on the grounds that elections to the throne had long since ceased. We only need to note that, even according to the traditional story, the assembly in question possesses some curious characteristics, and in particular that of self-convocation.

The assembly of Huesca of 1162 was also concerned with the succession to the Aragonese throne. It was called by Queen Petronilla, widow of the last king, and was attended by prelates, *ricos hombres* and knights and envoys of the cities and *ville*. We know the names of the members of the first two groups, but not of the third one, and we know that, in ratifying the king's last wishes (expressed orally), all of them recognised and acclaimed as their sovereign Alfonso the Chaste, eldest son of the prince whose succession was in dispute. Once again we find ourselves in the presence of one of those extraordinary reunions which are not and cannot be included in the general category of parliamentary institutions, because of the exceptional nature of their aims, the plenary character of their composition, the personal and direct pledges sworn by their members, and the solemn oaths which accompanied and followed them.[9]

These plebiscitary reunions of a political character were usually held in both Aragon and Navarre in order to acclaim a new sovereign, or to exchange the oath of loyalty on his formal accession to the

[9] We have already spoken of these assemblies, which were only parliamentary in a purely formal sense. The very fact that they were concerned with dynastic matters, even the founding of new dynasties, meant that they stood outside the normal constitutional framework of the state.

throne, or to celebrate a royal marriage, the signing of a treaty of particular importance, or the publication of particularly significant laws. But apart from such extraordinary reunions there is no evidence that town representatives participated in the great national assemblies in the 12th or during most of the 13th centuries. In these extraordinary reunions, the representatives of the cities and of even the smaller centres fluctuated greatly in number, but were always more numerous than in real parliamentary assemblies. The participants swore oaths and signed their names. Their presence was purely passive – to listen and obey, or acclaim in a disciplined manner. This would seem to be the explanation of their presence when agreements were made by the king or by the lay and ecclesiastical grandees.[10]

Aragonese history in the 13th century – even more than Castilian – is full of violent episodes and civil or foreign wars. The sovereigns were almost always in sharp conflict with the most powerful barons, who were usually led by a prince or an illegitimate offspring of the royal house who felt slighted in his ambitions. The clergy supported the sovereign, until they fell under pontifical censure over the invasion of Sicily; thereupon they abandoned him. The barons acted and made public statements in close understanding with the principal cities, such as Saragossa, Jaca, and Huesca. This agreement or Union was not only real in substance, but had a formal character: it was not a conspiracy, but a publicly acknowledged covenant. It dated from the earliest years of the reign of James the Conqueror, and had its own assemblies of the two orders, which displayed a clear awareness and consciousness of their representative functions, and which carried them out repeatedly and in a fairly regular manner. The assembly of Huesca of 1247, for example, is regarded by Spanish historians as offering an example of a regular convocation. It was attended by the *ricos hombres*, *infanzones*,[11] knights and barons,

[10] One of the most famous of these assemblies was held at Lérida in 1214, when prelates, *ricos hombres*, barons, knights and ten representatives of each city recognised the very young Infante James I as their king, pledged their fealty and swore to defend his person and the state. On this occasion an agreement "of peace and truce" was drawn up with the counsel of the bishops, prelates, citizens, "bourgeois" and inhabitants of both Aragon and Navarre.

[11] The *infanzones* or *hijosdalgos* were the same as the *capitanei et valvasores* of Italian and other texts, according to Alfonso X in his famous *Partidas* (II, i, 13). Elsewhere they were identified with the *infantes, ricos omnes* or *otros homens poderosos o generosos*.

and the citizens and representatives of the towns who were sent with instructions by their respective communal councils; they carried out so total a revision of the old *fueros* or customs and passed so many and such wide-ranging decrees as to create in practice a new organic corpus of law. But despite its undoubtedly great importance, this assembly still offers no proof, nor any new evidence, to give it a true parliamentary nature in an unequivocal manner. Parliamentary characteristics only appear beyond dispute in the later assemblies of the Union mentioned above (*Jura de la Unidad de Zaragoza*), one of the strongest and most tenacious leagues (*coniurationes*) of this period, which lost its factious character and assumed the character and authority of an official organisation of the state; indeed it received official ratification from the very holders of the throne, in particular from the unfortunate Alfonso III.

A notable, but not yet decisive, victory had already been achieved by the Union in 1283 with the promulgation of a general privilege (*Privilegio General*) by Alfonso's father, Peter III the Great. The king accepted the petitions of grievances which had been presented, and declared that before he made war or peace he would take counsel with the *cortes*, which would be convoked at least once a year in Saragossa. However, the practice of triennial convocations was soon adopted, following the example of the neighbouring state of Catalonia. This became customary about 1307.

Shortly after the first recognition of the new constitutional order, Alfonso ratified the *Privilegio de la Unión*, and accepted its request that he no longer act as judge in cases where the king was involved personally. In such instances judgement was to be made by the *cortes* itself, together with the *Justicia*, a newly created constitutional magistrate possessing great independence and authority as the emanation and personification of the parliament. Even more, the king accepted a request for which the representatives of the Union had long been agitating, that his councillors be chosen from the orders represented in the *cortes*, and in fact be nominated by the *cortes* or by a majority of their members, so long as they included representatives of the city of Saragossa. Alfonso guaranteed these very large concessions in the most concrete manner by recognising the right of his subjects to rebel if he broke his promises, and even by handing over as a pledge the fortresses and military focal points of the country to the leaders of the political coalition. As a complementary guarantee of the right of rebellion and of the personal immunity of all the members of the nobles and cities in the league, Alfonso recognised their right to transfer their allegiance to other sovereigns. Alfonso's successor, James II, carried out a partially successful reaction in defence of monarchical power. But by now the institution of parliament, with communal representatives participating in its work and regular annual sessions, had risen above the alternating fortunes of the political struggle and represented a fundamental part of the structure of the Aragonese state. Peter IV, the Ceremonious, reasserted the pre-eminence of royal power in 1347 and suppressed the *Privilegio de la Unión*.[12] But by the last years of his reign he was slowly forced to yield and restore the *cortes* to a position of primary importance in the state.

In discussing the kingdom of Valencia we need to bear in mind its late creation, following upon its conquest (or liberation) by James I the Conqueror.[13]

The oldest document offering reliable evidence of the convocation of the *cortes* of the kingdom of Valencia dates from April 1261. The sovereign, James I, publicly recognised the financial aid given him by the "good men" of the city of Valencia for his expedition to the Holy Land and for the confirmation of their customs or *Furs*, and promised both to respect these customary laws and to pledge his successors to swear to observe them within a month of their accession to the throne. When Peter III followed his father on the throne, he convoked a great assembly at Valencia in 1276, which the famous chronicle of Muntaner described as a *cortes*. But this in fact derives from a confusion with another assembly held on 1 December 1283 when the same sovereign reaffirmed the agreement of 1261 that the customs of the kingdom be confirmed within thirty days of an

[12] The effect of the suppression of the *Privilegio de la Unión*, which took place in the *cortes* of Saragossa, was to revive the *Privilegio General* (as it had been modified by James II), and consequently the authority of the sovereign.

[13] The origins and early parliamentary history of Valencia were first studied seriously in the latter part of the 17th century by P. Belluga in his *Speculum principum ac iustitiae*, (Brussels, 1680), dedicated to Alfonso the Magnanimous, and by Lorenzo Matheu y Sanz in his *Tractatus de regimine regni Valentiae* (Lyon, 1677) and *Tratado de la celebracion de Cortes generales del* Reino *de Valencia* (Madrid, 1677). In a sense, all these works, and particularly the last, were protests against the failure to convoke the *cortes* since 1645.

accession to the throne. Naturally historians have described even earlier assemblies as *cortes*, such as reunions held in 1238, 1250, 1266 and 1271. But no evidence has been produced, any more than for the assembly of 1276. While it is clear that several great assemblies were convoked or held, they all seem to be political manifestations of one sort or another, and not sessions of a true parliamentary character, despite the names attributed to the meetings. This at least is as far as we can go, given the extremely poor documentation.

Serious doubts even exist about the legitimacy of the title of *Cortes generales* which Matheu y Sanz attributed to the meeting of 1283. It was called a *general cort* in 1482 by the editors of the *Furs*, Pere Hagenbach and Leonardo Hutz; and we also know that the king sanctioned various petitions from Valencia and other places, which were then proclaimed as Privileges (*Privilegis* or *Fors*). Nevertheless, we know nothing about this meeting except for a royal statement or declaration which is by no means conclusive. This document, which was drawn up only one month later, states that the king was present and seated in the cloister of the church of Santa Maria de Valencia, "publicly in the presence of a congregation of the people there". But this expression of the participation of the "people" is too vague and equivocal to prove that even a brief parliamentary session of the "three estates", or even of one "estate", of the kingdom was held.

Even the solemn reunion of Valencia and Burriana of 1286, when the "syndics" of the cities of the kingdom pledged their oaths in the presence of the newly elected King Alfonso III (who was also king of Aragon) was probably not a true parliamentary meeting. In fact, the title can probably only be used legitimately for the first time for the meeting of Valencia of 1302, which was attended by the prelates, *ricos hombres*, knights and communal representatives. Already in 1292 James II had decreed that the *cortes* of the kingdom be called at least once every three years in January. But this assembly is inadequately documented and additional information is only available for the assemblies of 1329 and 1330, for which we possess the names of the participants. But the documents offer no more details about the chronology, procedure, or results of these assemblies.

Parliamentary institutions reflect the life of a country vividly and directly. The kingdom of Valencia represented no real political force and was of little significance within the crown of Aragon. This situation was inevitably reflected in its *cortes*. Nevertheless, in the course of the 14th century even the Valencian *cortes* emerged as a concrete reality, perhaps following the example of the Aragonese and Catalan institutions. This could be seen at the moment of the *congreso* of Caspe, when the representatives of Valencia took their part in voting for a new king of Aragon.

Despite the frequently inadequate detail of this account, due to lacunae in the source materials, even so summary a survey clearly brings out the importance of these initial experiments at parliamentary institutions in Spain. There can be no question that they merit study as much as the far better known English parliament of the 13th century, because of the significant light they throw on the problem of the origins of representative institutions in Europe.

2

England

Few chapters of the historiography of the last century arouse such interest as the study of the origins and early history of the English parliament. The great wealth of material, for the most part published; the number and differing attitudes of the historians, who have explored not only the parliamentary documents themselves, but all sources of even marginal relevance, from the annotations of chronicles to references contained in legislative texts; the high quality of the critical apparatus applied to the documentation – all this reflects the advanced state of studies on English parliamentary history.

But to a foreigner, the most singular characteristic is to be found in the curious and determined re-evaluation of the positivist method employed almost a century ago by William Stubbs, if not the first, certainly the greatest of English parliamentary historians. Stubbs sketched the outlines of the origins and evolution of English constitutional history in a manner then considered, almost unanimously, exemplary. The subsequent re-evaluation seems to be accompanied by an apparent decrease of our overall knowledge of the argument.

For Stubbs, the large collection of documents he utilized – and had in part assembled – spoke a clear, unequivocal language. Perhaps it is true – as has been suggested – that he believed that it was the mission of the English people to create a parliamentary regime. It was in any case something of a commonplace, following on the romanticised history of the English parliament traced rapidly by Montesquieu, or the hardly less imaginary accounts of Hallam and Freeman, who thought that history should be written as if human affairs had developed on purely rational principles. Indeed, two Spanish writers, Martínez Marina and Sempre y Guarinos, had in analogous manner relived and interpreted the fortunes of the Spanish *cortes* in a somewhat sanguine light. It is undoubtedly true that Stubbs projected the image and reality of the constitutional monarchy of his age into the past, so that at a certain point his history seemed – at least to one German critic, Riess[14] – too beautiful to be true. It is not my purpose – and it would be out of place here – to indicate in detail the weaknesses of Stubbs's interpretations and those aspects which have been most strongly attacked or criticised by Riess, Maitland, Adams, Pasquet, Pollard, Petit-Dutaillis, and so many others. The important fact to note is that in recent decades English parliamentary historiography – even of such distinguished exponents as H. G. Richardson and G. O. Sayles – has radically changed its approach and adopted Maitland's criterion of "describing, not explaining". In order to avoid the dangers of premature synthesis or excessive value judgements, this more recent school of historiography has gone to the other extreme and has dedicated itself to researches of extreme erudition and merit, but for the most part so minute and fragmentary as to seem at times remote or impenetrable.

It is true that more recent English and American literature on the subject has in part attempted to adopt a more constructive approach.

[14] L. Riess, "Der Ursprung des englischen Unterhauses", *Historische Zeitschrift*, n.f., XXIX, 1888.

But the gap created by the methodical demolition of that part of Stubbs's work dedicated to the formative period of the English constitution is still far from being filled. The road is not merely strewn with natural difficulties, but is rendered treacherous by a long series of detailed studies, for the most part lacking in any logical links and difficult to pull together into an overall view.

Perhaps few other European countries experienced such agitated and dramatic events in the 13th century as England. The political struggles between the monarchy and feudatories, which took place throughout Europe in that period, assumed quite remarkable aspects in England. For the frequent rebellions of the barons found greater justification here than elsewhere. It was not merely a question of exercising the right of resistance to the arbitrary acts and illegalities of a sovereign which characterised feudal society. It was also a problem of protecting the country against the excessive influence of foreign ministers in the government, and of protecting it by remarkable measures in situations of extreme gravity. The very complexity of the royal administration and the inadequacy of the bureaucratic organisation made collaboration between the sovereign and leaders of the country indispensable.

In over a hundred years (1199–1366) England had only three sovereigns. A French historian, Petit-Dutaillis, has repeatedly pointed out that these sovereigns were lacking in adequate qualities of character, equilibrium and sense of responsibility for so high an office. Even if one does not accept Petit-Dutaillis's severe judgement that King John (1199–1216) was mentally ill, it seems necessary to recognise that he pursued an unstable and illogical policy with only one consistent thread – that of persistently opposing the desires of his people. On the other hand, one needs to take into account Lady Stenton's recent assessment that John was an excellent organiser, but unfortunate in that he found his kingdom in disastrous financial conditions at a time when he had to compete abroad with exceptional adversaries such as Philip Augustus and Innocent III. The reign of Henry III (1216–72) was filled with a continual series of struggles between the sovereign and the greater part of the magnates and barons. The latter refused to tolerate the systematic repetition of abuses and injustices by his officers, the king's obstinacy in retaining confidence in extremely unpopular ministers and councillors, his attempts to eliminate hitherto respected immunities and franchises. It seems probable that Henry III wished to revoke the excessive concessions made by his father, but was never sufficiently strong. Edward I (1272–1307) was a conqueror who engaged in enterprises beyond his own strength.

As elsewhere in the same period, the English sovereigns, with all their positive and negative qualities assisted by ministers of greater or lesser ability, struggled to free themselves from their dependence upon feudal society, but were not always adept in their choice of weapons or fortunate in achieving their aims. The barons were – or believed themselves to be – within their rights in opposing a policy which, according to current concepts of monarchical power, could well be considered as premeditated and reactionary aggression. As is well known, the fundamental episodes of this great struggle between the sovereign and leading vassals were the concession of the Magna Carta and the Forest Charter extracted from King John in 1215, and the promulgation of the Provisions of Oxford, dictated to Henry III by the rebel barons in 1258–9. The various withdrawals and confirmations of these concessions marked the alternating phases of the continual political struggle, and reflected an almost ostentatious concern for legal forms; but in the process these concessions underwent substantial amendments, which considerably modified their original importance.

Curiae, colloquia, tractatus, concilia and parliaments summed up and reflected the various phases and aspects both of this unstable political situation and of the more or less solemn meetings between the king and his council, officers, judges and the country. The traditional view, which goes back to Stubbs but is shared by a great number of historians, is that all these assemblies should be placed on the same plane of particularly solemn meetings between the king and his council, composed of lay and ecclesiastical dignitaries and other barons or magnates. According to this view, they were enlarged royal councils, held irregularly in various ways, occasionally with the participation of the knights of the shires, representatives of the cities and boroughs and legal experts or others with experience in matters of public interest. The various terms were apparently used indifferently by Englishmen of the 13th and 14th centuries to describe either the reunion itself or the whole body of the participants or the deliberative organ. This series of assemblies, convoked by the sovereign for a wide range of motives (sometimes alluded to in general terms as "deliberations on matters of common interest") of course would include the frequent meetings, *curiae, placita, assisae regis* and the like held by the sovereign with the prelates, bishops, abbots, and magnates or barons, as well as occasionally with a limited representation of the knights of the shires. These meetings had the duty of doing justice (*rectum facere*) in response to the complaints of subjects (*clamores regni*).

Such a view of the 13th-century English parliament would seem extremely plausible and convincing, because it would settle doubts and problems about the continuity and progressive nature of the great national consultations – which culminated, as we shall point out later, in the famous "Model Parliament" of 1295 – and anticipates the remarkable realisation of the English parliament of later centuries. But this almost idyllically progressive image of the constitution presumed by Stubbs has been often and severely criticised: in recent decades by Richardson and Sayles.[15]

These two authors maintain that it is a grave mistake to place all these parliaments without distinction among the great assemblies of the English monarchy. For the assemblies were sometimes consultative and sometimes deliberative. According to them, "parliaments" were something separate and different from the customary assemblies. They had the aspect and functions, if not of true courts of justice, at least of assemblies convoked primarily to allow subjects to complain of abuses and obtain satisfaction. As Richardson and Sayles point out, the overall physiognomy of the institution was clearly delineated towards the end of the 13th century in the words of the unknown author of the treatise of medieval English law called *Fleta*: "in his parliament", says this text, "the king in council holds his court; doubts which have arisen in the course of judgements are settled, necessary measures are adopted to reform abuses which have come to light, justice is administered to each according to his merits". "Parliament" is the place and occasion for demanding reparation for an injustice, for laying complaints before the judges

[15] H. G. Richardson and G. O. Sayles, "Parliaments and great councils in medieval England", *Law Quarterly Review,* vol. 77, 1961; H. G. Richardson, "The origins of parliament", *TRHS*, 4th ser., vol. XI, 1928.

and officers of the king's council and awaiting their reply and providing a remedy either by justice or pardon. The right to present such petitions belonged to the subjects and parliaments were convoked specifically for this purpose, as could be seen in the statute of *Rageman* or *de Justiciis assignatis*, which conceived of parliament as the centre of a system to repress abuses of power by officers of the local administration, or in the statutes of Winchester, and elsewhere. This specific administration of justice was then often accompanied by a more general discussion and followed by the promulgation of statutes or laws.

According to these two authors the Englishmen of the 13th and 14th centuries, in fact, were well aware whether they were dealing with "parliament" or with another great assembly convoked for different purposes: both the writs of summons and of expenses stated clearly and uniformly whether they were for an assembly of the first or the second type. People with judicial problems knew that they had to turn to "parliament" and not to a royal "colloquium", *tractatus*, or great council. The confusion was not really to be attributed to Stubbs except in so far as he accepted uncritically the hasty conclusions or affirmations of the Committees of the House of Lords which had been given the task of searching for the first signs of life of parliament. In fact, if Stubbs had concerned himself with reaching critically valid conclusions, he would not have forgotten that the first criterion in qualifying an assembly or institution is not its structure or composition, but the end or purpose for which it has been summoned. The idea of the "Model Parliament" of 1295, in fact, goes back to the House of Lords' Report. But a considerable number of assemblies possessed both the name of *parlamentum* and had basically legal–judicial functions, whether or not representatives of the shires and boroughs took part. A "parliament" could be of any size, and could be formed by the representatives of the most varied social groups, but if it was a "parliament" it remained such – and this had a fundamental influence on its method of working, often in small groups rather than in a single body.

The council, colloquium, *tractatus*, great council or the like, was a different matter, whether it was a greater or smaller body. The term and the institutions were quite distinct and unequivocal. There are examples of the same people attending a "parliament" and a *tractatus* at extremely short intervals of time; in these cases they never failed to specify their reasons in claiming their expenses for such attendance. Over a longer period we can also see that, because of their duties, the "parliaments" often remained in session longer than the other great assemblies. The parliaments were convoked on fixed dates – by the time of Edward I for the most part at Easter and Michaelmas – so that a member who was present at one of them had no need of a writ of summons for the following session. But the other assemblies were held by special summons, whenever there was need, and the writs were only valid for that particular session. Apart from these general characteristics, there is no way of stating precisely in what ways a "parliament" differed from a national assembly (or "great council", as the two authors described it), except by distinguishing them on each occasion by the "pedestrian method of description" – that is, by describing without hazarding an explanation.

This distinction made by the two authors seems to me well founded. The meetings in which the king, the members of his council and a few others did justice or discussed legal matters belong to one species. All other assemblies belong to another, for here the king, together with all the lay and ecclesiastical magnates and frequently also the knights of the shires and representatives of the cities and boroughs, discussed the administrative, political and financial problems of the country, exchanged opinions, made claims and concessions, and put into practice the principle of consent. Nevertheless, however important this observation, it is not adequate to overthrow all previous interpretations. In fact, even in the works of Richardson and Sayles it is possible to see that, while the term "parliament" was not synonymous with a great national political assembly in the period from the mid-13th to the mid-14th century, on more than one occasion some of these parliaments did act as political assemblies and were so considered. Nor is this surprising. Indeed, specific examples of such mixed functions, which cannot be ignored, had already been published by Stubbs in his *Select Charters* in 1870. For example, Henry III asked and obtained a subsidy for a journey (*peregrinatio*) he was about to undertake from a "great parliament" held soon after Easter 1253. Two years later in 1255, again at Easter time, the king held *parlamentum suum* at Westminster and made a new and formal request for financial aid from the bishops, abbots, earls and barons of the kingdom assembled there; this time the request was without success because of disputes which arose and which led to the postponement of the matter to another parliament; this was held a few days after Michaelmas day, but again without result. In 1257, Henry was once more in urgent need of money for his Sicilian enterprise and because of his sizable debts: he held a "great parliament" in Lent to which he sent his son Edmund, the claimant to the Sicilian throne, dressed in Sicilian costume in order to arouse enthusiasm and so obtain the continuation and increase of certain taxes, but again without success. A new parliament at London, still "about the affair of the kingdom of Sicily", was held on the second Tuesday after Easter of 1258, and marked a new royal defeat.

When the barons forced the king to accept the famous Provisions of Oxford, in the same year 1258, he undertook to convoke three parliaments a year. According to Richardson and Sayles, the rebel barons spoke of "parliaments" in the technical sense of the word; the very regularity invoked by the barons was equivalent to a definition: "there cannot be a periodical occurrence of something that is not defined".[16] However, the same authors are also ready to admit that the rebels spoke of "parliaments" in the popular sense of the word, as referring to some sort of enlarged royal council, although this had not yet become official.

But even if we leave aside how the barons may have conceived of parliaments in their claims and demands, it remains quite clear that the Provisions of Oxford laid down that regular parliaments be held to "look after the state of the kingdom and treat of the common interests of the king and people" (*voier le estat du reaume et . . . treter des communes busoignes du roy et du reaume*). Once again we have an example of parliaments which do not fit too precisely into the classification of our two authors. In fact, Richardson and Sayles do not deny that other structurally identical assemblies coexisted with these parliaments, which could, if they so wished, deal with matters normally dealt with by the latter, given that the power of the king in council with his barons was always the same, whatever the purpose originally assigned to the assembly.

[16] "Parliaments and great councils", cit., p. 221.

In 1311 an analogous situation to that of 1258 occurred, when the weak Edward II was called to pay the price of the autocratic policies of his father and forced to accept a committee of magnates "to order and settle the affairs of the kingdom . . . according to law and reason". Alongside other measures, the Lords Ordainers decreed that one, and if necessary two parliaments a year be held. For our authors, the most important point was that by insisting on the regularity of the meetings the magnates confirmed their belief in the vitality of these legal–judicial parliaments. Moreover, they state, the ordinances in question reasserted the belief that the aims and functions of these parliaments were the restoration of law and the examination and answering of petitions. But here, too, one needs to note that other articles of the ordinances contemplated the assembly's participation in the discussion of matters relating to war and peace, the exercise of executive power, the appointment of royal officials, and the control of the court. As Richardson and Sayles state, the Ordainers were certainly aware that the basic purpose of "parliament" was to give justice to whoever requested it. But equally certainly the Ordainers were claiming that the king consult and reach agreement with his barons "in matters of consequence". There can be little question that parliaments so conceived were not only judicial and administrative assemblies, but also political and constitutional. They were and must be considered as forerunners of parliament in the widest sense of the word.

From the time of the dynastic crisis which culminated in the deposition of Edward II in 1327, "parliament" became something more than the preceding "parliaments". It is difficult to distinguish it from the old *colloquia* or *tractatus* or great councils, as like them it takes the form of a convocation of the prelates and magnates of the kingdom. This can be seen even more clearly in the reign of Richard II, when he stated in 1386 that his controversy with the king of Aragon, Peter the Ceremonious, should be deferred "to our next parliament or great council". In fact, by then the only difference would seem to be the procedure used in the two types of assemblies: by the last decades of the 14th and early 15th centuries the "great council" – consisting, like the other parliaments, not only of prelates and barons but also of "commons" – would seem to be considered as both quicker and more suitable "in offering a rapid remedy to the said needs or least vexations of our people". We have no means of seeing how this evolution took place. "Parliament" and council coexisted without merging; they were, however, so close to each other as to constitute more or less a *bis in idem*, different forms with the same content. The only certain fact is that from the accession of Edward III petitions were no longer sent by individuals to the king, but to the Commons, and then by the Commons to the king, his Lords and officials as common petitions.

This outline is by no means equally clear or certain in all its phases, and the ambiguity or lacunae of a large part of the documentation easily explains the great diversity of opinions among historians. It is impossible to decide with certainty, for example, whether the assemblies of 1290, 1306 and 1307, or indeed those of 1258 and 1311, were "parliaments" or "great councils"; other meetings, such as that of 1325, are called "parliaments" but are inadequately described.

Nevertheless it is clear, at least in general terms, that many of the assemblies held in England in the 13th and 14th centuries under the name of "parliaments", with a larger or smaller body of representatives, had their own physiognomy and functions which distinguished them from the long and rich series of courts, councils, colloquia and *tractatus* of the English monarchy. They cannot be placed, *a priori*, outside the mainstream of constitutional history, because on more than one occasion they extended their judicial functions to political, financial and other more general matters. But these were not their main purpose, as had long been believed. Theories of steady progress, such as Stubbs put forward, need to be treated with extreme caution, for like all patterns imposed for logical or rational considerations, they tend to take insufficient account of the complexity and illogicality of historical accident.

But even if we leave aside the judicial–bureaucratic aspects of these parliaments, the history of the relationship between the English monarchy and the great forces of the country, as expressed in their complex social and administrative structure, still presents a rich and varied reality.

Many assemblies attended by various groups – both corporative bodies and individuals – witnessed the exchange of mutual pledges between king and subjects on the accession of a new sovereign to the throne. Other assemblies, more restricted and better ordered – in the sense of a more uniform composition – counselled the king (as in 1191) "on the most important and arduous matters"; they judged controversial questions of a varied nature, and were present at the promulgation of new statutes by the king; they took part in the apportioning of feudal aids, or confirmed the legitimacy of analogous requests for extraordinary subsidies – or in exceptional cases even denied them or granted them on conditions, as in 1258; they put forward requests and grievances (*querelae, peticiones, griefs*) to the king on behalf of groups or individuals against abuses and errors of the administration or of the king himself, and demanded their redress. In 1261, when one such assembly was convoked in the absence of the king, it is he who made his protests (*greuances*), above all against the irregular holding of a meeting without his presence. Although the permanent officials of the court or *concilium* normally exercised such functions, occasionally these assemblies also took part in giving judgement in trials which must have had an impact on public opinion, such as those against extortionate officials for acts of treachery or felony, or over disputed feudal successions.

The king was not obliged to obey the decisions of the assemblies. But in practice it would have been difficult, impolitic or even dangerous for him to ignore them.[17] It was his council, in fact his "great council"—he could not disown it openly. As a result, no oath from the king was required to give such assemblies authority. Indeed, when the barons made Henry III swear in 1237, it was specifically because that council had been held as a result of their threats and because they wanted to ensure that the king should accept it.

The sessions lacked any regularity. They had the same name even when their composition appeared notably different. But they always had a central nucleus in common, consisting of the council of the leading officials, and especially of the permanent councillors of the king, even though these varied in number. They consisted of prelates, earls and barons, sometimes of the representatives of the country clergy and chapters of religious orders, fairly frequently of

[17] In 1255, after failing to persuade the bishops, abbots, earls and barons to grant him an aid in the Easter Parliament, Henry II imposed a *taylagium quod dicitur horngelth*, a tax on horned cattle. But his financial position was disastrous, and he was already at loggerheads with the barons.

knights, and later also of representatives of the boroughs and cities. They were summoned by royal order to the place where the royal court was assembled, usually – as in the past – on the occasion or about the time of great religious festivals. The meetings were of short duration, and were held within the court, in fact as a session of the royal court. As has been mentioned, the prelates and barons varied in number each time, while the other groups were only summoned if it was in the king's interest to do so. Not only the composition of the assemblies, but the nature and fullness of their discussion varied according to the variation of the subjects to be discussed.[18] A basic problem which remains to be resolved is when and how this limited participation in public life ceased to be – as it had long been – a privilege and duty, a natural obligation on the members of the higher clergy and group of great feudal lords, the immediate vassals of the sovereign (*tenentes in capite*), the *prelats, countes et barons de la terre,* or, more briefly, the *episcopi et barones*.[19]

The first to be summoned together with the magnates to assemblies of various kinds – above all local assemblies – were the representatives of the important and politically conscious class of the small nobility, the knights of the shires, who were too numerous for all to be called in person. Since the previous century the knights had been members of the borough councils and county courts (organs with administrative, judicial, fiscal and representative functions in general) and of the special inquests occasionally summoned by the sovereigns. Their military character had gradually disappeared, and more than anything else they had been transformed into a large class of local nobles with special qualities and experience in administering public affairs and with taxable resources.

At a later stage, the summons were extended to the representatives of the "communes", the unprivileged inhabitants of the cities and boroughs, artificial entities according to Maitland, created by the government as local centres of administration, but always active and with a vitality of their own. This extension of the franchise was

[18] The writs were more concerned to emphasise the obligatory nature of the summons; for the most part the powers of the assembly were described in a vague and general manner by such phrases as "to treat", "to listen", etc.

[19] After three summons, absentees without excuse could be declared contumacious, or even rebels. The first known case of sanctions was that against Robert Mowbray in 1095.

determined not so much by legal reasons or by a desire for uniformity (to offer, for instance, the privileges which the city of London had long enjoyed to the smaller towns) but rather by a prudent and conscious use of the royal prerogative to call whomsoever it wished to, or before, its council. There was, in fact, no reason why the local centres should be treated differently from those which had already achieved recognition through commercial or industrial activities or through the presence of a particularly large population. This development resulted not only from demands of an administrative, financial or political character, but also from a new conception of the relationship between king and subjects, and from the royal desire to weaken the power of the magnates and great feudal lords.

The presence of representatives of this new element in national life was for some time merely tacit and submissive.[20] Initially it was perhaps conceived of mainly as a means of propaganda to facilitate the formation of public opinion in favour of arguments or decisions of particular importance, and to give necessary publicity to the solemn declarations of the sovereign, or to legal decrees, judgements, and royal declarations and requests in general. Moreover, by issuing writs of summons to boroughs located within the possessions of the feudal lords (summons to communities on the royal demesne were only issued later, from 1322), the king gained greater freedom and authority in his relations with his immediate vassals, not least from a financial point of view. In fact these summons to feudal boroughs may have seemed arbitrary, as they contrasted with the principle that vassals were to be protected and defended (and hence also represented) by their immediate lords. But without doubt a fundamental reason can be found in the desire to facilitate the levying of taxes.[21]

[20] A totally different opinion is to be found in J. C. Russell ("Early parliamentary organisation", *AHR*, XXVI, 1941), who maintains that in the 13th century the knights and commons possessed an aggressive political sense as representatives of the *communitas Anglie*, asserting the principle that what affected all should be approved by all.

[21] Lady Stenton rightly observed (*English society in the early Middle Ages (1066–1307)*, Harmondsworth, 1951, pp. 54–6) that the enormous constitutional significance of this enlargement of the franchise escaped the notice of contemporary chroniclers, even of Matthew Paris, who failed to realise that "a new institution was being born". "The knights and burgesses were not yet a necessary part of a true parliament, nor is there any evidence of their talks together from which the House of Commons ultimately grew. But the germ of all future growth was there."

The summoning of representatives of the knights to assemblies occurred for the first time in 1213, when King John declared that he wished to consult them about the affairs of the kingdom. The king ordered the sheriffs of each county to come to the assembly together with two, and in some cases four, of the most worthy and capable knights (*de legalioribus et discretioribus militibus*). It is not certain, but seems extremely probable, that this first assembly of 1213 never took place. Nevertheless, the precedent was not forgotten and the knights were subsequently summoned to numerous and various assemblies (including many which do not belong to the "type" of assembly which interests us).[22] The summons was repeated in 1231, when Henry III wanted to give evidence of his magnanimity and sense of justice, and declared that he desired to ascertain the truth about real or supposed transgressions of the Magna Carta. Such summons were certainly or very probably issued in 1254, 1261 and 1264. Writs went out in 1265 on the occasion of the famous parliament held by Simon de Montfort – which included representatives of the boroughs as well – in order to mobilise as wide an array of opinion and resources as possible against the king. Further summons in 1269 and 1273 (the latter to mark Edward I's formal taking possession of the kingdom) were followed by increasingly frequent and more regular writs. However, until Edward I such summons had not been at all regular: indeed the "community" (*le Commun*) of the kingdom which rose up against the king in 1258 had been personified by the magnates alone. We have noted how a few years later, in January 1265, the representatives of the boroughs were also summoned together with the prelates, feudal lords and knights. But this assembly was less of a normal parliamentary reunion than one of those virtually plebiscitary meetings which took place on the occasion of an oath of fealty to a new sovereign, or to confirm a treaty or legislative act of particular importance. On this occasion, in fact, it was called to take note of a new constitution, the form of the government of the lord king and the kingdom "agreed

[22] As D. Pasquet stated (*An essay on the origins of the House of Commons*, Cambridge, 1925, pp. 66–7), the summons of 1226, 1227 and October 1258 may not have been "parliamentary" convocations in the sense that the word was later to acquire, but contemporaries were probably hardly aware of such subtle distinctions; the fact that the knights were summoned to state their grievances about transgressions of Magna Carta was more or less equivalent to their convocation in 1265 to treat with the king and his council about important matters of the kingdom.

on" between Simon de Montfort, earl of Leicester, steward of the kingdom and head of the insurrection, and the king.

Similarly, the assembly held on the accession of Edward I on Saint Hilary's Day 1273 possessed a wholly exceptional and plebiscitary character. In fact, one cannot be certain of the attendance of representatives of the cities and boroughs in great national assemblies until April 1275. The next instance is the assembly of November 1295: it was this meeting that Stubbs – unaware of the precedent of April 1275 – described by the suggestive but much disputed and inadequately proven title of "Model Parliament".[23]

It is generally held that the presence of representatives of the boroughs implied the existence of a genuine public opinion, in the sense that it presupposed the participation of various classes of the population. But in fact it may have represented something far more important. For although the new members attended under conditions of inferiority, they formed part of an assembly which by tradition possessed the right to accept or deny the sovereign's request for financial aid, according to their judgement of the validity of his reasons, and which also decided the apportionment of any sum granted among the various social orders.[24] Nevertheless, either because of the slowness and irregularity of this development, or because of the very conditions of inferiority assigned to these

[23] The writ of summons for the 1275 parliament was only published nine years after Stubbs' death in 1910. There are, of course, various decisive objections that can be made to the description "model parliament", besides the precedent of 1275. In the first place, the writ of summons was so general that it included (according to the *Premunientes* clause sent to ecclesiastical leaders) representatives of the lower clergy, who were summoned, however, not to parliament, but to their own separate convocations. In the second place, the representatives of the cities and boroughs were only summoned in November 1295 "to do what shall be ordered by common counsel about the matters discussed"; they were not invited to express consent until 1313. Thirdly, the request that representatives be given full powers was already clear, if not explicit, in writs of summons before 1295. Fourthly, the number of cities and boroughs convoked in 1295 was 110, whereas at later assemblies only an average of 75 to 85 were convoked; in fact, some of the boroughs summoned in 1295 were not summoned later, while new boroughs were convoked to later parliaments. Finally, even after the 1295 parliament, it remained somewhat unusual – at least until Edward III's reign – for boroughs to be convoked.

[24] According to G. Post ("The two laws and the statute of York", *Speculum*, XXIX, 1954), when searching for the origins of parliament, one needs to look less towards the feudal structure of society and more towards the principles of Roman and canonical law relating to sovereign authority, communities, representation and mandates, the state, common utility, etc. He would seem to suggest that the principle of *quod omnes tangit*, or consent within an assembly, had validity – even at a formal level – in England as in the rest of Western Europe.

representatives in the writs, this enlargement of the membership of parliament passed by almost wholly unobserved, as if it were a natural and logical matter. But whether or not natural or logical, it was certainly no triumphal entry – rather an entry by the kitchen door. In fact the writs only included an invitation to express consent in 1313. All the same, the participation of borough members represented the hesitant beginnings of a great future reality.

Let us for the moment merely take note of this completion of the formative process of the great English assemblies with the participation of two "of the most discreet and laborious" inhabitants of every city and borough, who were summoned to carry out what was decided and ordained by "common council",[25] that is by the original and basic nucleus of the great assemblies, consisting of officials and great lords. For a considerable time after this event, at the end of the 13th century, there was no indication, no real sign of new developments within these great assemblies, nor of autonomous activities by the knights and borough representatives.[26] But their very participation – undoubtedly useful to the crown as offering an additional guarantee of fairness in the assessment and levying of the taxes – came to constitute something far more, in a manner wholly independent of the royal will. For their participation not only provided the missing integrative element required to ensure the solemnity and generality of the assemblies which the documents refer to so frequently, but also the sort of friction from which, to borrow the words of Maude Clarke, the spark was generated that makes co-operation dynamic. In short, it also represented an important factor in achieving that awareness and sense of their unity, that consciousness of their functions, whose psychological, political and constitutional importance we have already noted as marking a

[25] As various historians have observed, the commons were not vocal and possessed no vote throughout the reign of Edward II. A. R. Myers (*England in the late Middle Ages*, Harmondsworth, 1952, p. 34) has observed that the knights and burgesses were not even considered part of parliament, but were summoned to listen or reply to what was asked of them. Nevertheless, from the point of view of interesting and informing wider circles of subjects about affairs of state, the convocation of the knights and burgesses could not but have far-reaching consequences.

[26] It is worth noting that later writs – such as those of 1335 and 1336 – limited the functions and powers of the representatives of the counties and boroughs to carrying out what was asked of them. It is extremely probable that these were not parliaments in the technical sense of judicial meetings, as defined by Richardson and Sayles, but in the broader sense of general assemblies of the country.

crucial moment in the transformation of the great councils into true parliamentary assemblies.

The English constitution developed with extreme slowness, in response to immediate contingent needs rather than to predetermined patterns. Despite the precedents we have already noted and the repeated declarations of Edward I that he wished to follow the principle that what concerned all should be submitted to the judgement of all (*quod omnes tangit* . . .), the parliament of Westminster in the early months of 1305 continued to be described as "full and general" even after the prelates, earls, barons, knights and citizens had departed, leaving an assembly which consisted of only the king and his council. As far as we know, neither the assembly of November 1295 nor those that followed in the reigns of Edward I and Edward II differed substantially from their predecessors. Nevertheless there can be no doubt that it was in this period that the concept of "the community of the realm" (*communaute du roiaume, communitas regni, communitas terre*), which originally included only the nobility, was gradually extended in law and practice (albeit with interruptions and regressions) to include the knights and representatives of the cities and boroughs as well. By the time of Edward II the tendency to regard such an extension as normal had become more marked, while under Edward III it became the habitual way of thinking. During the reign of Edward II, the two rival factions – king and magnates – competed in their attempts to win the support of the commons and insisted on their presence in parliament. They sought to use them for their own purposes and as a result placed them in a favourable position to decide the most serious questions for themselves.

Because of the slow nature of the development it is impossible to point with certainty to any particular moment when the process of transformation of the old great council into the new representative institution was completed. The novelty lay not only in the fact that a new sector of the community now took part in parliament, but in the position of the assembly in relation to the sovereign and the country. Hence we cannot accept the viewpoint of historians who consider the entry of the "third estate" into the assemblies as the necessary and adequately qualifying element which marks the transformation. A series of significant dates can be pointed to:

1275 or 1295 when the "third estate" made its first parliamentary appearance; 1313 when the writs of summons for the first time invited the representatives to attend in order to give their consent;[27] 1327 when the commons gained the exclusive right to present petitions, grievances or the like in the name of the "community" of the kingdom. But it was only considerably later that the knights and representatives of the cities and boroughs, working together, achieved, or were near achieving, either a collective awareness or an absolute fullness of powers within the parliamentary sphere. It is one thing to observe the presence of the third estate among the privileged and responsible orders of the country; it is entirely another matter to show that a representative assembly – which fulfilled the requirements we outlined earlier on – existed at that date.

The evolution, although not complete, was nearing its completion by the last years of Edward II and during the first decades of the reign of Edward III. The new institution, which in a certain sense had been anticipated momentarily by some of the preceding great assemblies, now grew almost by leaps: it appeared, disappeared, only to reappear fully developed as a true parliamentary institution, a central and fundamental part of the constitution of the state. According to a well-known passage of the statute of York of 1322, everything relating to the state of the king, the kingdom or the people could only be settled in parliament by the king, with the consent of the prelates, earls, barons, knights and the "community" of the realm. One can reasonably doubt whether these words, or such a legislative act, represented the birth certificate of a true parliamentary institution. According to more than one writer, the statute did no more than confirm what already existed in practice. Nevertheless, the great significance of the document remains, especially in a country like England where the written document has always been regarded as of fundamental importance.

At the same time, other equally significant facts need to be taken into account: the request made by the representatives of the City of London in 1327 that assemblies be held at regular annual intervals;

[27] "Mes les choses que serount a establir pur le stat de nostre seignur le roi et de seis heirs et pur le stat du roialme et du poeple, soient tretes, accordees, establies en parlement par nostre seignur le roi et por lassent des prelatz, countes et barouns et la communalte du roialme, auxint come ad este acustume cea enarere." *The statutes of the realm,* London, vol. I (1810), 189.

the fact that only a few months before parliament had pronounced the deposition, subsequently changed into abdication, of Edward II; the fact that in 1340 Edward III made a formal renunciation of the right to impose or levy aids or other charges, "if it be not by the common assent of the prelates, earls, barons and other great men and commons of our . . . realm of England, assembled in Parliament"; the statement in 1341 that peers of the realm could only be judged by their peers in full parliament; the rejection of a proposed law in 1382 because it was not approved by the commons. From a formalistic point of view, the royal "concession" of 1340 did not differ much from that contained in the *confirmatio chartarum* of 1297, which had eluded rather than given satisfaction to most of the protests and petitions against the *maltôte* on wool, expressed in the famous so-called statute *de tallagio non concedendo*. But alongside the formal reference to parliament there was also the new and fundamental reality of an alert and authoritative national body of representatives – a body which only thirteen years before had dethroned the king because of the abuses and arbitrary actions of his government. The "constitutional monarchy" which Stubbs and more than one writer found in the period of the great King Edward was indeed becoming a reality.

Nevertheless in 1383 the speaker of the commons stated that only the king and the lords of the kingdom could decide about expeditions beyond the sea, "as seems fitting to them". At this date, in fact, the vote of the commons in the national assemblies still remained limited and subordinate.[28]

[28] In 1348, when requested to give their opinion about the conduct of military operations, the commons replied that they were incompetent and incapable of discussing such matters. In 1399 the commons stated that the judicial activities of parliament lay within the exclusive competence of the king and the lords. In fact, in the reign of Edward III, as Richardson and Sayles have clearly pointed out ("Parliament and great councils", cit., pp. 18, 19, 40), the petitory procedure changed radically: petitions were presented to the commons, which examined them and commented on them; but the decision was left to the lords and leading officials of the royal council.

3

France

As we have already seen, France possessed an old tradition of great "synodal diets", such as, for example, the council of Compiègne of 816, when Louis the Pious solemnly received the Saracen ambassadors. This tradition still existed in France in the 13th century. The great and solemn assemblies held at Paris in January 1226 by Louis VIII and at Bourges in September 1240 by his son St Louis seem to be half parliaments, half councils. This practice combined and confused government and administration with ecclesiastical or religious problems and organisation.

But outside this tradition, the sovereigns still summoned great assemblies of feudal lords and high ecclesiastical dignitaries, perhaps with greater solemnity and dignity than in the past, because of the increased power of the feudatories in the 13th century. Alongside these lords or sometimes even in place of some of them, the kings occasionally summoned the representatives of the cities (especially of the cities which possessed their own statutes, the so-called *bonnes villes*) or even experts in economic, commercial or financial matters. They did so whenever they felt the need to examine specific problems with them, or wished to emphasise their authority before the restless and by no means always obedient vassals, or the country in general.

We know extremely little about these assemblies. Direct references to them are extremely rare; we do not even know the dates of some of the assemblies. We know nothing about their functions, their composition, the arguments they discussed and so on. But we do know that under St Louis (1226–70) a certain number of great assemblies took place, sometimes consisting only of the feudal barons and secular lords (as in 1235 and 1246), sometimes of both barons and prelates. However, St Louis repeatedly called the inhabitants of the independent cities to his court or curia, in order to take counsel with them, particularly on matters relating to the exchange rates of the increasingly debased coinage.

From the middle of the 13th century our information about these great assemblies is more detailed. We know for example that some of them aroused considerable interest, as the documents state that great numbers of the inhabitants flocked to them (*en grant foison*, in the words of the chroniclers), although naturally without taking a direct part in their work. The sources which refer to them for the most part speak of a *concilium* (*concilium celebre*, *concilium magnum*), a *parlamentum*, a *curia generalis* or the like. As elsewhere, they represented and constituted solemn sessions of the curia or of the royal *concilium* or *très grant conseil*.

At least three of these assemblies deserve to be rescued from the obscurity of time. The first is the assembly of 1267 when St Louis, about to embark on his crusade, pronounced his farewell to his subjects and made arrangements for the period of his absence and the eventuality of his decease abroad. The second is the assembly of Bourges of 1283 when prelates and barons examined the invitation and proposals of the pope for a crusade against the kingdom of Aragon, considered responsible for driving the French out of Sicily and rebelling against the pope. The third assembly, held in Paris in 1284, was more or less the continuation of the second. The prelates and barons, after a long discussion of the arguments for and against the pontifical proposal, announced their favourable opinion to the king. The historian is struck by a detail of the assembly's organisation, which was destined to perpetuate itself: the prelates and barons met in separate rooms of the royal palace. Soon after, the king (Philip III the Bold, son of St Louis and father of Philip the Fair) communicated to the assembly his own support for the pope and that of his brother Charles, the king of Sicily. Another of these great reunions, composed of the members of the three groups mentioned earlier, must have been held in 1289–90: otherwise one cannot explain the meaning of Pope Nicholas IV's letter to Philip the Fair in March 1290 that he had received the envoys of the counts, barons, and "universities" or communities of the kingdom.

Although the inadequate documentation does not offer any conclusive proof, the relative frequency of similar great assemblies would seem to be confirmed by the words of a most reliable ecclesiastical dignitary, Humbert of the Romans, general of the Dominican order in St Louis's reign. According to a copy of the sermon he pronounced at the inauguration of such an assembly (for these assemblies were always preceded by religious ceremonies) the kings were accustomed to hold great assemblies, attended by laymen and prelates, on fixed dates every year. For the most part these parliaments were called for three reasons: in the first place, to carry out a useful and serious examination of questions which deserved weighty attention; in the second place, to receive the accounts of the administration (and, although it was not stated in the sermon, to request more financial aid from the country); in the third place, to decide whatever else was necessary. The preacher added that bad ministers were far worse than bad sovereigns: this judgement could be regarded as another, implicit justification of national consultations.

The presence of communal representatives in the parliaments or sessions of the royal curia had clear and well-founded precedents in the local assemblies of the *sénéchaussées* of Beaucaire and Carcassone, convoked frequently under St Louis and Philip the Bold. One can point in particular to an ordinance of St Louis of 1254, aimed at checking and suppressing the abuses of seneschals, which decreed that, before adopting measures to limit the free commerce of mass consumption produce, the seneschals should listen to the opinion of assemblies of prelates, feudal lords and representatives of the "good towns".

We have seen how the principle of consent developed in England through the concessions of more than one king, through force of circumstances rather than through enlightened judgement. In France, the personality and actions of the sovereigns are such as to exclude any impression that they consciously accepted the principle of consent, or searched for the collaboration and consent of their most qualified subjects, convoked and assembled in meetings called specifically for this purpose. On the contrary, one is left with the feeling that the sole or principal purpose of the convocation of these subjects was to corroborate and give greater prestige to royal views. Nor can there be much doubt that such an attitude persisted under Philip the Bold's heir and continuator, Philip the Fair. Indeed for this very reason the great and solemn assemblies convoked by Philip the Fair became a political element of exceptional importance, greater than in the past.

The major events of Philip the Fair's reign (1285–1314) are very well known and have been much discussed. But from the point of view of constitutional development they are by no means clear, partly because of the contradictory opinions of historians about the value and parliamentary nature of Philip the Fair's clamorous initiatives.

No less autocratic and quarrelsome than his two predecessors and namesakes Philip II Augustus and Philip III the Bold, Philip the Fair inherited from his grandfather and his great-grandfather not only a strong and well-established tradition, but considerable and extensive power, far more effective than that possessed by any of his predecessors. In the last years of the 13th century, as much owing to temperament as because of any real need arising from the war against England, Philip had requested – or rather exacted – heavy contributions even from ecclesiastics, despite their self-proclaimed immunity from state taxes. He had even imprisoned the papal legate, found guilty of defending the clergy of the kingdom. As relations with the pope grew tense and bitter and Boniface VIII threatened the king with the gravest sanctions, Philip played his trump card and summoned the barons, prelates and envoys of the cities to Paris on 15 February 1302. The writ of summons informed them that the king wished to treat and deal with them about grave problems of the moment. In fact it spoke of "many serious affairs", touching (*tangentia*) the king, the kingdom, the liberty of the Church, of ecclesiastics, of nobles and of all other inhabitants (*universi et singuli*) of the kingdom. The terms were detailed, although in a sense they kept to generalities; but they were nevertheless coherent with, and expressed the substance of the celebrated principle that *quod omnes tangit ab omnibus approbari debet.*

This assembly is traditionally described as the first reunion in France of the "estates general", of a parliamentary assembly or institution. But the tradition, in fact, is not very old: there is no mention of it in Bodin's writings in the 16th century, perhaps because the supporters of the antiquity of the "estates" (like Montesquieu later) preferred to trace their origins to the so-called "dark ages". Sismondi's discordant voice had little influence on 19th-century historians, and least of all on constitutional historians such as Boutaric, Picot, or Hervieu.

In the 20th century the controversy has grown more violent. In

1911 Langlois wrote[29] that the assembly of 1302 did not possess so novel a character as was habitually attributed to it: contemporaries had found nothing unusual about it; the name of "estates general" was only used much later; while in any case it was far from certain that the presence of a popular element in the assembly was unusual and exceptional. Langlois admitted that because of the unusual importance of the conflict between two such great antagonists as Philip and Boniface, the assembly of 1302 was not only larger than preceding ones but also "more remarkable and more remarked upon than any other", but he denied that it marked the beginnings of a representative institution in France. In contrast to Langlois, an equally famous legal historian, Esmein,[30] maintained that by uniting "everyone representing an authority independent of royal power in France", Philip had given life to the estates general. The controversy still continues: on the one hand Olivier-Martin has asserted the novelty of the assembly; on the other, it has been denied by such historians as Perrot, C. H. Taylor, Perroy and Fawtier.[31]

Perroy in particular has made the pertinent observation that the qualifying criterion of a parliamentary institution can only be that it be recognised, if only implicitly, as a representative and deliberative body legally and by the supreme organs of the state. In fact, the Paris assembly of 1302, like the Tours assemblies of 1308 and the later meetings until about 1340, possessed powers only of a plebiscitary nature, to acclaim the decisions of the sovereign without the possibility of opposing or modifying them.

Great assemblies continued to be summoned under Philip V (1316–22) and Charles IV (1322–8). The size of the assemblies varied, however, as they were occasionally held separately for the provinces of *Langue d'Oil* and *Langue d'Oc*. After usurping his niece Jeanne's throne, Philip convoked the barons, prelates, citizens and lawyers in 1317 to ratify the *fait accompli*, on the grounds that *femme ne succède au*

[29] C. V. Langlois, *Histoire de France* (ed. E. Lavisse) Paris, t. III, vol. 2 (1901), pp. 260–1.

[30] A. Esmein, *Cours élémentaire d'histoire du droit français*, 11th ed., Paris, 1912.

[31] F. Olivier-Martin, *Histoire du droit français*, 3rd ed., Paris, 1948, pp. 365–6; E. Perrot, *Précis élémentaire d'histoire du droit français public et privé*, Paris, 1932, p. 456; C. H. Taylor, "The composition of baronial assemblies in France, 1315–1320", *Speculum*, XXIX, 1954; E. Perroy, *Histoire de France pour tous les Français*, Paris, t. 1 (1955), p. 164 f.; R. Fawtier, "Parlement d'Angleterre et états-généraux de France au moyen-âge", *Comptes-rendues des séances de l'Académie des Inscriptions et Belles Lettres*, 1953, p. 281 ff.

royaume de France. According to Hervieu,[32] this assembly, and similar ones, were "estates general" of magnates and barons (*barons et grantz hommes*). Nevertheless, he adds, one should be wary of accepting the 15th and 16th-century tradition which idealised both the exclusively baronial assembly of 1328 and the more open one of 1338 as prototypes of independent and virtually sovereign estates general.

In fact, there do not seem to have been any significant novelties in this period. None of the far from numerous documents proves that as early as these first decades of the 14th century the kingdom of France possessed a representative body, with definite and recognisable attributes and a deliberative power more or less accepted in public law. These characteristics only seem to emerge in the course of the agitated assemblies of 1355 to 1357 when King John II (1350–64) was a prisoner of the English while the dauphin Charles acted as regent.

From the first the "estates" of 1355 displayed that curiously uncompromising, almost revolutionary attitude so often repeated in French history. Instead of endeavouring to discover and provide the means for the defence of the country, the estates, incited by able agitators and barely responding to patriotic appeals to oppose the invader, made claims that no other assembly had ever made nor perhaps had even taken into consideration. Even before they had studied the measures and agreed to the sacrifices asked of them by the chancellor and other royal ministers, the *bonnes gens* of the *trois estas* demanded of the king direct participation in the government, periodic convocations of the estates, and immediate responsibility for the exaction and control of taxes in order to avoid speculation and ensure that the amounts exacted corresponded to the concessions. Only on these conditions did they pledge themselves to find the necessary means to raise an army of 120,000 men and 30,000 horses. The money was to be raised from the income of the salt *gabelle*; there were to be no exemptions, even in favour of the king or royal family. The exaction of the tax was to be entrusted to the estates, who were to appoint a special staff (*Receveurs et Ministres, Receveurs génereaux*) under the control of "superintendents" and "generals" who were to be members of the assembly, until such

[32] H. Hervieu, *Recherches sur les premiers états-généraux et les assemblées représentatives pendant la première moitié du quatorzième siècle,* Paris, 1879, p. 132.

time as a following assembly (to be called in March 1356) regulated the matter on the basis of the first accounts. The royal ordinance which authorised the decision of the estates not only accepted the general application of the new tax, but also recognised the right of subjects to resist arbitrary exactions. But this universal application was a total failure, as entire regions, as well as many individuals, refused to recognise the validity of the new law or escaped paying the tax.

Resistance to this tax voted by the estates general undoubtedly assisted the English invasion. Indeed, the following assembly attempted to rectify the situation by proposing a new tax on commerce and by deciding to meet again in November to examine the situation. In the meantime, however, in September 1356, the king was captured by the English. The dauphin, who assumed the functions of lieutenant, asked the estates to keep their promises. The archbishop of Rouen, Pierre de la Forest, chancellor of the kingdom, harangued the assembly when it met in Paris on 17 October, but received a cold reception. Then the dauphin himself spoke to the members with no better success. Seduced by the promises of the emissaries of Charles the Bad, king of Navarre, and urged on by the partisan Robert le Coq, bishop of Laon, the estates suspended their session for a month. On their reunion in November they asked the regent to dismiss his ministers and appoint a council in their place, consisting of representatives of the three groups, with powers to *tout faire et ordonner au royaume aussi comme le roi*. The prince dismissed the estates, but they met again irregularly. A few months later, Charles was forced to convoke them once more, when parliamentary and popular favour seemed to turn towards another turbulent agitator, the provost of the Paris merchants, Etienne Marcel.

In February–March 1357 the estates confirmed their intention of supplying a military contingent. The royal ordinance of 4 March accepted their control over the exaction and utilisation of the revenue of the tax, and agreed that they meet without further convocation whenever seemed necessary. The dauphin also promised a series of reforms: he recognised the assembly's right to increase or diminish the amount of the subsidy; he pledged himself not to make peace with the enemy without the consent of future assemblies; and so on. But this predominance of the estates – or rather of the mob – was already on the decline. A new session of the assembly was due to be convoked on the second Monday after Easter (17 April). But the king publicly proclaimed from Bordeaux that, as he had concluded a truce with the English and was about to be freed, he had no more need of the subsidy or of the assembly, and forbade its convocation.

In order to avoid this threat, Robert le Coq and Etienne Marcel extracted from the lieutenant by promises or threats (*par conseil ou par contrainte*) both a disavowal of the royal letter and confirmation of the convocation of the *gens des trois estas*.

Our source of information for this new meeting of the estates is a sort of proclamation of the dauphin-lieutenant, Charles duke of Normandy, about the subsidies voted for the continuation of the war. All that was necessary for the needs of the situation had been "counselled and ordained by the three estates by common consent and will" and "praised, approved and willingly ratified" by the lieutenant himself. In particular the estates had postponed the subsidy, once more entrusted to its own organs, and had decided to examine the situation again in the course of another assembly. It was decided that the new meeting be called on 22 July with the task of "ordering and advising on the said subsidies and on whatever touched on the honour and profit of the said kingdom of France and of the said lords and their subjects". From the point of view of the leaders of the assembly, the most important points were to keep control of the public finances and to maintain a check on the work of the regent's counsellors.

We do not even know if the assembly of 22 July was really held. These frequent assemblies and the accompanying agitation ultimately tired out both public opinion and the majority of what we should nowadays call members of parliament. The popularity of the agitators diminished steadily and their supporters abandoned them. The fairly widespread reluctance to pay taxes was symptomatic: many "did not want to pay", and in some places this refusal was accompanied by episodes of violence. Equally symptomatic were the appeals to the lieutenant from his subjects in Normandy and from many of the estates of the provinces of *Langue d'Oc* that he free himself from the humiliating tutelage in which he was held. However, the *bonnes villes* and many other parliamentarians continued to support Marcel, and once more the dauphin was forced to give way. But this time the situation changed rapidly. Another assembly of the estates held at Compiègne overthrew and disclaimed Marcel and his followers. From then on the supporters of the sovereign's authority gained the initiative.

We should not claim to explain better than French historians why and in what way the work of the estates of 1355–8 was weak and unpopular. There can be no doubt that the moment had seemed to be and was exceptionally favourable for a definitive affirmation of their authority, because of the weakening of the coercive structure of society with the imprisonment of the king and the critical financial situation. According to Professor Fawtier, the estates' projects of reform were a model of wisdom, their political clairvoyance was incomparable. It almost seems as if, up to 1789, France only knew how to fight absolutism in one way – by violent actions followed by deep collapse. In fact, the history of the French "estates" is not so much the history of an institution as of single episodes and moments of history, all to some extent spectacular and sensational; in the words of a French historian, "in a sense, such assemblies are incidents in French history, even accidents",[33] an observation, says Fawtier, so true that "the estates general, because they were so rare, never formed a true political body".[34]

This is not an overall critical judgement on the history of the French estates, whether general or local, but rather an assessment of their legal significance. The situation was not perhaps very clear, but it reflected a new attitude and was of consequence. This legal significance was certainly not to be found in the assembly of 1302, nor in those of 1308 or 1317. But it can be seen quite clearly in these assemblies of the 1350s, when the sessions of the estates were so closely linked together that they cannot be considered apart. At this point, in fact, the expression the "three estates" begins to be natural because they represent a consistent – if somewhat turbulent – reality, a power, perhaps the greatest power in the kingdom in terms of efficiency. These estates did not succeed in imposing themselves upon the government, or even in substituting their own members for it; nevertheless, they represented, in practice, the voice of the

[33] P. Viollet, *Histoire des institutions politiques et administratives de la France,* Paris, vol. III (1903), p. 178.

[34] Fawtier, "Parlement d'Angleterre et états-généraux de France", cit., p. 280.

country and, apart from a few exceptions, their decisions inspired the laws or ordinances of the king and his lieutenant. *A priori*, no law gave them powers of deliberation and decision, but they did deliberate and their decisions were accepted and confirmed as laws. In the words of the ordinance of 26 May 1356, "we have granted (*octroyé*) to those who have granted (*octroyé*) financial aid to us . . . as follows". The reciprocity of the concession – and hence, in effect, the equality of positions – was openly recognised in this clear and unequivocal statement. Nor is this all. In the course of the reunions of the estates, the dauphin and his lords not only recognised the utility and importance of the decisions taken by the estates, but were also concerned to sanction and underline the need for an accord between all three "estates" in order that the deliberations be confirmed.

It is extremely probable that this recognition did not derive from any clear concept of a constitutional nature, but rather from the contingent circumstances of this isolated occasion. The precedent, in fact, failed to take root. Neither the king and his court nor his successors conceived of, or were prepared to admit, the division of responsibility and power with representatives of the country, particularly as the latter had shown themselves overbearing, anything but conformist and not even conciliatory in the recent dramatic events. Nor did public opinion accept the enforced acquisition of the estates' authority in these tragic years as establishing a legal standard. It was an abnormal situation, a precedent not to be repeated. Nevertheless, in the estates of Tours of 1484, authoritative representatives of parliament did not fail to recall and try to utilise this precedent in their attempts to recreate more or less what had been the programme of Robert le Coq and Etienne Marcel in 1355–8.

In fact, after this critical period, even the power of taxation and financial functions returned to the "three estates" of the provinces and *bailliages* which had exercised them in the preceding decades. Indeed, the capacity for organic and constructive work in financial and administrative matters, as well as the true and sole image of representation and consent in assemblies, is to be found in these provincial and local estates, which we tend to describe nowadays by the general and more accurate name of *états particuliers*.

It should be noted that from the beginning of the second or third decade of the 14th century the assemblies began to take this new name of *trois estas* or *trois états*.[35] It is in this period, in fact, that the name of *parlement* (or *parlamentum*) – which in the previous century had been used to describe the great assemblies, alongside such words as *concilium* – assumed a different and precise significance. It was a specifically judicial organ, which had evolved from the complex of the old royal curia, and which was regulated at various times, especially in 1318–19, by royal ordinances.

4

Germany

Compared with Spanish or French assemblies of the post-Carolingian period, the German assemblies of the 13th and 14th centuries present few novelties. They were meetings of notables (*Notabelversammlungen*), and were called irregularly, without order or fixed rules. Although the meeting might be described as a *curia generalis* or a *curia solemnis*, these adjectives were merely chancellary usage. On the occasion of the accession of a sovereign or when decisions of a military character had to be reached the meetings tended to be larger; on such occasions they retain their original name of parliaments. The most frequent assemblies – which the princes attended with a sizable "armed company" – were not called at regular intervals, had no fixed seat, and served not so much for true purposes of government as for political and legal ends, such as the settlement of feudal lawsuits or cases directly interesting the greater feudal lords.

Some assemblies were general – of the empire; others were restricted to the barely unitary kingdom of Germany. One of the most solemn of the general assemblies must have been that held at

[35] At least from 1355 the royal *ordonnances* began to speak with a certain frequency of *bonnes Genz de notre royaume . . . de tous les trois estaz*, or of *trois estaz*, or of *tres estatus Prelatorum, Nobilium et Communitatum*, etc. They never mentioned an "estates general" or "provincial estates".

Mainz in 1235, when a peace settlement of great importance was promulgated which, according to the Emperor Frederick II, had been drawn up "with the counsel and assent of the prince electors, both ecclesiastical and lay". At another important assembly held at Nuremberg in 1274 in the presence of Rudolf of Habsburg and attended by magnates, notables, laymen and prelates, new pacts were proclaimed. The fact that appearance was compulsory was indirectly confirmed by the condemnation for contumacy of the absentees Otokar king of Bohemia and Henry duke of Bavaria, who were summoned to a later curia. It was further decreed – although it is not clear how or by whom – that henceforth documents were no longer to be drawn up in Latin, but in the vulgar tongue. A great crowd of people (*magnus populorum cetus*) apparently attended the next curia, but the envoys of the two princes – who did not recognise the validity of Rudolf's accession – spoke only to the magnates (*in medio magnatorum et principum*). Another solemn court was held at Augsburg in 1286 and was attended by Rudolf, the prince electors, both lay and ecclesiastical, dukes, counts, nobles and lords from various parts. The king asked that his two sons be raised from the rank of counts to that of dukes, and those present accepted. We note that – as in earlier centuries – the royal court and ecclesiastical council were sometimes held contemporaneously in the same place.

The counsels and deliberations of these German courts were frequently asked for and followed by the emperors. But they never included communal representatives. The assembly of Nuremberg of 1294 was attended by the king of Bohemia, prelates, bishops, abbots *praepositi*, dukes, marquises, counts, knights and barons – in all five thousand persons – but not a single representative of the cities. The evolution which in so many other countries was more or less completed by the inclusion of the third estate did not seem to develop fully in Germany. The court continued to be a court of princes and lords, a strictly feudal assembly, an assembly of territorial princes, who as sovereigns in their own territories (although with precise limits and duties) attended the meetings because they were directly concerned through their particular legal position. In consequence, it was an assembly lacking any organic representative functions. In a sense, the omission of the third estate was all the more curious as many flourishing cities were in existence, which asked for and obtained franchises in return for payment, supplied money and arms when requested, organised themselves into confederations and more than once were able to express their opinion on the gravest problems of the moment, even without participating in the courts.

In fact, even though they were absent from the courts, the representatives or envoys of the cities were present at more than one *colloquium*. These *colloquia* possessed the same formal and practical characteristics of the other courts, except for the fact that they were also attended by the envoys of the cities. Typical examples were the *colloquia* called in Italy by Frederick II in Terra di Lavoro, in Ravenna in 1231, Piacenza in 1236, Cremona in 1247; or the self-convoked *colloquia* of the Rhine Confederation in 1255 and later years, or of Cologne in 1259, or of Worms in 1269. Once again the terminology is by no means unequivocal and helps little in distinguishing the real nature of the great assemblies. The documentation on these assemblies would hardly justify us in ascribing deliberative powers to them, but would rather seem to indicate a summons to take note of royal decisions. Nevertheless, the constant use of two different terms, court and *colloquium* – in fact three, if one includes "parliament" – might be a hint of something substantial which as yet, given the present state of our knowledge, we are unable to demonstrate.

It was commonly believed by historians of the last century that parliamentary institutions arose in the Middle Ages because sovereigns found themselves constantly in need of financial aid, and were consequently obliged to summon the representative orders and come to terms with them. Nowadays this theory is less fashionable. It has rightly been pointed out that parliamentary assemblies were of more use to the privileged classes to defend their own interests than to the sovereign to break them.[36] In fact one cannot

[36] E. Lousse ("La formation des états dans la société européenne du moyen âge et l'apparition des assemblées d'état. Questions de faits et de méthodes", *BICHS*, V, 1933, p. 250 ff.) argues extremely plausibly that votes on taxation were not necessarily related to the origins of parliamentary assemblies, and that indeed it was necessary for such assemblies already to possess a certain consistency to be able to vote taxes. Almost always, the assemblies predated the earliest subsidies. Hence, once the principle "no taxation without redress of grievances" had been established, the concession of subsidies was the most effective defensive weapon and thus the main attribute of parliaments.

accept this explanation of the origins of parliament, as it is too simplified and dogmatic, too unilateral and restricted to explain so complex and natural a phenomenon. Nevertheless, however inadequate, the explanation is not wholly to be rejected, as it does reflect at least one aspect of the origins of the assemblies. It is extremely probable that the late development of representative institutions in the kingdom of Germany, or their failure to develop, was due, at least in part, to the position of superiority and independence – including financial independence – of the emperor, who had more ways of raising money (outside his kingdom as well) than any other sovereign of his time.

The "general curia", and perhaps also the *colloquia,* of Germany in the 13th century were thus much more similar to the great assemblies of the preceding centuries than to the contemporary *colloquia* or parliaments and *cortes* of England, Spain, and the kingdom of Sicily. Princes, electors, lay and ecclesiastic lords, no less powerful in the 13th century than in the past, formed a compact body which on more than one occasion successfully thwarted the ambitions of various emperors for absolute power. But this struggle was not transformed into constitutional terms, nor did it give life to an organ consisting of and representing both the particular and the general interests. Such a development only came much later. In the 13th-century struggle, both sides maintained their own positions or, if forced temporarily to give way, sought to recover lost ground.

The adoption of a term different from the normal one to indicate assemblies attended by the cities, and the extremely limited number of the cities, would seem to show that their regular participation in the direction of state affairs – even if limited to consultative functions – was not yet even conceived of. This needs to be emphasised, even if it seems to be immediately contradicted by a decision of the "solemn curia" held at Worms on 1 May 1231 and ratified by the emperor.[37] According to this well-known constitution (*sententia de iure statuum terrae*), the princes were ordered not to introduce legislative innovations or initiate extraordinary taxation without first consulting and obtaining the consent of the most representa-

[37] According to H. Mitteis, the concessions of 1220 and 1231 were not a definite renunciation of his authority by Frederick II, but temporary concessions dictated by contingent circumstances.

tive elements (*meliores et maiores terrae*) of their respective populations.

A possible explanation of this apparent contradiction is that the decision approved at Worms applied only within territories of various cities and lands dependent on the emperor, but not to the actual empire, not to the territories of the German princes, whether or not they were electors, who were subject to the king-emperor. Within the territories of the German princes, the emperor's rights were so limited as to be virtually non-existent. If they expanded later, this was through the consent of the territorial princes themselves or through the decision of the curia of the empire, which from 1495 assumed more definite characteristics and its definitive German name of *Reichstag*.

5

Italy

a. Sicily

As in other states of Western Europe, the assemblies or courts acquired a certain importance and frequency in the kingdom of Sicily also in the 13th century. Some of these assemblies were undoubtedly of political character, as a result of the antagonism between the popes and the Swabians and subsequently of the discreditable policy of Charles of Anjou towards his subjects.

Besides the general courts of the kingdom, we need to note the provincial assemblies which Frederick II planned, giving them the same name of curias: they were his invention, based on his initiative. Enlightened, as he said, by the "solemn colloquy" held previously at Lentini, he promulgated a constitution at Messina in 1234 to correct and impede abuses by his officials or by others in their favour. Special solemn or general courts were to be held twice a year (at the beginning of May and November) in five localities of the kingdom, corresponding to each of the great territorial circumscriptions: at Piazza for Sicily; Cosenza for Calabria; Gravina for Puglia and Basilicata; Salerno for the Principato, Terra di Lavoro and Molise; Sulmona for the Abruzzi. These assemblies were to be presided over by special royal representatives, and attended by the counts and barons, ecclesiastical dignitaries and two or four envoys "from the more important towns", who were to be honest, of good fame and non partisan (*qui non sint de parte*). Any ecclesiastic or layman was to feel free to state his grievance concerning injustices or abuses of the *giustizieri* (high judicial and administrative officials) or their dependants, or even of persons outside the administration. Once the grievances had been heard, the royal representative, together with two prelates and two of the most qualified laymen, was to carry out an enquiry and then refer the results of the enquiry and recommended measures to the king.

This control over the actions of officials, based on complaints and grievances expressed directly by the injured parties, was aimed at guaranteeing the correct observance of justice and an honest administration. This new institution was more useful than the former Byzantine "syndicate" set up to check dishonesty, as it was quicker and more directly in touch with the public. But it was also of greater importance and significance because it was not an internal act of the administration, but represented and created the right of subjects to be governed according to justice and to claim redress of abuses and errors.

It was the king's function and duty to redress injustices and abuses, and as we shall see the sovereigns held special assemblies for this purpose (the first, perhaps, to bear the name of parliament). In France, St Louis had decreed that three general assemblies a year be held to administer justice and suppress the abuses and mis-government of the *baillis* which had emerged in the so-called grand inquest of 1247–8. In England, the famous Provisions of Oxford of 1258 also demanded three parliaments a year and other appropriate measures for the same purpose. But even if we leave aside these analogies, the provincial curias decreed by Frederick II cannot but be considered as extremely similar, at least from the structural point of view, to the courts or *cortes* elsewhere which met for different purposes. However, one needs to note that these Sicilian courts probably remained on paper, because of the exceptional political circumstances which kept the emperor far from Sicily and engaged on other matters, and perhaps also because of defects in their planning.[38]

The assemblies of the kingdom of Sicily in the 13th century, both as institutions and in their structure, were only the continuation of those of the preceding period. They were, however, more frequent, and were no longer bound up with dynastic events, as had been almost all those of the Norman period. They served the interests of the country, or at all events of its government and administration, rather than the person of the sovereign. Thus they were, or tended to become, larger and more national.

The first of these assemblies was held in 1208 at San Germano (Cassino) in order to provide for and aid Frederick (who was still a minor) in the work of pacification carried out by Pope Innocent III as tutor to the young sovereign. The pope came in person to this "general curia" and issued important measures with "many of the prelates and magnates of the kingdom". A statement by the anonymous chronicler of Monte Cassino that envoys of the cities took part together with the lay and ecclesiastical lords remains unproven, for it is not confirmed by any other source. Nevertheless it is not contradicted by a later document which stated that in May 1225 Frederick convoked prelates, magnates and "other faithful" to a solemn colloquium.

The account of another equally solemn colloquium held at Melfi on 12 June 1231 describes how a tax of a twelfth on the incomes of domanial lands was decided upon by the king on the basis of the counsel and corresponding vote of the prelates, counts, lords and *multorum civium regni*. Did this refer to "many citizens" or to "citizens of many cities"? If the latter, was it pure coincidence, or the result of the decision adopted at the curia of Worms on 1 May of the same year which, as we have seen, ordered the *domini terrae* not to modify the laws or system of taxation except in agreement with the *maiores et meliores*? It does not seem very likely, as Frederick II wanted to

[38] A 15th century Neapolitan jurist, M. De Afflictis (*In utriusque Siciliae, Neapolisque sanctiones et constitutiones novissima praelectio*, Venice, 1606, f. 136 v.) lamented the fact, asking why so useful a measure should not have been followed up (*et minor, quare tam bonus ordo non servatur*). But, in fact, Charles of Anjou may have had this precedent in mind when he took the initiative in holding "general parliaments" to redress grievances and abuses.

be lord of everyone and everything in the kingdom of Sicily; in any case, there were no *domini terrae* under him in the kingdom – there was only the *dominus* himself, the king-emperor.

The chronicler Riccardo di San Germano stated that the cities and castles were invited to send two of their *meliores* to the assembly of Foggia in September 1232. The general colloquium of Foggia of April 1240 was also attended by envoys of the castles and cities subject to feudal law: forty-seven cities were invited to send their nuncios. Similar examples of participation by the cities are to be found in the assemblies of Foggia of 1258 and 1265.

There were many more assemblies in this period, but the convocation of the *meliores terrae* was neither a constant nor a normal event. The Swabian kings used them to give publicity to their judicial or legislative measures, relying on them to ensure, or maintain, the favour of the people. It is impossible to say more than this, given Frederick II's enlightened but despotic character: it is difficult to imagine that he intended to admit his subjects to an active participation in the administration of power, or to give executive authority in the kingdom of Sicily to the regulations decreed in the kingdom of Germany by the constitution of Worms.

The typical function of the Sicilian assemblies of the Swabian period was – in the words of the summons of 1240 – to permit the subjects to "contemplate the majesty and serenity of the sovereign and hear his word". Nevertheless, more than once the participants did not limit themselves to witnessing the publication of judicial decisions or the promulgation of legislative measures. As far as one can deduce from other writs of summons, they decided measures of a general nature together with the king. This was certainly the case at the assembly of 1208 (when Frederick was still a minor), at the colloquium of Foggia of 1225, and at the solemn curia of Melfi of 1231 when the tax on the income of domanial lands was fixed "by the counsel of the prelates, counts, barons and many citizens".

What remains obscure about the activity of these assemblies and their members was their capacity to judge, or at least to listen to, petitions against violations of the laws and customs and abuses of power in general by royal ministers and officials. On the occasion of the Foggia colloquium of May 1225 Frederick had invited all the members to put in writing the "grievances or complaints" of which they were aware. In 1234 he had decided and decreed the method by which the general curias would be relieved of this burden; but we do not know whether or not he was successful.

These facts are not sufficient to allow us to conclude that these assemblies displayed any initiative, or that they corresponded to the concept of a parliamentary institution as we have defined it. In fact we are of the opinion that, despite their composition and solemnity, these assemblies merely constituted pre-parliaments, limited episodes, rather than real collective bodies with their part in the structure of the state.

However, there remained the political fact that the clergy, nobility and representatives of the cities and towns were convoked frequently, and that in time this became almost normal even if the actual organisation changed. This state of affairs certainly prepared the grounds for a transformation – as always, by a voluntary act of the sovereign – into an established custom, an obligation. But the new fact, the recognition of this practice did not come either from the king or from the assembly. It came from the overlord of the kingdom, Pope Clement IV. On hearing of the unjust domination of Charles of Anjou (1266–85), who at first had seemed a liberator to some, Clement IV repeatedly appealed to him not to exact illegal taxes but to lay his financial needs before the "prelates, barons and community" in order to obtain their counsel and aid in his difficulties and regulate his affairs with their consent.

The invitation – or rather warning – of the pope was only accepted in small part. Charles preferred to follow French customs rather than papal exhortations and the precedents of the Swabian period. He created a general *curia* of *giustizieri* and other officials to do justice, by summary procedure, to the wrongs denounced by subjects, to ask them for an account of what they had exacted for the treasury, and to "treat of what he had decreed" – a clear indication that these assemblies, which he called parliaments, were of an exclusively administrative, bureaucratic and fiscal nature. Only after the outbreak of the Vespers did his son, the prince of Salerno, lieutenant of the kingdom, decide, with unexpected obedience, to call a general parliament of the region of San Martino in Calabria Citeriore. The assembly, which met in 1283, and was attended by prelates, nobles and envoys of the cities and towns, aimed at and partially succeeded in giving a new and more equitable order to the affairs of the country. Forty-seven legal decrees were approved, while the assembly proclaimed a return to the good customs of the time of William II; an embassy was sent to the pope, begging him to define the new customs, but only a vague record of this survives. In fact, this completion of the decrees and laws by the pope only occurred in 1285 when an *Edictalis Provisio ac Constitutio* of Honorius IV defined the limits of royal authority in relation to the subjects in its most important points, especially in matters of taxation.

We know nothing about another general parliament summoned to Foggia on St Martin's day 1284, and it was probably never held. The writ of summons to the general parliament of Naples of 1289 is of particular interest as it contained a clear reference to the principle of representation. In the writ, the sovereign stated that by legal fiction (*de interpretazione benigna*), it was as if the whole community were present through the presence of the *maiores et meliores*; the writ even referred to the election of representatives (*pari voto communiter eligendi*).

Another extremely large and solemn "parliament" was held by Charles Martel, vicar of the kingdom, at Eboli in September 1290, which was attended by a considerable number of dignitaries, and even by the papal legate, as well as by the prelates and barons of almost all the provinces of the kingdom. The assembly lasted for five days, while its members examined the most important political, financial and military questions. Various important *capitula et statuta super regimine regni* resulted from this meeting.[39]

It is possible that another parliament was held (in August 1296?) by Charles II on his return to the Regno after a long absence. We know that another "public parliament" held at Naples at the end of 1297 or the beginning of January 1298 agreed without difficulty to give Prince Robert, vicar of the kingdom, a subsidy for an expedition against the "Sicilian rebels", equivalent to the sum total of an annuity of the *colletta* or general aid.

[39] Clause 14 of the *capitula – Demum ut ordinatio premissa regulata non claudicat* – laid it down that parliament meet twice a year in March and September in order to look after the state of the kingdom and all needs created by the war (*disponimus parlamentum ac de statu regni et guerre conditionibus ordinare*); cf. E. Gentile, "Parlamenti generali nel regno di Napoli nel periodo angioino", *Studi in onore di* R. *Filangieri,* Naples, vol. I (1959). It is clear that these were not meant to be judicial assemblies; but there is no evidence that such paper dispositions were ever put into practice.

Thus by the end of this century the Angevins, learning more from their Sicilian experience than from papal admonitions, did not ignore the possibilities inherent in parliamentary convocations. Indeed they took care, especially during the absence of Charles II and the minority of Charles Martel, not to repeat the gravest excesses of which they had previously been accused, and sought to govern legally and so preserve the loyalty of the population.

The reigns in Sicily of Peter I of Aragon (1282–5) and his son Frederick II (1296–1337) were marked by a distinct increase in the frequency of convocations of parliamentary assemblies and by the direct, immediate and close contact of these assemblies with the sovereign. An anonymous chronicler of a later period maintained that the accession of the king of Aragon to the kingdom of Sicily had in fact been preceded by an invitation sent him by Sicilians meeting in a parliament at Palermo in August 1282. Whatever the reliability of this chronicler, it seems certain that Peter of Aragon held a general reunion at Palermo soon after his arrival, which was also attended by the "better men" (*millors*, according to the Catalan chronicle) of the cities and villages; its purpose was to announce his possession of the kingdom and to confirm the laws and customs of the times of good King William. All those present immediately swore an oath of fealty; subsequently, the communes which were not represented at the reunion swore an oath through special envoys (*sindici*).

A general *colloquium* was also held at Catania in November 1282, when the *sindici*, "of their good and spontaneous will", offered the king a subsidy for the war, while the king decreed the abolition of the *colletta* and the *marineria* tax; another colloquium met at Messina in April 1283 shortly before the departure of King Peter. However, these meetings are insufficient to prove that regular periodic convocations of parliament began in Sicily with this reign. The next parliamentary assembly we know about was held on the occasion of the coronation of King James in February 1286, when the new king issued various important constitutions in 23 *capitoli*, inspired in part by Pope Honorius IV's bull of 1285 against the arbitrary government of the Angevins. We can deduce that another general colloquium was held in 1288, as King James published various legal decrees in that year, for the most part rendering justice to the complaints laid before him by representatives of the villages of the region on the hither side of the Salso river. It seems probable that other later assemblies, held in King James's absence by his representative, the Infante Frederick, were also not general assemblies but limited to one or the other part of the island, which was divided into two circumscriptions by the Salso river.

As is well known, when King James failed to maintain his promises, he gave way to papal pressure and renounced his rights over the island. But with the general consent of the kingdom, on the request of the "counts, barons and *syndici*" of Sicily, these rights were taken over by his brother Frederick, who adopted the royal title and responsibility for the war against the Angevins.

The constitutions announced by Frederick of Aragon in the general colloquium held on the occasion of his coronation in 1296 were not drawn up by this parliament, but were merely promulgated by it. Nevertheless with these constitutions or *capitoli* the young sovereign swore not to abandon the country, even if offered another kingdom, nor to make alliances, war or peace without the consent of the Sicilians. He confirmed the practices, privileges and liberties conceded by Frederick II of Swabia, Manfred and the first kings of the house of Aragon.[40] He decreed that a general curia be held every year on All Saints' day, and that the counts, barons and suitable and adequate representatives (*syndici*) of the *università* (cities and villages) be called. This annual assembly was to be called to look after the interests of the king, the island and its inhabitants; to punish abuses and errors by the *giustizieri*, judges and notaries denounced by the representatives; to control the actions of royal officials; to order and decree laws and regulations together with the king, which the latter would then observe faithfully, "it being most just that the king be bound to observe his own laws"; to proceed to the nomination of twelve nobles and "prudent men" by the counts, nobles, barons and *sindici*, who were to judge criminal cases against feudatories and vassals. Besides these constitutions, further ones were decreed by Frederick II in the general colloquium of Piazza on 20 October 1296, and were confirmed at Messina in the following

[40] It may be that the provincial parliaments were related in their origins to more ancient assemblies and to traditions common to the various territories of the Italic kingdom-empire.

month. They included a decree prohibiting the forced eviction of people who owed the *colletta*, and other measures which attempted to inhibit feudal abuses, etc.

These two sets of constitutions seem to me sufficient to support the conclusion that a new legal regime was about to arise, or had in fact arisen. The continuous demonstrations of their attachment to the fortunes of their country, and the political initiatives demonstrated on so many occasions by the aristocracy and cities and villages of Sicily, guaranteed and proved that the new order reflected a deeply felt need, a stage of evolution in the political life of the island in which the barons, clergy and cities now participated actively together with their king.

b. The States of the Church

We have already seen that the principle that what touches all must be approved by all began to circulate in the 13th century. Not surprisingly, some application of the same criterion of justice and popular sovereignty was to be found in the states of the church, where a succession of active popes had revived the fame of the former capital of the Roman world.

Unfortunately our documentation is not adequate to provide precise details about the various colloquies, *tractatus* or *parlamenta* which were held either for the whole territory of the papal states, or for specific provinces, or even parts of provinces in this period. We know even less about the origins or prototypes of such meetings.

One of the first of these great assemblies was that called by Innocent III in 1200. Suitable representatives (*responsales idonei*) of the communes of the Marches were summoned in order to treat of the "settlement of peace" and the "defence of the land" and to swear an oath of fealty: the pope's decisions were adopted "after a diligent meeting", in which the counsel of these procurators was heard. Another important "solemn curia" was held at Viterbo in 1207, attended by the clergy, aristocracy and communal representatives of the March of Ancona, the duchy of Spoleto and Tuscia; those present swore fealty to the pope, while the latter examined and in part accepted their "complaints and petitions", besides promulgating various statutes to maintain the public peace and tranquillity of the country. Other meetings of the same kind were clearly aimed at re-establishing contact in the intermittent phases of peace in the midst of the continuous rebellions and civil wars of the period: the repetition of the oaths of fealty are symptomatic. Such meetings were held by Honorius III in 1220 at Orvieto to mark the return of the duchy of Spoleto "to the hands of the apostolic see"; in 1270 and 1271 at Viterbo, where Clement IV, threatened by the advance of Manfred's troops, convoked the envoys of the cities of such provinces as remained faithful to him (the Patrimony, Tuscia and the duchy of Spoleto) for "counsel and to treat"; in 1279 at Viterbo to confirm renewed pontifical sovereignty over the cities of the Romagna and recognition of this sovereignty by Rudolf of Habsburg; and finally in 1296 under Boniface VIII to study how to re-establish peace once more in the Romagna.

Although the documentary evidence of these assemblies is extremely scanty, there can be no doubt that they were of an exceptional nature and of little importance in the legal and political structure of the states. In the same period, and particularly in the second half of the century, provincial parliaments were convoked province by province by the pontifical legates and rectors. These assemblies were usually summoned for the appointment of new rectors, the publication of constitutions, to raise an army – the most direct link with earlier assemblies, also called *parlamenta* – and to request financial contributions. The duty of attendance at such parliaments convoked by the provincial legate, rector or other pontifical officials repeated and confirmed the obligation for members of the feudal hierarchy to participate in the earlier type of parliament mentioned above. This quality of obligation for the most part continued in the provincial assemblies of the following century, even when the assemblies had become so frequent, normal and functional as almost to assume the character of an organ of provincial government.

These were clearly not parliamentary institutions as we defined them earlier, nor did the later assemblies acquire parliamentary characteristics. Nevertheless, at least in some provinces, these extremely limited assemblies acquired certain fixed characteristics and so tended to become sufficiently stable and definitive to distinguish themselves from those of the preceding centuries.[41] They

[41] The stability and permanency of assemblies does not, of course, wholly meet our

were and remained *parlements manqués*. They failed to become purely administrative organs in the full sense we have given to the term. But they possessed by no means negligible functions: they legalised the actions of the provincial rectors (or corresponding magistrates); they formed an executive body to carry out orders received from the pontifical representatives; and they possessed consultative capacities in a broad sense. They were by no means useless or without importance or responsibility.

c. Friuli

The first signs of life of a parliament in Friuli are to be found in the 13th century, but in the course of the century the assembly rapidly acquired clear outlines and great authority.

In 1077, the county of Friuli had been recognised by the Emperor Henry IV as the possession of his "faithful" patriarch Sigeard. From then until 1420 Friuli formed part of the patriarchate of Aquileia. Nevertheless, it always preserved a distinct physiognomy and organisation among the patriarchal possessions. The period was characterised by continual struggles, wars with neighbouring states, and a succession of weak prelates. Patriarchal authority had so declined that the help and collaboration of the subjects was essential for survival. Such a situation favoured the rise and early development of a parliamentary institution.

In searching for the origins of the Friuli parliament, its leading historian, P. S. Leicht, refuted the theory that it was derived from

---

criteria for parliamentary institutions. Nevertheless, by giving the assemblies legal recognition, on a formal level at least, they tended to assimilate the assemblies to parliaments. The proof of this is to be found in a formulary drawn up in 1298, which numbered among the rights of the papal curia that of "calling a colloquium and ordering the publication and observances of all that shall be agreed upon relating to the regulation of the state". Official recognition of these assemblies had reached the point that the formulary contained specimens of the writs to the assemblies: those sent to the bishops, abbots and other prelates ordered them to attend under pain of spiritual sanctions, which, in the case of the abbots, could even arrive at excommunication; those to the cities ordered them, in accordance with their oath of fealty and under threat of a fine of a hundred marks of silver, to send their mayor, an orator "legitimately elected, with four ambassadors chosen from the better men of the land, to hear and to do what shall be treated, ordered and decided upon"; those to the smaller centres ordered them to send the mayor or castellan, an ambassador and two envoys. Cf. P. Fabre, "Un registre cameral du cardinal Albornoz en 1364. Documents pour servir à l'histoire du patrimonium Beati Petri in Tuscia au XIVe siècle", *Ecole française de Rome. Mélanges d'archéologie et d'histoire,* VII, 1888, p. 133 ff.

the ancient Lombard ducal assemblies, or from the old *curia vassallorum*, a feudal organ with judicial powers. In Leicht's words,[42] "the curia of the vassals of Aquileia possessed a life of its own, wholly independent of parliament, to the extent that a judgement of the latter could be appealed against in the former. The presence of the vassals in the feudal curia was obligatory, while there is no record of any specific obligation of participation in parliament, except for the general obligation of all subjects to obey the summons of the prince." The members of parliament, he added, paid for themselves, while those of the curia attended at the prince's expense. Leicht also rejected the alternative thesis that the Friuli parliament derived from the council of the patriarch's court. In the first place, he stated, a council of feudal vassals (*fideles*), such as is presumed underlie the origins of this parliament, could not, by its very nature, have imposed compulsory decisions on the country; we can see, on the other hand, that the Friuli parliament, according to the earliest accounts which have survived, possessed certain notable constitutional characteristics, which rendered its deliberations binding, whether they concerned taxes or legislative measures. For example, in 1228 the patriarch Bertoldo described the requisition of workers and wagons as made by the counsel of "the prelates, vassals, *ministeriales*[43] and citizens". Again, in 1231, certain restrictions were abolished by the patriarch with the consensus of the cathedral chapter of Aquileia, the prelates, freemen and *ministeriales*. The second objection, according to Leicht, was that the *fideles* of the court, the "*ministeriales*" who assisted the patriarch in the most important affairs of state, remained in office even after parliament had been definitely constituted, whereas "if parliament's roots were to be found in this gathering of nobles at court, once it had been constituted, it would have arrogated to itself the functions which in former times had belonged to the court". Given these premises, it is not surprising that Leicht arrived at the conclusion that the most important of the various factors which determined the initial

[42] P. S. Leicht, *Parlamento friulano*, vol. I (1228–1420), pt. 1, Bologna, 1917 (R. Accademia dei Lincei. Commisssione per la pubblicazione degli atti delle assemblee costituzionali italiane, ser. 1, sez. 6); *idem*, "Il parlamento della patria del Friuli – Sua origine costituzione e legislazione (1231–1420)", *Atti dell'Accademia di Scienze Lettere e Arti di Udine*, X–XI, 1903.

[43] The *ministeriales* were small nobility holding office.

development of parliament was – for Friuli as for all the assemblies of this period – the need for the patriarch and the princes and leading lords of the province to reach agreement in order to impose taxes and apportion the military levy.

However, at least one episode, which Leicht has noted, offers the possibility of a broader interpretation, in the sense of an extension of the range of arguments normally discussed in consultations between patriarch and subjects. This episode took place in 1260, when the patriarch Gregorio of Montelongo called the prelates, cities and feudal lords for counsel, before restoring their lands to certain strong supporters of Frederick II, the counts of Prata.

Despite my great respect for so learned an authority as Leicht, I cannot but disagree with his views which clearly do not accord with my general interpretation of the birth of parliamentary institutions as a transformation, but even more a derivation from the consultative state assemblies of the post-Carolingian epoch. There seem to me to be certain weaknesses in Leicht's arguments. In the first place the binding nature of the decision of the two assemblies of 1228 and 1231 is not at all certain: all that emerged from these assemblies was a counsel to the patriarch or agreement with his decision. Secondly, there was and is no logical or legal necessity that the convocation of a parliamentary assembly, possibly only as an occasional or momentary enlargement of the sovereign's council, should lead to the extinction of that council. Indeed, what should have resulted was a consolidation of the old institution, a true constitutional evolution. In the third place, the Friuli assembly was asked to express agreement to financial impositions for the first time only in 1287.[44] Finally, requests for aids or subsidies, or in general for financial contributions, could have been made without recourse to collective summons or special assemblies or the reunion of such assemblies.[45]

There can be no question of the obscurity surrounding the origins

[44] However, according to a document of 1282 (Leicht, *Parlamento friulano*, vol. 2 (1420–50), pt. 1, Bologna, 1956, n. 1, p. CI), the "consent and counsel of nobles and others" over "statutes relating to the state of the land" was regarded as regular practice since the time of the patriarchs Bertoldo and Gregorio; such meetings were known "by public voice and fame".

[45] As for the expenses of those who attended the sessions, it is clear that the feudatories and ecclesiastics paid for themselves, while the city representatives were indemnified by their respective communes. Friuli did not differ in this from other states.

and the early signs of life of the Friuli parliament. It is difficult to make positive affirmations, given the lack of documentation. This is especially the case if one does not belong to the school which celebrates the birth of a parliament in a given country every time a document states that members of the aristocracy and town representatives were called to court by the sovereign.

A true parliament, in fact, did not come into being in Friuli until somewhat later (as we shall see shortly), and then most probably it only emerged as the result of conditions generated by the bitter political struggles, by the part played by the Friuli cities, and by the lack of energy of more than one patriarch. The contemporary chronicler, Canon Giuliano, relates that in 1283 the patriarch Raimondo della Torre, fighting against Venice for the dominion of Trieste, convoked prelates, freemen, "ministerials" and communes.[46] A commission of twenty-four people – six for each of the groups – was charged to discuss the question with power to make effective decisions. Nor was this an isolated event. An important detail, which the same chronicler of Cividale narrates, is that in 1287 the patriarch turned to the same assembly for a subsidy. It was one of those events which created a precedent; thenceforward innumerable examples are to be found. Finally, a decisive recognition of the new sharing of sovereignty is offered by the declaration apparently made in 1303 by the patriarch Ottobono de' Razzi in a letter to the allied cities of Padua and Treviso: all decisions about peace were referred to the parliamentary assembly or to such "wise men" (*sapienti*) as the assembly might wish to appoint. In 1310 Henry VII had asked for honours and help from the patriarch of Aquileia as the temporal lord of the state: the patriarch conceded the request only after he had discussed the matter with his vassals (*vassallis francis et danesmanis*) and with the ambassadors of the communities. It was in this period that the assembly began to work regularly, attended by members of the three privileged classes and by envoys of the cities of Aquileia, Udine, Cividale and Gemona.

With these events we have moved somewhat beyond our chronological limits. But it was necessary in order to offer a really significant

[46] The previous year the cathedral chapter of the church of Aquileia had complained to the patriarch about certain legislative measures he had adopted without listening to the "counsel of the nobles and others".

and explicit date for the transformation of the Friuli assembly from a consultative organ of the patriarch within the administration of the county (*colloquium domini patriarchae, Ecclesiae Aquileiensis*, as the first documents state) into a deliberative and representative organ (*colloquium generale terrae Forjulii* or *totius patriae*). It was deliberative because it was representative; in fact, in describing the assembly the documents speak figuratively of the "reunited Friulani" or of the Friulan people. Naturally these dates and isolated facts are merely indicative of a changing situation. Consequently we would not place great emphasis on the fact that the word *parlamentum* is to be found for the first time in a document of 29 April 1346.

It might be observed that these, like many other historical events, are merely the external manifestations of pre-existing situations, even though they were not easily recognised as such; that they represented the fortuitous but inevitable and expected breakdown of a merely apparent equilibrium; that they constituted a natural phenomenon which contemporaries lived through and felt before they realised or understood them. Once the patriarch had begun to listen to, and to follow the point of view not only of his personal counsellors, but of the most important people in the country and the cities, it was natural that he should continue such general consultations, and extend them to more important and serious discussions, for instance about subsidies. It was equally natural that the representatives who were consulted should profit from these changes in situation, and become more authoritative and influential to the point of becoming the true inspirers and moderators of the patriarch's policy. This development from an ordinary consultative organ convoking the feudal lords and vassals – a normal and habitual procedure for military questions – into a parliamentary institution, which brought together other politically influential elements for political and administrative purposes of good government, was slow and perhaps not clearly realised by contemporaries. Nevertheless it undoubtedly occurred, even if the two institutions were substantially and fundamentally different.

d. The Lands of Savoy

Given their representative function, parliamentary institutions only tended to arise in states which were so large or encumbered with such difficult communications as to hinder or discourage recourse to direct consultation of the people, that is of those persons and classes who took an active part in political life. The representative nature of parliaments is a direct consequence of this geographical fact and is exemplified in another small outlying Italian state, the Piedmontese-Savoyard possessions of the counts of Savoy, divided into two separate parts by the Alps. Unfortunately, little documentation exists about such institutions in the 13th century. The first manifestation of life traditionally claimed for the future parliament of the *patria cismontana* only dates back to 1286. In that year Aimone di Boczosel, general vicar of the count of Savoy Amadeus V, who lived in Savoy on the other side of the Alps, was charged by his lord with sending a circular letter of summons to the "nobles, citizens and bourgeois" of Piedmont inviting them to meet together to swear an oath of fealty and homage to Amadeus who, following arbitration, had acquired the dominion of the territory.

The reunion, which lacked an official denomination, was held on 24 May in the open in a meadow near Giaveno, in the presence of forty-five castellans, nobles and "ambassadors" of the lands of Piedmont, Val Susa, Turin and Moncalieri. Two letters were read – of Ludovico of Savoy and Guia of Burgundy, widow of Tomaso III of Savoy – calling for obedience to Amadeus; those present listened and promised fealty to their new lord. The notarial account which has survived would seem to attribute to the meeting "the character, hardly befitting a parliament, of a reunion in which those present did not intervene and were only asked to listen to the two letters, memorize the mandate contained in them and go home".[47] We know little or nothing of other reunions held in 1297, 1298 and 1299, except that the second was a *colloquium* with the "ambassadors" of Piedmont about the war with the dauphin of France and that similar "ambassadors" participated in all the reunions.

Given these bare facts, one hardly needs to be very critical to reject the thesis – more than a century old – that a Cismontane Savoyard parliament existed in the 13th century. Indeed, to accept this hypothesis we should be obliged to describe all the various

[47] A. Tallone, *Parlamento sabaudo,* t. 1, pt. 1, *Patria cismontana,* vol. I (1286–1385), Bologna, 1928 (R. Acc. Lincei. Commissione per la publicazione degli atti delle assemblee costituzionali italiane, ser. 1, sez. 5) p. CXVII.

assemblies of the post-Carolingian epoch as parliaments, because the mention of the presence of municipal "ambassadors" (in this case balanced, so to say, by the absence of the clergy) is hardly adequate to differentiate the Cismontane assemblies from any others. In fact, the most recent and serious historian of the Piedmontese parliament, Armando Tallone, was virtually forced to recognise this, however much he endeavoured to persuade himself to the contrary. He did not pretend that a meeting held nowadays and described in no more than the words used by the notary in 1286 would justify the assumption that other speeches or other arguments than those contained in the memorandum were made or discussed. However, he insinuated that "the act should not be considered as a verbal account of the meeting. It should be interpreted simply from the point of view of the purpose for which it was probably drawn up, because the notary's intention was to take down not everything that happened, but only the reading of the mandates, which was the main concern of the official representative of the count. But that could not have been the only purpose of the reunion."[48]

Tallone also based his argument on a rather dubious analogy of the failure to convoke a new assembly in similar circumstances in 1294, when a partial redistribution of the Cismontane territories took place between Amadeus V and his nephew Philip IV. As in 1286, so in 1294 Amadeus's new position had been notified by means of circular letters. It was useless to convoke an assembly in 1294, because the matter to be discussed had already been communicated singly to the participants. Hence, in 1286 "it must have taken place for other reasons, such as the usual (?) debate, if not about subsidies, about requesting counsel or other matters". Tallone was aware of the objection that the 1286 reunion occurred by order of Amadeus, whereas the circular letter of the same year came from Ludovico. But, he added, "there always remains the substantial fact that the communes which were convoked were being informed of an event of which they were already officially aware, and of a command which they had already officially received". Finally, he replied to the criticism that holding the meeting in the open was hardly appropriate for a true assembly with orators, that "it is not possible that Aimone di Boczosel did not add something else in the

[48] *Ibid.*, p. CXLIX.

name of his lord, and that none of the most notable persons present replied".

This is all very suggestive, but far from persuasive. We can leave aside the purely secondary question of whether the count's vicar and those present could or could not have exchanged ideas on different topics from those recorded in the reunion held in the open air on 24 May 1286. It was possible, as it was also possible that the conversation turned around arguments which were hardly parliamentary and not at all of an official character: it was already quite an achievement to collect the participants together in order to read the two messages to them, draw up the account, call them one by one to swear the oath of fealty, and so on. If the colloquium had dealt with some other important matter there can be little doubt that some information would have survived either in the notarial document or in some other source. The observation that the meeting could not have been purely for the officially documented purpose, because that could have been achieved without a meeting, is of no real force, and contradicts the consideration noted by Tallone himself that the letters read to the assembly were not sent by the person who had summoned the convocation. We have already pointed out numerous examples of how sovereigns were accustomed to convoke the largest possible number of subjects in an assembly when they gained their throne and possessions so as to exact an oath of fealty from them. It was more than natural that Amadeus V should have acted in this manner: the convocation is easily explained, even without unconvincing interpretations.

Apart from any other consideration, even if we accepted Tallone's interpretation, we should still be moving within the framework of an assembly of the type which – as we have seen – very generally constituted the starting point of parliamentary institutions, but which lacked the formal and substantial characteristics of real parliamentary assemblies: it was not the assembly which swore fealty, but only the individual members, each on his own account.

We have similar doubts and reservations about Tallone's attribution of the title "parliament" to various other assemblies of the 12th and 13th centuries in the transalpine Savoyard territories.

With his usual diligence, Tallone collected evidence – for the most part taken from French chroniclers of the 15th century, such as Cabaret, Du Pin and Servion – of various and variously composed assemblies which, beginning in 1148, met of their own initiative without previous official convocation, and which usually counselled their bachelor or widower princes to marry or remarry, or – on rare occasions – recognised the new sovereign and swore fealty and homage. The most interesting point is that these chroniclers (not so much Cabaret as his continuators) spoke constantly and in the most natural way of reunions of the "three estates" (*III Estas, Troys Estas*). If this expression had been found in documents of the 13th century, it would have anticipated the description by two or three centuries. The only contemporary document (1150) spoke of *consilium cum suis*. Peter II's preamble to his statute of 1265–6 referred to the "will and consent of the nobles and non-nobles" of Savoy and Burgundy, but this is too vague and imprecise to allow one to think of anything but a mass gathering, which acclaimed without discussing or perhaps even knowing the substance of the twenty-nine articles which Peter was promulgating. The members of the gathering were acting in a blind manner, as always in such circumstances, according to the ancient tradition of the *acclamatio*, the political and legal substitute for true and free consent. The expressions of the chroniclers are in fact gratuitous, irresponsible and unreliable. Their references do not help us to discover either the momentum or the genesis of representative assemblies in the Savoyard state on either side of the Alps. In fact, the most that such chronicles can tell us is that, according to the point of view of their authors, the Savoyard parliamentary assemblies grew out of gatherings of the court council of prelates and nobles (*prelas e barons*) and that these meetings took the initiative in speaking to the princes, seeking to persuade them to marry, in true or imaginary assemblies of the three estates, or more probably merely by assent.

I do not believe that the assemblies of the Savoyard "estates" had any direct link with the meetings described – or imagined – by the chroniclers as existing before the 14th century. By the time these chroniclers were writing, in the 15th century, French characteristics were tending to emerge and become explicit in the new assemblies by a process of imitation, derivation or importation from the French provincial estates.

PART IV

Italian parliaments from the 14th to the 16th centuries

I

Sardinia

The origins of the Sardinian parliament are traditionally traced back to the assembly of 1355, whose sessions were described by contemporaries as "*general curias*". Nevertheless, there can be little doubt that the assembly belonged to the category of extraordinary meetings, of political rather than constitutional significance.

The singular nature of this great assembly, which was held at Cagliari in February–March, 1355, was evident not only in its composition and structure, but in the part played by the Aragonese sovereign, Peter the Ceremonious, and his spokesmen. The king wanted to be recognised as the legitimate sovereign of all Sardinians. As a result all inhabited centres, however small, and almost all feudal territories – although they were already officially represented by their respective lords – were ordered to send their representatives. These representatives were elected in the cities and villages by popular assemblies called by the town-crier in the traditional manner, to the sound of church-bells or trumpets. In order to emphasise the solemnity and comprehensiveness of the occasion, the constitutions promulgated by the sovereign were signed and sworn to even by subjects with no parliamentary qualifications. There could be no doubt about the propagandist purpose of the meeting. But even so, the assembly was hardly a success. The summons was not obeyed by the king's political opponents, who included the powerful judge of Arborèa and various feudatories, including the representative of the commune of Pisa, deprived of most of its domains but still in possession of a few fiefs.

The publicity surrounding so large a convocation did not perhaps appear as the sole aim of this singular parliamentary session. The king wanted to impress Mariano, judge of Arborèa, and all the other rebels into recognising and respecting the new regime. No alternative explanation can be offered for so lengthy a session (lasting at least a month), which achieved such limited results. This would also explain why a criminal lawsuit, technically in the exclusive competence of the feudal group, was held before the entire parliamentary body: it was clearly a political trial.

One of the most remarkable aspects of this assembly was the declaration by the royal clerks in the preamble to the constitutions presented by the king to parliament. It states that the constitution had previously been examined, discussed and agreed upon by the parliamentary *brazos* or estates. But one can hardly take this statement at face value. No other document referred to a division of the members of parliament into *brazos*; and indeed the declaration did not even specify whether there were three *brazos* as in Catalonia, or four as in Aragon. Moreover, the statement is extremely unconvincing about the character or degree of participation in the assembly. All the constitutions – particularly the fifth one, which was presented to a small group of Cagliari notables who remained after the parliament had ended – consisted of political decrees, threats, warnings or police measures. It is obvious from their content that they could never have been initiated by the Sardinian and Catalan members of the assembly. The third constitution, for example, decreed that the Sardinians were to deliver up their sons or other suitable persons as hostages whenever ordered, and to send their children to special fortified places. It is quite possible that there was a discussion among the members, but it must have been very limited. The initiative and decision inevitably came from the king and his government. At most, one can presume, members did their best to limit or modify such draconian measures.

Once these "general curias" had been convoked and assembled, the king asked them for a subsidy or financial grant and a tax or customs duty must have been voted and accepted. Nevertheless, the assembly must be judged extraordinary and anomalous. Finally, it should be pointed out that there is no evidence at all that the assembly possessed either the character or self-consciousness of a representative and deliberative organ. This stands out even more clearly if one compares the 1355 meeting to the parliamentary sessions held in 1421 or even later.

It seems probable that the tardy development of parliamentary institutions in Sardinia depended, at least in part, on the tendency of Catalan–Aragonese official circles to consider the island as a possession of the crown rather than as an autonomous kingdom.

Moreover, from the mid-14th century until 1420, the Aragonese occupation of the island was purely military, and of extremely limited influence. Only after the viscounts of Narbonne, heirs of the judges of Arborèa, ended their resistance in 1420 did Sardinia re-enter the Aragonese world.

At that moment it was important to convoke a general assembly in order to conciliate the political forces of the country. The ruling class consisted for the most part of Catalan and Aragonese lords and citizens of Spanish origin. Participation in parliamentary assemblies was customary in Catalonia and Aragon. For some time Sardinian lords – clearly of Spanish origin – had taken part (irregularly) in the *cortes* of the states of the crown of Aragon. Moreover the cities of Cagliari and Alghero – the majority of whose population was of Spanish origin – had more than once demanded the right to participate in the Catalan *cortes*. In fact, the *cortes* possessed a position of importance and authority within the Aragonese structure of government. The new ruler, Alfonso V the Magnanimous, may have been authoritarian, but the very fact that he had convoked parliament immediately after his conquest of the island of Corsica in 1420 had already borne witness to his acceptance and recognition of the institution.

Thus it was logical that a parliament should have been called in Sardinia in 1421: its purpose was as much to end the civil war and reconcile the former rebels as to obtain financial aid. This assembly was one of the most important events in Sardinian history before the 18th century. It established laws that long retained their validity and initiated a practice of consultation and agreement between sovereign and estates which characterised the political life of the country until the late 18th century. The procedure of this parliament also confirmed the corporative character of the institution: the population was considered not as a collection of individuals, but as groups or categories, organised in orders, estates or *brazos*, which collaborated with the sovereign in administering the general affairs of the community. Nevertheless, it cannot be claimed that the 1421 parliament established definitively a new constitutional order. The subsequent meetings of the institution still lacked any regularity. On two occasions the military *brazo* (or *stament*) acted alone as if it represented the entire parliament.

Once initial protests of the cities of Cagliari and Iglesias had been overcome, the parliament of 1421 rapidly agreed out of its own generosity (*sola e magnifica liberalitat*) to make the king a financial grant to be raised from a customs tax for five years. In return it requested approval of the petitions or *capitula* put forward by all three *staments,* by single *staments* or even by individual cities. The customs duty (*dret general*) was to be collected under the control of three representatives of the same *brazos*, according to the practice of the *Generalitat* of Catalonia.

In the following decades, Alfonso and his Sardinian administrators exacted further taxes without consultation, claiming at least some of them as feudal aids. But discontent with the royal representatives increased, until Alfonso finally authorised the military *brachium* to meet in 1446, and ordered his officials not to interfere. He accepted that the decisions of the military *brazo* were to be adopted in the public interest, and confirmed that the vote of the majority (*sanior et nobilior et maior pars*) bound the minority. Indeed he affirmed a representative principle by stating that the decision of the "magnates, barons, feudatories and *heredati*"[1] present at the assembly bound not only those present and in agreement, but also the minority and those who had neither attended nor agreed. Difficulties arose in the end which annulled both the donative offered by the military *braccio* and the thirty-one *capitula* approved by the king. It needed a further meeting of this single *braccio,* held in 1452, for agreement to be reached on the basis of an increased grant in return for confirmation of the *capitula.*

The concessions made by the king included a promise not to exact money with specious justifications as had occurred in previous years, although the principle of the sovereign's right to demand contributions for coronations, marriages, ransom or foreign invasion remained intact. He further authorised the *bracci* to meet separately or together without opposition from royal officials, so long as the meetings were held in the presence of the king's procurator or one of the governors. He even allowed the military *brazo* or *stament* to meet of its own initiative, subject to the same conditions as the meetings of the three *brazos.*

It is difficult to explain why no further parliament was called for

[1] The *heredati,* called *heretats* in Aragon, were lords with hereditary titles.

almost forty years, particularly in the two peaceful decades preceding the revolt of the marquis of Oristano in 1470–8. The probable cause was the viceroys' hostility.

Certainly when parliament was finally called in 1481 the enmity between the viceroy Ximenes Perez and the leading feudatories dominated the proceedings.

This new parliament was called by Ferdinand the Catholic because he needed money. He wanted to ensure a continuous regular income by imposing a general hearth-tax (*fogatge*), and justified it in terms of the defence of the island against the Turks. He instructed the viceroy to assure the local leaders that he intended to confirm the island's "franchises, liberties, immunities, *capitula* and privileges". Nevertheless, he let it be understood that the new tax was not to be regarded as an alternative, but as a substitute for the customary feudal aids.

The parliament lasted from 1481 to 1485. By the time it ended, it had established in practice (though not in writing) that grants were offered by parliaments in exchange for royal acceptance of parliamentary requests. For the first time it had also clearly subordinated the taxation system to parliament by limiting the period of the grant to ten years.

Thus the convocation of a new parliament a decade later, in 1495, seemed logical and necessary. In fact Ferdinand summoned parliaments throughout his kingdoms in the same year in order to meet the Turkish threat. He instructed his viceroy to avoid friction and resultant delays, but to try to persuade opponents that he was only asking for a modest customs duty. Nevertheless, he also insisted that there was no question of a voluntary *donativo*, as the Turkish threat constituted one of those occasions when subjects were legally obliged to assist their sovereign, even if no assembly were called. The opposition finally gave way, but controlled the exaction of the tax through a committee of *elects* of the three *staments* (or *brazos*).

Another parliament was called in 1497 and continued with interruptions until 1511. It was in practice not one but a group of parliaments. By 1511 the obligatory character of the grants, which had been inherited from the parliament of 1495, had once more been transformed into a reciprocal agreement, typical of an ordinary general parliament in which grants were made as a counterpart to royal concessions. By then the assemblies had established themselves: after 1511 ten more sessions were held in the 16th century, and twelve in the 17th. Even if they did not all possess the same characteristics and political significance (two or three seem to have been meetings called for special purposes), they represented a new order, a new constitutional reality in the country. The members of parliament were undoubtedly aware of this. Thus the military *stament* repeatedly insisted that the sovereigns confirm its right of self-convocation. At the end of the 1543 parliament, the cathedral chapter and clergy of the diocese of Suelli asked that assemblies should be convoked not every nine but every three years, as in the other Aragonese states. In 1559 all three *brazos* made the same demand, although to no effect.

This development of the Sardinian parliament occurred in the very period when the Spanish rulers were attempting to limit the autonomy of local institutions. Ferdinand the Catholic's decision in 1495 to summon concurrently all the parliaments in the empire against the common Turkish threat may well be regarded as symptomatic of this drive against local individuality. But the Sardinian parliament undoubtedly managed to retain some of its newly acquired authority: even Philip II convoked it not merely to gain financial aid, but to hear the counsel and proposals of its members on legislative and administrative matters. Its attempts to assert its authority against the viceroys can be seen in the procedural battles of the 1543–4 parliament, and in the initial protests against Don Alvaro de Madrigal's delayed convocation of parliament in 1558.

But the theory and practice of negotiated laws, sanctioned "by force of contract, to possess perpetual validity", was inevitably weakened by the new concept of the monarchy. Already in the 1484–1511 parliaments the royal "replies and decisions" to parliamentary requests had been mostly confirmations of existing *capitula*, but with considerable reservations and restrictions. The last time a king accepted the *capitula* of the *bracci* with the formula of a negotiated law was at La Coruna in 1520, and even then only with the gloss that it was owing to his "habitual benevolence". Nevertheless, even if the Sardinian parliament suffered from the absolutism of the Spanish monarchy, it was never subjected to such autocratic and definitive restrictions as were imposed on the Castilian *cortes* at Tarazona in 1592.

The structural, functional and procedural characteristics of the Sardinian parliament, as it was to emerge in the 16th century, were already clear in the 1421 assembly and the later meetings of the 15th century. Although many of the acts of these assemblies have not yet been published, there is sufficient material to provide a fairly accurate outline of these characteristics.

The documents of the assemblies of 1481–5 and 1495 in particular shed considerable light on the problem of the different categories in which the parliamentary convocations and sessions should be classified. A Catalan parliamentarian of the 15th century, Tomas Mieres, had theorised and distinguished two different types of convocations and assemblies.[2] The first consisted of the *cortes* or *curiae generales*, which were summoned to enable necessary measures to be taken for the good order of the country and to permit the sovereign to redress grievances. Attendance was, in principle, obligatory. The second consisted of parliaments summoned for some specific need of the sovereign or country, although the summons merely stated that the assembly was for counsel and aid; attendance was not obligatory. The acts of the Catalan *cortes* are for the most part still unpublished, so that we are in no position to test Mieres' theory against the experience of Catalan parliamentary history. But on the basis of these categories, it has been maintained[3] that the Sardinian assemblies – although described in some documents as *curiae* or *cortes* – were only partial, limited and inferior examples of "parlia-

[2] *Apparatus super constitutionibus curiarum generalium Cathaloniae* (Barcelona, 2nd ed., 1621), vol. 2, col. 10: "subjects, prelates, barons, men of the cities or villages of Catalonia are held obligatorily to attend convocations to general curias, but only voluntarily to parliaments. A general curia is held for the good order of the entire commonweal and that the lord king may settle grievances in due manner. A parliament is held by the prince for some necessity or utility of the lord king or the commonweal; it is convoked for certain not-specified reasons, as the prince wishes to hold a parliament with the prelates, barons and men of the cities and villages . . . and he warns and requests and requires that they come to the said parliament in the said city or village, and that they give him counsel, aid and assistance; and that they send their procurators with powers to the said parliament. The difference between a general curia and a parliament is that a curia is held about general matters, whereas a parliament is held about certain, specific matters affecting the prince."

[3] R. Di Tucci, *Istituzioni pubbliche in Sardegna nel periodo aragonese*, Cagliari, 1920, p. 54 ff., regards the Sardinian parliament as a less important type of representative institution than the *cortes* of the Iberian peninsula and as corresponding to the "parliaments" defined by Mieres. For an opposing interpretation, cf. A. Marongiu, *I parlamenti di Sardegna nella storia e nel diritto pubblico comparato,* Rome, 1931, p. 212 ff. and A. Era, *Il parlamento sardo del 1481–1485*, Milan, 1955, p. XCII.

ments". Consequently they were incomplete institutions, held without regularity, lacking in authority and initiative and without specific attributes recognised by the state.

The publication of the acts of the parliaments and assemblies of 1421, 1446, 1452 and 1481–5 has now made it possible to see that two types of parliaments may also have existed in Sardinia, though different from Mieres' theoretical models for Catalonia.[4] Some of the Sardinian parliaments possessed the character of general parliaments, similar to the *cortes* of the Spanish peninsula; but others were special assemblies, even if also described as parliaments. On some occasions, in fact, the king and his ministers distinguished between parliaments "by grace" – in which both sides made concessions by voluntary agreement – and all other parliaments, where the king demanded his due without any legislative counterpart or redress of grievance.[5] This distinction was apparently not noticed by the early editors of the parliamentary acts. But they did note a difference caused by the urgency of royal requests and certain formal characteristics (for example, convocation by the viceroy without a special royal mandate), which led them to distinguish between what appeared to be "normal" parliaments – meetings held fairly regularly and periodic-

[4] A. Boscolo, *I parlamenti di Alfonso il Magnanimo,* Milan, 1953, "Acta curiarum Sardiniae", vol. 3; A. Era, *Il parlamento sardo del 1481–1485*, Milan, 1955.
The latter author ("Contributi alla storia dei parlamenti sardi", *Studi sassaresi,* XXVI, 1954) distinguished between the two different categories of parliamentary sessions in Sardinia in the following terms: first, "general parliaments", in which the sovereign asked for a *donativo* or *servizio,* and in return offered to listen to grievances (*greuges*) and grant *grazie*; such parliaments were held with a certain regularity. Secondly, reunions of the *stament* or *brazos* called at exceptional moments when it was necessary to raise a sum of money, which did not pledge the sovereign to any reciprocal concession. But the term "parliament" is extremely ambiguous in Sardinia, as elsewhere: it would seem clearer to distinguish between ordinary parliaments, similar to the Iberian *cortes* once they had achieved their full maturity, and extraordinary or pseudo-parliaments – irregular meetings with some only of the characteristics or prerogatives of true parliamentary institutions.

[5] Ferdinand the Catholic offered a clear instance of this distinction in a letter to his viceroy of 21 August 1495 (Era, "Contributi", cit., p. 26): "This is an instance of a *servizio* or a *donativo* not made to us, but for the defence of the kingdom, and hence which all inhabited villages of the island are held and obliged to grant; we could have exacted the necessary means for this defence even without proceeding to a regular convocation of parliament, as our predecessors the Aragonese sovereigns did in the past." Another example is offered by the protest made by don Ludovico di Castelvì on 21 July 1483, in his own name and that of the other judges of grievances, that the assembly then being held was not a parliament "by force", but a free parliament (*com aquest parlament no sia de forsa mas de libertat*), which entitled all members to express their opinions freely (Era, *Il parlamento sardo,* cit., p. 97).

ally, at least from the 16th century – and extraordinary meetings.

It would be dangerous to construct any elaborate theory on the basis of this evidence. All we can say is that certain of the parliamentary convocations and sessions were undoubtedly extraordinary in character and procedure. The royal ministers – either for reasons of principle or merely through careful management – reduced their functions to a purely formal registration of the overbearing demands of the sovereign and to determining the distribution of the sum to be paid.

Whether ordinary or extraordinary, the parliaments were composed of all three *brazos* or *staments* – military, ecclesiastical and royal – each of which deliberated by majority vote,[6] but all three *brazos* had to be in agreement for their vote to be considered as the vote and deliberation of the whole parliament.

The military *brachium* was composed of feudatories and lords of vassals (*barones et feudatarii seu heredati*). Members were convoked individually by royal writs; so were the female holders of fiefs, who could not attend personally and were obliged to appoint procurators. Ecclesiastics or corporations in possession of fiefs were also represented by procurators. The holders of certain high judicial or administrative offices attended parliament by virtue of their office, but did not sit among the members of the *staments*. On certain occasions the military *brachium* formed not only part of parliament, but acted as its representative and substitute, in so far as it spoke and acted for the good of the whole kingdom.[7] When a feudatory could not attend personally, he was permitted to nominate a procurator. But no single member could accumulate more than four votes.[8]

In terms of status or protocol, the military *stament* came second to the ecclesiastical estate, although in practice the reverse was true. The ecclesiastical *brachium* consisted of all archbishops and bishops with sees in Sardinia, abbots, priors and cathedral chapters or vicars.

[6] The question of a majority vote, as against a unanimous vote, was discussed by the military *stament* in the 1481–5 parliament. But there is no evidence that any deliberation was annulled through lack of unanimity or because of disagreement among the *maior* or *sanior pars* of the voters.

[7] The representatives of the military *stament* claimed this when asking for permission to hold separate reunions in 1421, and during such reunions in 1446 and 1452.

[8] This was laid down by the parliament held in 1575 under the presidency of the viceroy Don Juan Coloma.

However, this full membership only became stable quite late, and in the 15th century writs of summons were by no means always so general or complete. The higher clergy, and particularly the archbishops and bishops, were gradually chosen exclusively among Spanish priests, who acted dutifully towards a sovereign responsible for their present position and on whom their future hopes depended. Hence the ecclesiastical *brachium*, for both personal and political reasons, was normally moved by a desire not to create difficulties for the viceregal government. Prelates who did not attend personally were represented by their dependants or fiduciaries with power of attorney. Ecclesiastical bodies, such as cathedral chapters, were represented by procurators with full powers (*plena potestat a tals actes acostumada*).

The Sardinian parliament also included the so-called royal *stament* or *brazo*, composed of the cities, villages, *terre* or *contrade* which were not enfeoffed and hence belonged to the royal demesne. Normally the councillors and jurors of the villages (*maiores et iurati*) chose their representatives, who possessed a regular mandate or notarial act of nomination (*instrumentum sindacatus*). These representatives were called *sindaci* (*sindichs* in Catalan), procurators, or even, exceptionally, messengers (*missatgers* in Catalan). Their instructions contained the customary full powers: in the words of the instructions of the city of Oristano of 13 June 1483, "the fullness of power, so broad that they shall say what they think". They were not representatives of their respective local administration, but of the entire city (*terra*). Despite the amplitude of these mandates, in exceptional circumstances not only municipal representatives, but even those of cathedral chapters, asked and obtained a suspension of the parliamentary session in order to discuss the situation with their electors or nominators (*principals*). However, this may not have been a legal necessity but rather an obstructionist tactic calculated to create difficulties for the viceregal government.

The representatives of the capital, Cagliari, were in a unique position. They had continually to consult a parliamentary committee elected by the city council and also to obey its instructions. The committee first appears in the parliament of 1481–5 as the *quinzena de cort* or "fifteen of parliament", but was subsequently reduced to thirteen members (*tretzean de cort*). At times this body seemed directly to represent the civic council in its relations not only with the municipal *sindichs* but with the entire parliament.

The members of parliament who, according to official doctrine, represented the whole kingdom, were convoked by the king either personally or by mandate through the viceroy.[9] The writs of summons, similar in form to a judicial writ, contained the somewhat unusual order to attend infallibly (*infallibilter*). No specific sanctions, however, seem to have been imposed for failure to appear. The general threat of a condemnation for contumacy appears to have been used as a warning against waverers and latecomers rather than as a punitive sanction. In fact, once the criterion of a unanimous vote had been abandoned total attendance was unnecessary. For if the majority of those present could pledge both the minority and the absentees, as in 1446, the latter were no longer of importance. At the same time it seems extremely probable[10] that no number was specified as necessary for a quorum either for holding sessions or for deliberations. However, the use of powers of attorney offered a method of ensuring an adequate attendance at the assemblies.

Writs of summons were usually extremely vague and elusive, because of such formulas as service to His Majesty, "for the good of the kingdom", etc. But they also included a request for counsel and aid, and promised to carry out whatever was judged opportune for the good of the kingdom. More than once these writs emerged as the conclusion of negotiations between the viceroy and authoritative leaders of the ruling classes. But already before the mid-16th century parliaments (and the grants they made) had acquired a decennial pattern, so that no elaborate preparations were necessary – at least for the "ordinary" parliaments. On three occasions – in 1543–4, 1559 and 1579 – parliamentary groups or leaders requested that the assemblies be held every three or five years. In the eyes of the parliamentarians at least the institution was judged as possessing a certain utility in itself, besides offering an occasion to examine the

[9] However, even if no special mandate had been sent, as in 1481, parliament could be convoked, held and ended by the viceroy on the basis of his diploma of nomination, or by subsequent ratification by the sovereign.

[10] If this had not been so, the threat of declaring absentees contumacious would have been far more severe. The acts of the parliament of 1481–5 show that at a certain point the power of the *bracci* was concentrated in extremely few hands.

conduct of the viceregal administration and redistribute the taxes among the population.

Members who attended personally only had to prove their identity or produce their writ of summons on appearing in parliament. Procurators, *sindaci*, had to show their powers of attorney to the royal representatives, the viceroy and his collaborators. In 1559, following a proposal by the military *stament*, the control of titles was assigned to a special committee, analogous to a committee of the Catalan *corts*. The committee consisted of six *habilitatores* or "habilitators": three government nominees and three parliamentarians, one for each *stament*; parity of votes signified non-acceptance. In order to accelerate the procedure it was agreed in the parliament of 1575 that all titles to attend parliament which had been acknowledged by 29 November 1574 should be permanently recognised. Soon after, all three *brazos* agreed that nobody could accumulate more than four powers of attorney.

Until the examination of titles had ended, it was impossible to hold valid deliberations. Nevertheless the assembly was opened with full ceremony in the presence of the king or viceroy, and the members sat in separate groups, according to their respective *brazos*. There was no fixed rule where parliaments should be held, but it soon became uniform practice to hold them in the capital, Cagliari. Sassari never succeeded (as did Messina in Sicily) in providing an alternative centre for the viceregal government and parliamentary sessions.

In the first or second meeting the sovereign or his representative, seated on the throne, read a declaration to explain the purpose of the summons. This *propositio,* however, was hardly less vague than the writ of summons. After a symbolic discussion, the "leader" of the parliament, usually the archbishop of Cagliari, made a short deferential reply. From then on parliament as a unified entity was little more than a constitutional fiction brought to life only by a series of brief ceremonies or prorogations. During this stage the only unifying activity was the exchange of messages between the different *brazos* and the viceroy's announcement of the nomination of each *brazos*' representatives on the various committees. In fact, real parliamentary work was concentrated within the individual *brazos* and in the committees.

The first committee to be nominated was that of the "habilitators".

Although its powers were theoretically only technical and legal, the committee could be a powerful weapon to delay or even refuse the admission of political opponents.

Another even more important committee was that of the *tractadors*, which dealt with financial, fiscal and legislative matters. It was a mixed committee of officials and parliamentarians, characteristic of Sardinian parliaments. It was this committee which decided on the voluntary grants or *donativos* and drew up the requests to present to the king and his government as conditions for the grant. At first, with twenty-four members (three royal nominees and seven for each *stament*), it was a clumsy and inexpert body. But by the reign of Ferdinand the Catholic it was working regularly. Its membership finally settled at four viceregal officials and twelve parliamentarians. Its authority was great because it dealt not only with the total amount and distribution of the *donativo*, and requests for laws originating from parliament, but also with the assignment of indemnities to the viceroy and members of almost all committees except that of the "habilitators". The actual power of decision lay exclusively with the *brazos*. On the other hand, the committee's resolutions and proposals, especially if unanimous, were undoubtedly extremely influential, as they formed both a necessary and an adequate basis for further deliberations by the *brazos*. In practice, it was the committee of the *tractadors* which gave the *brazos* (the Catalan *bras*) the necessary knowledge and arguments to back up parliamentary requests before the Supreme Council of Aragon, whose judgement was often decisive,[11] and ultimately before the king.

Another parliamentary committee of analogous composition, which usually consisted of the same members, was that of the judges or examiners of grievances, the *provisores gravaminum* (called in Catalan manner, *iutges de greuges, iutges esgravadors*).

The Sardinian parliament was born adult. Behind it lay the precedents of Catalan and Aragonese parliamentary customs. One precedent was its right to claim redress of grievances, to impugn government actions and judge them in an appropriate committee. Even more characteristic and significant was the fact that such protests or *greuges* had to be settled before any other matter was

[11] The Council of Aragon was created by Ferdinand the Catholic as the supreme organ of government and continued to function throughout the period.

discussed. In this sense the "grievance" justified its Catalan name and synonym *dissentiment*. For it implied opposition, a veto on all further activities of the assembly or *bras*. Alfonso the Magnanimous had ably eliminated such grievances in the parliament of 1421. But they appeared again in 1481 and in the subsequent sessions. The viceroy could do nothing to check or settle these demands for redress, even though they held up his entire programme. More than once the *greuge* was a protest and remonstrance against the viceroy's actions as president of the parliament; in this case, probably to avoid complicated procedural problems, the appeal was sent directly to the sovereign or his Supreme Council. Logically this should have led to a suspension of the parliament. But if the viceroy declared the grievance to be "frivolous", manifestly unfounded, such a suspension might not be decreed.

Before the session began the viceroy and each of the three parliamentary greoups proceeded, "as is the custom of parliament", to nominate "the examiners of grievances presented or to be presented in parliament". In 1483 the *bras* asked the viceroy to use his authority to settle grievances not only according to justice but rapidly; if the judges did not terminate their work within four months of their nomination, they were to be incarcerated in a monastery until they finished. But this request can only be regarded as a curiosity; it does not create a precedent.

The committee of "judges of grievances" did not consist of a fixed number of members, and this in turn created other *greuges* and questions. The judges nominated by the government were usually in a minority (normally three against six). However, a grievance could not be accepted as well founded unless a majority of the committee including at least one of the royal nominees agreed that it was. In the absence of any rules, appeals were made to precedents, to general legal norms or to comparative law, but above all to Catalan parliamentary customs.

In 1511 the appeal to the Catalan example was legitimised. In 1559 an attempt was made to demand Catalan practice, so as to acquire triennial sessions: but Philip II rejected the claim.

Apart from such subsidiary regulations new questions were often discussed and decided both by the viceroy and his council and by the *brazos*. For example, in the 1481–5 parliament a problem arose because the city of Cagliari withdrew two of its three representatives. This was calculated to cause difficulties for the viceroy Ximene Perez, because the representatives of the capital were also members of various committees, and their substitution would have caused enormous delays. The viceroy annulled the withdrawal and justified himself by the criterion of *perpetuatio iurisdictionis*. The Cagliari council opposed the annulment on the grounds that the decision could not be taken by the president alone but only in collaboration with the *bras*, especially given the precedent of various other cities which had changed their *sindaci* without any viceregal opposition. The subsequent recognition by the viceroy of the city's freedom to choose the representatives it wanted – without prejudice to the question of principle – must have been determined by his desire to hasten the conclusion of the parliament and by his awareness of the military *brazos*' support of the city's protest.

Once a name is believed to carry with it certain rights it is difficult to eliminate such connotations. Even the obligatory or executive parliaments – such as those of 1495 or 1626 – which were in a different category from ordinary parliaments – bore witness to the idea and substance of discussion and consent among the members. Naturally this was clearer and more easy to insist upon in the ordinary general parliaments or *cortes*. Consent or agreement constituted both a formal and a practical criterion: it applied to the parliamentarians in each of the *brazos*, to the three *brazos* in their relations with each other and to the three *brazos* acting as a single organ in their relations with the viceroy and Spanish government. As no separation of powers existed, every act and decision was a complex matter in need of consent. The king needed the consent of the *brazos* as a legal and practical necessity in order to impose taxation. But the consent and collaboration of parliament was extremely desirable for many other matters as well. In general it facilitated matters. But officially prompted proposals, adopted through the collaboration of the representative organ, also appeared more acceptable and less onerous to those most directly affected. Public opinion is no invention of our times, but a permanent reality. The survival of traditional attitudes and attachment to old privileges – easier in an island with poor communications than elsewhere – tended to act as a defensive buffer as governments at Madrid and their representatives in Sardinia became more overbearing and demanding. It is significant that the first *Capitols de cort* or *Acta curiarum* of the kingdom were published in the last quarter of the 16th century, when appeals to precedent were made frequently.[12]

Already by the late 15th century, the entire administration was beginning to act according to certain fixed, publicly recognised rules and regulations which made arbitrary action difficult. Moreover, the bureaucracy was filled with Sardinian lawyers (*letrados*) who were numerous and authoritative, although they did not occupy the highest posts, and who were by no means always inclined to obey the orders or plans of the viceroys or oppose parliamentary requests. In the course of the 16th century, as a growing number of the Sardinian ruling class acquired some knowledge of the elements of jurisprudence, the *staments* showed themselves increasingly ready to resist viceregal demands.[13]

This legal training and belief in the value of regulations and precedents enabled the Sardinian élite to entrench itself in its old positions, which – in a legalistically-minded environment – could not be disproved. The rights of the country were believed to be represented in an assembly expressing and focalising all possibilities of political life and action. Hence, to members of parliament the very mechanism of the institution still appeared valid and efficacious. In the sessions of the *tractadors*, collaboration between government and parliament conditioned and determined the solutions to the problems of the moment. Political and psychological obstacles to rapid and satisfactory solutions were transformed into legal difficulties and hindrances of such magnitude that the very frequency and possibility of holding sessions became blocked by a grievance or *greuge*.

Theoretically, and according to practice, the reciprocal concessions between *bras* and government – ordinary and extraordinary grants in return for acceptance of parliamentary proposals – were dependent upon the personal relations and minor concessions made by the viceroy and leaders of the three *brachia*. At the closure of each session a small shower of rewards, honours and indemnities fell upon the

[12] F. Bellit, *Capitols de cort del stament militar de Sardenya,* Cagliari, 1572; P. G. Arquer, *Capitols de cort del stament militar de Sardenya,* Cagliari, 1591; J. Dexart, *Capitula siue acta curiarum regni Sardiniae,* Cagliari, 1645.

[13] Many of their members had studied at the university of Pisa.

viceroy, his most important collaborators, even upon agents of the administration and leading figures of the three *bras*. Service to the king (such as the voting of a grant) was identical to service to the state, so that the most active and zealous parliamentarians were publicly praised and rewarded, despite the official secrecy of debates and votes within the *bras*. Agreements were contractual in character and wording (the *donativo* was an act of liberality; the single laws or measures were contracts). Nevertheless, such arrangements could be substituted or added to by a financial contribution offered by one or all of the *staments* in order to facilitate the adoption by the government of measures entailing an increase of public expenditure.[14] These contributions were necessary to avoid upsetting the equilibrium of positions and concessions made by the two powers (government and parliament). But legally speaking, they also confirmed in a useful manner the equal importance of the contracting parties, and the reluctance of either side to change the *status quo* without a specific compensation. The king, personifying the state, in his relations with the country, represented by parliament with its three *brazos*, repeatedly and systematically employed a contractual form. The form assumed the character and value of a fundamental law. It was generally and openly stated in the 15th and 16th centuries that the king had no right unilaterally to abrogate any contract he had entered into with parliamentary bodies. Such an abrogation would have been an act of force and hence legally invalid.[15]

The dialogue between the viceroy and his officials and the parliamentary *bras* or committees did not end, however, with the consent of the former to the final deliberations of the latter. The later Spanish phase of this dialogue was extremely significant. It was naturally important that the viceroy approve the decisions and proposals of the *brachia*. But the final decision could come only from the king, or from his consultative organ, the Supreme Council of Aragon. It was here that the parliamentary representative or *sindacus*[16]

[14] For example, in 1562 the "Supreme Magistracy of the Royal *Audiencia*" was created at the expense of the inhabitants of the island.

[15] Even Charles V's attacks against the Castilian *cortes* and those of Philip II against the Aragonese *cortes* used as their instrument and means of expression parliamentary votes and decisions.

[16] There was usually one representative. But in the parliament of 1481–5 and in the separate reunions of the military *stament* of 1446 and 1452 a small group of representatives was sent.

was able to test the sincerity of viceregal consent. It was necessary to convince the councillors and royal courtiers by patient and energetic explanations as well as by gifts and promises.

After agreement had been reached between the viceroy and the *bras*, parliament was prorogued. Then, often after an interval of some months, it was recalled to listen to the formal and solemn pronouncement of the definitive agreements, equivalent to a promulgation of royal decrees. Parliament was then dismissed, the executive measures which had been passed became effective, as did the exaction of the *donativo* granted or renewed by parliament, and controlled by parliamentary delegates. The grant usually lasted ten years, until the opening of a new parliament.

2

Naples

The most striking aspect of the parliaments of the kingdom of Naples is that they do not correspond to the concept of parliament as we have outlined it in the course of this study. The only common feature of these assemblies of the Angevin period is that they were all meetings between sovereigns and the baronial class (for the cities or "universities" rarely appeared). Some of them were purely casual, but all of them in any case were wholly separate and remote from any idea or claim to represent the country. There was no awareness of a representative function, no sense of that solidarity which transforms groups of individuals into collective bodies or communities.

The king decided when and where meetings were to take place and instructed his officials in the various provinces to inform those who were to attend. These writs of summons in no way acknowledged that the community or its ruling classes possessed any political force, status or corresponding constitutional position. The sovereigns held the meetings purely in their own interest, to give greater prestige to their appearances in public, to communicate and promulgate orders for which widespread publicity was judged opportune, and to demand subsidies and contributions. They did not ask or await a reply; they ordered and imposed.

Regular meetings were not arranged either theoretically or in practice. This would have presupposed that once a subsidy had been received, exacted and spent, it was necessary to obtain its renewal. But the king imposed and exacted "general subventions" (*collette*) and subsidies irrespective of whether or not they fell within the criteria of the papal bull of 1285,[17] without worrying about the consent of his subjects, and with no intention of allowing an assembly of those concerned to judge whether the request was justified or not.

In consequence, the convocation of great assemblies, although they were called "parliaments" or "general parliaments", was neither obligatory nor customary. There was no parliamentary institution with its place in the structure of the state. There were only more or less solemn reunions, all of an extraordinary character; they were composed of magnates and barons (including ecclesiastical dignitaries) or of town or local envoys, whose presence at the most important royal declarations or at the swearing of an oath of fealty to the king or his heir was judged useful but not essential. In fact, general reunions or constitutional assemblies were not necessary for these purposes.

Throughout the 14th and indeed the first half of the 15th century these assemblies continued and followed the same pattern of the feudal assemblies of the 13th century: they were military gatherings, of individuals with no collective representatives or deliberative character. It is difficult to believe that they were so passive that no one dared to express his own opinion or even object to royal impositions. But until the time of Alfonso of Aragon (1443–58) there

[17] In order to end the "onerous exaction of *collectae*", which not only the Neapolitans but his own predecessors had complained of, in 1285 Honorius IV decreed, in agreement with the college of cardinals, that henceforth the kings of Naples could only exact *collectae* for four specific cases and then only for fixed amounts: for a serious invasion of the island; if the king was made prisoner and had to be ransomed; when a royal prince was knighted; for the marriage of a princess. The bull sanctioned the decisions of the parliament of St Martin's day 1283, which had regulated these four cases, but added that more than one *collecta* could not be exacted in a single year. But these limitations remained on paper: not only were *collectae* exacted without legitimate justification, but so-called "gifts" were extorted, arbitrary fines or confiscations followed false accusations of crimes, etc.

is no trace of objections, or of votes which would presuppose deliberation and agreement.

The most that can be said about these so-called parliaments is that they were called to take part in the formulation of laws. But even this was a passive role, as the assemblies received and approved the laws decreed by the sovereign by acclamation. Such were the assemblies of San Martino di Calabria in 1283, Naples in 1289 or Eboli in 1290.

A second purpose of these meetings might have been to inform the king of the needs, desires and complaints of the population and to request appropriate measures. The circular sent to the *giustizieri* together with the writs of summons for a "general and public parliament" in 1318 stated that its purpose was to publish solemnly the *capitula* and decrees for the good of the country and to listen to and redress the petitions and grievances of those who had suffered injustices and abuses. Two prelates for each judicial circumscription and two or three *sindaci* for each city or "famous place" (*terra famosa*) were to appear for this purpose to state their requests or accusations and listen to decisions "of common utility".

Other assemblies in 1327 and 1332 had the character of extraordinary meetings called for military purposes. Sometimes parliaments were convoked to enable the sovereigns to make particularly important declarations as, for example, the assemblies of 1342, when Robert announced the choice of his niece Joanna as heir, and 1347, when Joanna released her subjects from their oath. In 1366 a similar parliament was held by Cardinal Egidio d'Albornoz to promulgate his constitutions. In 1382 and 1390, as on other occasions, the term parliament was used to describe exclusively feudal meetings, which were no longer representative but called to give counsel and aid according to feudal practice. But the assemblies of the city of Naples, as for example those of 1390 and 1495, also called themselves general parliaments. In short, all these meetings were not parliaments in any true sense, but extraordinary political assemblies.

It need hardly be said that the accession of the Aragonese to the kingdom of Naples did not inaugurate true parliamentary activities or a representative institution. Nevertheless, the assemblies did assume a relatively new character and strongly influenced the whole life of the country. This new activity, stimulated by the sovereign, lacked any continuity or regularity. It was still fragmentary, episodic and uncertain. But each episode was related to a clear precedent, and taken together they presented a different and more consistent image than in the past.

The first sign of this trend was the "general parliament" of "all the princes, dukes, marquises, counts and barons of the said kingdom" and of the procurators of the absentee barons, which began at Benevento and closed at Naples in 1443. Here for the first time in the history of the kingdom of Naples a great national assembly acted as a single body and requested, granted, petitioned and in practice negotiated with the sovereign and his government. Even if we ignore its composition, the assembly's procedure and methods of deliberation were extremely similar to those of the *cortes* of the possessions of the Crown of Aragon. On the one hand, there was the offer and acceptance of a conspicuous contribution (naturally not from the whole kingdom, but from the barons alone); on the other, the royal approval or *placet* of a series of parliamentary *capitula*. Alfonso rejected or modified many of the *capitula* and, even more significantly, agreed to the others by his "gracious will" and not as contractual laws. This was no conquest of a kingdom, but neither was it an abdication of his powers by the king.

Successive assemblies, which were sometimes attended by the representatives of the communes or *università*, discussed *donativi* or *collette*. But these infrequent parliaments have no real history and belong to the series of financial measures which resulted from the diplomatic–military activities of the Aragonese king. The parliament of 1456 contained echoes of that of 1443, in the sense that the barons of the kingdom, in return for a few royal concessions, pledged themselves to pay new taxes "themselves and on behalf of their vassals, subjects and inhabitants of their lands".[18] As in 1443 it was only a parliament of "magnates and barons".

An almost permanent characteristic of these assemblies was the absence of ecclesiastical representatives, except for those holding

[18] The final declaration of this assembly spoke of "all parliament", but at the same time of the "magnates and barons". Alfonso carefully kept control: he reserved the right to send commissions or agents to carry out general or special inquiries, if he judged it necessary; and in reply to the request that he confirm his obligations to observe and enforce the observance of the local *capitula* and immunities, he reserved the right to break his pledge by "arbitrary letters patent" (*licterae arbitrariae*).

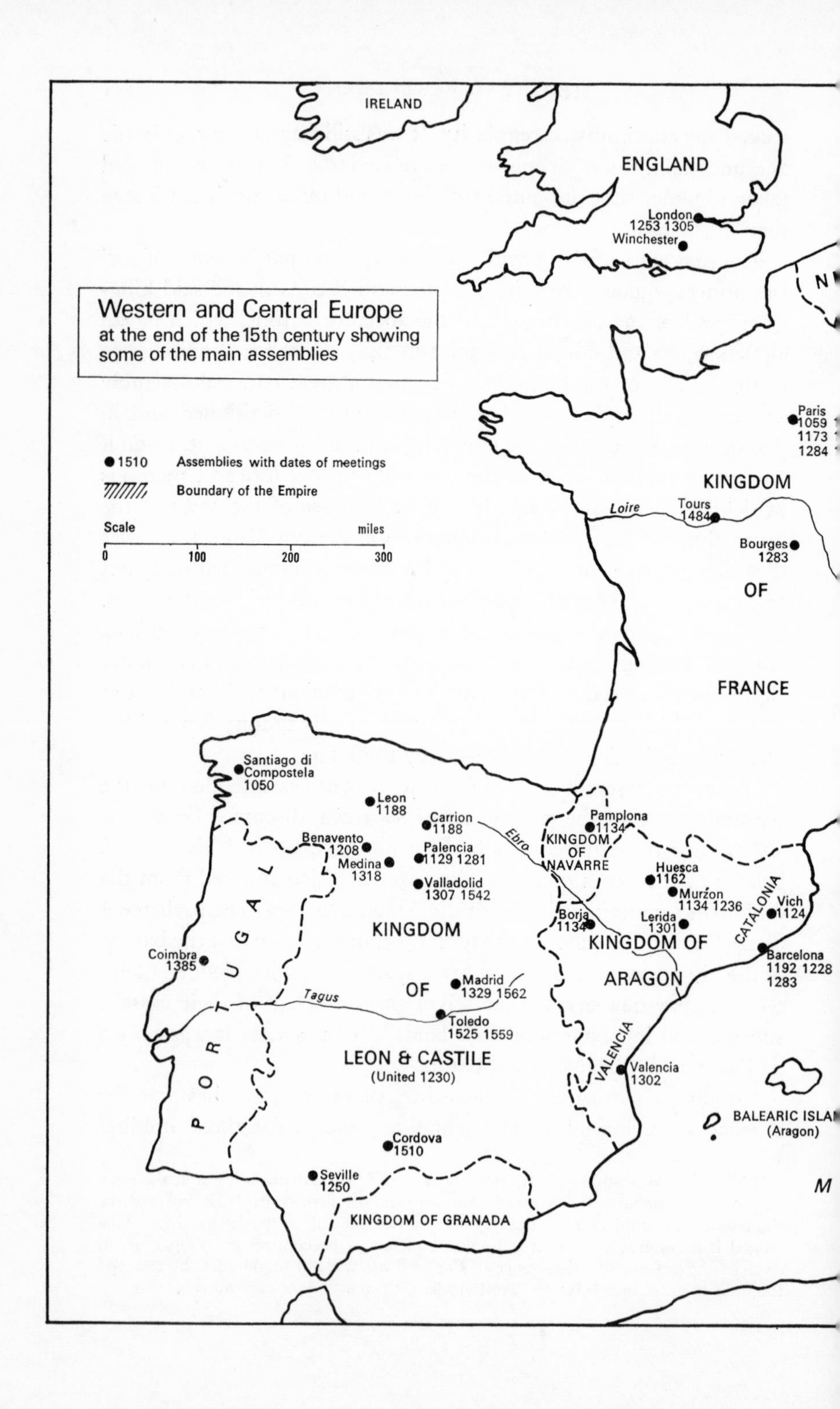
Western and Central Europe
at the end of the 15th century showing some of the main assemblies
1510 Assemblies with dates of meetings
Boundary of the Empire
Scale
miles
0
100
200
300
IRELAND
ENGLAND
London
1253 1305
Winchester
Paris
1059
1173
1284
KINGDOM
OF
FRANCE
Loire
Tours
1484
Bourges
1283
Santiago di
Compostela
1050
Leon
1188
Carrion
1188
Benavento
1208
Palencia
1129 1281
Medina
1318
Valladolid
1307 1542
Ebro
Pamplona
1134
KINGDOM
OF
NAVARRE
Huesca
1162
Murzon
1134 1236
Vich
1124
CATALONIA
Lerida
1301
Borja
1134
KINGDOM OF
ARAGON
Barcelona
1192 1228
1283
KINGDOM
OF
LEON & CASTILE
(United 1230)
Coimbra
1385
PORTUGAL
Tagus
Madrid
1329 1562
Toledo
1525 1559
VALENCIA
Valencia
1302
BALEARIC ISLA
(Aragon)
Cordova
1510
Seville
1250
KINGDOM OF GRANADA
M

Berlin
POLAND
Rhine
Cologne 1259
THE EMPIRE
EMBOURG
Mainz 1235
Worms 1269
BOHEMIA
Nuremburg
Augsburg 1286
Munich
Vienna
Danube
SWISS CONFEDERATION
AUSTRIA (Habsburg)
HUNGARY
FRIULI (To Venice 1420)
Udine 1287
UCHY OF SAVOY
Aosta
DUCHY OF MILAN
Milan
VENICE
Verona 1244
Venice
Trino 1305
Cremona
MANTUA
Giaveno 1286
Turin
Po
MON-FERRAT
Roncaglia 1136 1154 1158
Saluzzo
PIEDMONT
GENOA
MODENA
FERRARA
Ravenna
VENETIA
OTTOMAN EMPIRE
LUCCA
Florence 1284
FLORENCE
Ancona
Recanati
Macerata
Loreto
Fermo
arseilles
PAPAL STATES
SIENA
Orvieto 1220
Viterbo 1296
CORSICA (Genoa)
Rome
Foggia
Benevento 1443
Ariano 1140
Naples 1289
Eboli 1290
Sassari
SARDINIA (To Aragon 1327)
KINGDOM OF NAPLES
Cagliari 1421
Messina 1296
ranean Sea
San Martino 1283
Palermo 1130
Catania 1397
Syracuse 1398
KINGDOM OF SICILY (To Aragon 1282)

fiefs who attended as "barons". Ecclesiastics appeared in the parliaments of 1480 and 1481 and perhaps a few others, but always for a specific reason. On the other hand, the domanial cities appeared far more frequently than has generally been noted – at least ten times between 1444 and 1497. In 1456 Alfonso stated that he wanted the *sindaci* to be provided with ample powers. But once the city of Naples had acquired new privileges and immunities and isolated itself from the other cities and parliament, the convocation and participation of envoys of the cities would appear to have little importance.

These 15th century meetings still lacked any regularity. Nor were there any fixed rules about the place of the reunions, or about whom to summon. The assemblies were based on the baronial class and in general seemed to concern themselves only with their interests, and in particular with maintaining and, if possible, extending their acquisition from Alfonso of criminal jurisdiction (*merum et mixtum imperium*) over their territories. Naturally their class interests sometimes coincided with the general interest, as could be seen for instance in the attempt of the 1456 parliament to limit excesses in the administration of royal justice, or in the petition in 1443 that agreement be reached with the pope.

Thus, because of their limited composition and the long irregular intervals between convocations, these assemblies were of little importance in the latter half of the 15th century. They did not act, nor did they claim to act as the recognised and responsible representative of the country. In this sense, the assemblies of the Aragonese period, although more dynamic, vocal and better articulated than their Angevin predecessors, cannot be considered as true parliaments, but only as pre-parliaments.

Nevertheless the principle of consent by assembly undoubtedly existed, although not openly realised or recognised, and in part this was due to the great autonomy achieved by the administration of the city of Naples. It is true that all the parliaments, whether plenary or merely baronial, resulted in new taxes. But they also resulted in the elaboration, presentation and request for royal approval of the most common and deeply felt petitions and aspirations of the population, or at least of its political élite.

Paradoxically it was under Ferdinand the Catholic, when the kingdom of Naples became a Spanish province, that parliamentary activity developed and the representative institution became an important instrument of government. It seemed natural to the Spanish, mainly Castilian governors like Gonsalvo, that each possession of the crown should have its own parliament or *cortes* to offer the government aid and express opinions or requests. By now the Neapolitan leaders had also acquired experience of parliamentary practice. Moreover, parliaments were called throughout the kingdoms of the Spanish empire for the same reason: to supply the king with the means to oppose the Turkish threat.

A session in April 1504 was followed by another held in the presence of Ferdinand the Catholic in January 1507, and then by others attended not only by the barons and prelates, but also by representatives of the *università* and *terre* of the kingdom. The result of these sessions was to leave parliament with the tasks of deliberating and meeting the needs of the budget through a *donativo*, and of elaborating and presenting requests to be submitted for the sovereign's *placet*. These requests often related to the past, expressing respectful but firm protests against abuses or transgressions of local rights. The long list which followed each session was drawn up by the members of parliament together with the representatives of the capital, Naples. The latter were "elected" by the *piazze* or *sedili* of Naples and took no part in the actual assembly, as they were immune from taxation and did not even contribute towards the *donativo*. Instead they took part in the so-called parliament–senate of twenty-four members (twelve for the assembly and twelve for the city), and at the end of the session examined the proposals and prepared the text of the petitions of *grazie*, divided into *capitoli*, to be submitted for the sovereign's approval. This senate or deputation was presided over by a member of the group of nobles among the city's representatives.

The *donativi*, however, were discussed by parliament alone. The unusual feature was that the assembly was not divided into chambers, estates, "orders" or *brachia*, but met as a single body to deliberate and vote by simple majority. The *donativi* were anything but spontaneous, and were never granted without discussion. In the parliament of 1531–2 there was strong opposition to an increase in the customary amount proposed by the viceroy, Cardinal Pompeo Colonna. In 1536, despite the presence of the Emperor Charles V, there was bitter opposition because of the hostility to the viceroy Pedro de Toledo. By then, however, the tie between *donativi* and parliaments had become established. Parliaments had to be convoked periodically because the *donativo* expired. Of some forty parliamentary sessions in the 16th century, twenty-four belonged to the period 1552–98. By the middle of the century biennial sessions had probably become the rule. This was certainly the case by the time of de Ponte's publication in 1611.[19]

At the end of each session there remained the delicate problem of whom to send to Madrid as representative of both parliament and deputation to present the document containing the offer of the *donativo* and the text of the *capitula* of *grazie* to the Supreme Council of Italy and then to the sovereign. The viceroys tried to prevent such embassies by persuasion and threats, offering to take care of the matter themselves; they pointed out that embassies were useless and expensive, and that they themselves would be able to adjust matters far better. They only gave way when they were sure that the parliamentary representatives were not animated by bad feelings towards them. But as it was rare that the chosen representatives were well disposed, they not only opposed the despatch of such embassies, but got Madrid to send prohibitions, for the court was equally desirous of avoiding the quarrels and confusion which inevitably accompanied these representatives. At times, unofficial, almost clandestine envoys arrived and spoke forth. On other occasions the mere despatch of a written request for permission to send envoys was enough to transform the viceroys into active supporters of parliamentary requests.

The Neapolitan parliaments of the Spanish period have traditionally been condemned out of hand. This is unjust and arbitrary. It is enough to look at the long series of acts and votes of the assemblies to realise that they played an important, albeit hardly a glorious role. The testimony of a lawyer and royal councillor of the later 16th century, Marino Freccia, bears witness to this.[20] According to Freccia, what mattered were not the resolutions or who spoke but the number of members present who voted (*coetus et multitudo pro ratione*).

But if the number was considerable, the assembly possessed a

[19] G. F. de Ponte, *De potestate proregis, collateralis consilii et regni regimine tractatus,* Naples, 1611.

[20] M. Freccia, *De subfeudis baronum et investituris feudorum,* Venice, 1579.

certain influence. By the time of de Ponte in the early 17th century,[21] the situation had changed and seems to reflect Philip II's attack on local autonomies. According to de Ponte, the fiction of voluntary *donativi* no longer held good, especially after the royal decision of 1533 that *donativi* were legitimate because of the obligation of the country to meet its immediate needs and ensure its safety. On the other hand de Ponte refused to accept the official doctrine that the baronial class, as the "greater and wiser part" of the assembly, possessed representative functions. The third estate, the *universitates civitatum et terrarum*, had an adequate organisation and sufficient interests to express and represent itself separately. The effect of the absenteeism of the cities was to reduce what could have been a "sublime and supreme congregation" into a collection of individuals, of little use to the kingdom. In effect the assertion of royal omnipotence, supported by the Neapolitan lawyers,[22] weakened the parliament of the kingdom. This was reflected in the concentration by power of attorney of most parliamentary votes in the hands of an extremely small group.

3

Sicily

Inadequate documentation may well result from loss or destruction; but it may also indicate the insignificance of an institution. The contrast between the very poor documentation on the medieval Neapolitan parliament and the quantity of evidence about the Sicilian assembly would appear symptomatic of the far greater vitality of the latter.

The history of the Sicilian parliament can be divided into two phases: an indigenous period until the reforms of Martin I and II

[21] See above, note 19.

[22] According to M. De Afflictis (*In utriusque Siciliae, Neapolisque sanctiones, et constitutiones novissimia Praelectio*, Lyon, 1556, I, 22 v.) the purpose of legal doctrine was to aid the king to govern; lawyers were to assist the crown with their knowledge.

(1395–1410), followed by a period characterised by strong Catalan influence.

There are few signs of innovations in the earlier period although this view may result from the paucity of our sources. The basic organisation remained that laid down by the Aragonese Frederick II and the Palermo assembly of 1296. Parliament was to be called every year in order "to improve the lot of all Sicilians". It had powers to examine, judge and punish public magistrates, officials, notaries, etc. It was to examine and pass legal measures. It was to nominate twelve "noble and prudent men", who were to hold office until the following session and judge criminal cases against feudatories and vassals. Everyone summoned was obliged to attend: prelates and barons, *syndici* or other representatives of the towns who had regular mandates giving them full powers to make decisions and vote, and had their expenses covered by their *università*, or where this proved impossible by the royal treasury itself. The parliament or curia remained the king's court, and was presided over by the sovereign. Nothing was said about its methods of discussion and deliberation.

Such was the ordinance of 1296. There is no evidence that it ever worked in practice.

For almost the whole of the 14th century, the uncertainty over the future of the kingdom, which was contested by the Angevins and the papacy, the series of military expeditions, the incapacity of the sovereigns and the bitter strife between factions made parliamentary convocations and assemblies irregular, infrequent, ineffective, partial and partisan. Even reunions held to celebrate a sovereign's accession to the throne or his marriage were marred by these characteristics. The assemblies, in fact, could hardly have fulfilled the requirements outlined in the constitutions of 1296. They were not held regularly; they possessed no fixed seat; they lacked initiative and took neither a direct nor an indirect part in deciding political, administrative or financial matters.

All these assemblies were called by the same name of *generale colloquium*. They were composed of nobles or *primates* and representatives (*syndici*) of the *universitates* (*civitates et famosa loca*, in the words of a writ of summons of 20 October 1307), or indeed "of all Sicily".[23]

[23] Sometimes, however, assemblies were held in this period for the regions on either side of the Salso river.

Attendance was regarded as legally binding, similar to a feudal obligation. Town representatives were chosen by the *baiulus* and other local administrators "unanimously and amicably". Each writ specified the number to be sent (six from Palermo in 1312, two from Syracuse in 1314), requested that they be chosen from "the best and most suitable elements" and insisted that they attend the assembly with a regular mandate. According to the summons of 1314 the expenses of the representatives were to be reimbursed by the city council, or if this proved impossible by the royal treasury. Although we know very little about the procedure of the assemblies, it is probable that they lacked any power of decision. In fact, the chroniclers' descriptions of various assemblies seem to exclude such power. For example, the "general colloquium" of Messina of 1296 was apparently called to enable Frederick II to promulgate his "general and special ordinances". In 1316 at Palermo Frederick merely informed the assembly that he was arming sixty galleys, leaving it to the members to find the means. In the parliament of 1320 he announced that he had made an alliance with the Ghibelline exiles of Genoa and was imposing a customs duty in order to provide funds in case of war against the Guelph–Angevin coalition.

This lack of deliberative powers was not surprising. The Sicilian barons and *syndici* displayed moments of fierce activity – as when they drove out the Angevins – but otherwise they did not aspire to or succeed in forming a representative body. Nothing prevented members of the assembly from expressing their own opinions, especially if these were loyal. But the initiative and power of decision, even in matters of taxation, rested with the sovereign.

The parliament of 1296, in fact, was not so much a constitutional as a political event. The regime remained what it had been before; the assemblies remained substantially what they had been in the Swabian and Angevin period. Nevertheless, it may be suggested that the attitudes of both sovereigns and assemblies underwent a change: sentiments of devotion and solidarity tended to displace relationships of a formal judicial nature; *fidelitas* meant more than a precise legal tie. This state of affairs undoubtedly changed during the reigns of Martin I and Martin II (1395–1410).

Once assured of complete dominance of the island, Martin the Younger slowly reorganised the entire structure of the country, without renouncing any of his royal prerogatives. He revived and in fact created parliament *ex novo*. There can be little doubt that this parliament was totally different from its predecessors, although the gradual nature of the change and our inadequate documentation has made this difficult to perceive.

Martin's first parliament, held at Catania in 1397, was undoubtedly of extreme importance for the general history of the country and for its legal and administrative reorganisation. But it did not differ in character from its predecessors. The sovereign was still exploiting the assembly as a means of announcing his intentions and promulgating his laws. The most one can point to is the discussion of the *capitoli* which were decided "with the deliberation and consent of the prelates, counts, barons and procurators of absentee lords and barons, and the representatives of the *università*."

It was in the following parliaments, beginning with that of Syracuse of October 1398, that the parliament of Sicily began to acquire the functions and structural characteristics of the *cortes* of Aragon and Catalonia, with its own specific sphere of competence and control and deliberative powers. There were two fundamental innovations, one structural, the other procedural. Parliament was organised in three *bracci*: the domanial *braccio* made a series of proposals which became law through the approval of the sovereign. The ecclesiastical representatives may already have separated from the secular lords in 1320, when Frederick II sent them a special writ of summons convoking them to assist in resolving financial difficulties. But this single occasion did not seem to have created a precedent. Only after 1398 did the division into three *bracci* become clear. By the time of the parliament of Taormina of August 1411, which contested the regency of Martin's widow Bianca, the assembly was unquestionably divided into three *bracci*. It was from this parliament that there emerged the so-called "Regiment of Sicilians" (*Regimentu di Sichiliani*) – a government committee, of at least partially revolutionary intent, which attempted to elect its own king: the "Regiment" included a prelate among its members as representative of the ecclesiastical state (*lu brazu ecclesiasticu*). The practice of the *cortes* of the Crown of Aragon was also imitated in other matters, not only in the participation in parliament of senior royal officials and procurators of absentee feudatories, but in the internal organisation of the assemblies, the ceremonial orders of precedence and the creation of a permanent Deputation.

Under Alfonso the Magnanimous (1416–58) the recently developed reciprocity of concessions between king and parliament was maintained. The *donativi* or financial contributions demanded by the king were offered (*oblatio*) in return for the acceptance of parliamentary votes, which for the most part requested respect of the *capitoli* of the kingdom. Laws were no longer simple manifestations of the royal will and prerogative but were bilateral contracts, sworn under oath and revocable only by mutual accord (*pactionatae leges et inviolabiles contractus*).[24]

During the crisis over the succession, parliament's last-minute support for Alfonso's nephew Ferdinand the Catholic in 1460 won it further concessions, which contrasted sharply with Ferdinand's treatment of Catalonia. Abandoning Alfonso's policy of strict control, Ferdinand restored full feudal jurisdiction to the barons, revoking previous exemptions or concessions made to the barons' vassals. He even abolished all taxes on the island, except for the ordinary *collette*, and only twice (in 1474 and 1478) asked parliament to grant *donativi*. In 1478 the viceroy, count de Cardona y Prades, tried to collect taxes without a full consultation with parliament, using as his excuse that it was for the defence of the island. The effect of his bribes and threats was to create a coalition of the various cities (with the probable exception of Messina, the perpetual rival of Palermo), which protected themselves by sending their ambassadors with new mandates, which broke entirely with custom, "to listen to the viceregal proposal and refer back". The majority of the domanial *braccio* was backed up by the other two *bracci*, who delayed all decisions until finally the session was indefinitely prorogued.

Thus few changes were made in the structure or activities of parliament under Ferdinand. Nevertheless, the character of Spanish rule began to change. At first the contractual nature of the *capitoli* was officially denied, although in practice they remained the price the king had to pay for the *bracci*'s vote of the *donativo*. Then in the

[24] In the 1446 parliament the *bracci* offered Alfonso the Magnanimous 120,000 florins to grant the concessions and *grazie* they requested. The king accepted, provided the amount was increased to 125,000 florins. The final document contained the explicit clause that "his said majesty abdicates *omne posse* his power to dispense with the present orders and *capitoli*, which are contracts made with the kingdom for a price (*pro praetio*)".

early 16th century the threat of Turkish invasion obliged parliament to be more generous in its offers of *donativi*. Even so, a formal respect for the autonomy of the country remained and the dialogue or collaboration between viceroy and parliament continued. For parliament was regarded by the Sicilians as a guarantee of their rights. Undoubtedly its members became increasingly concerned to conserve their own privileges. But at the same time the "three *bracci* of the kingdom" made a systematic contribution to better administration and justice, to the defence of the country, to the distribution of taxes, to the preservation of the monopoly of civil, military and ecclesiastical offices for Sicilians and to measures encouraging economic or commercial progress. Parliament, in fact, remained the expression of both particularist and general interests in Sicily.

The structure and procedure of the Sicilian parliaments of the 15th and 16th centuries can be outlined with a fair degree of precision.

Parliament was convoked by the king or by the viceroy on receipt of a special royal mandate. Already before the end of the 15th century custom prescribed that parliaments be summoned at least once every three years, corresponding to the period for which *donativi* were granted. The sovereign (or viceroy) presided over the assemblies, including those which were occasionally summoned outside the normal triennial period for special reasons.[25] Extraordinary taxes tended to be voted in addition to the ordinary *donativi*, except on a few occasions (as in 1481 and 1567) when the granting of the latter excluded the former. Adequate time had to be left between the issuing of the writs and the opening of parliament in order to allow the participants to reach the city chosen for the meeting. The writ of summons was obligatory. Queen Blanche, in her writs for the parliament of 1411, warned those who failed to attend or send a representative that they "will show themselves public enemies of the royal house of Aragon and of the kingdom". It may have been in this assembly that for the first time absentees ran the risk of being declared contumacious. The custom was adopted of beginning parliamentary discussions only after a double prorogation: following Roman law practice, parliamentarians who had failed to appear

[25] The assemblies called to swear fealty to new sovereigns (at least from 1503) had a special character and possessed no deliberative powers.

by then and had not offered adequate justification could be threatened with sanctions.

Failure to appear thus implied disobedience to a legal ruling. But the writs of summons placed the emphasis on persuasion. For example, the writ of June 1478 stated: "We certify that the general parliament to which you are summoned will not treat of *donativi* or of granting any sum; do not delay if you cherish royal grace." The writ of 1411 varied the form for the different estates: for the ecclesiastical *braccio* it stated "we request, pray and command you" (though soon after it began to state simply "we exhort you"); for the military *braccio*, "we charge you"; for the domanial *braccio*, "we command you". But these were mere chancery terms, which changed nothing of the blandly coercive nature of the summons. In 1411, to assist obedience, a practice current in Aragonese territories was introduced: procurators were allowed to represent those unable to attend. This concession was continued and judged sufficiently convenient by the government for Ferdinand the Catholic to maintain it despite the protests of the parliament of 1481 that "often procurators accumulate six, seven, eight or more votes, which results in many scandals".

Special messengers delivered the writs and each recipient signed a receipt, enabling the Protonotary at the beginning of the session to count the number and judge the validity of explanations of failure to attend. The writ stated the reasons for the convocation in more or less precise terms, as well as the date and place of the assembly. Under Frederick II parliaments had been held in such minor cities as Piazza and Eraclea, and in the early 15th century they were still held at Catania and Syracuse. But it became the practice to hold them at Palermo – or in periods of disorder in the nearby Castellammare – or in the rival city of Messina.

The three orders of the prelates, barons and *università*, when in common session, were considered the representatives of the kingdom. The ecclesiastical *braccio* came first in order of dignity and precedence. It was composed of the archbishops, abbots (and originally of an archimandrite), priors and other clergy. But all its members participated not as priests, but as holders of fiefs or benefices under royal patronage. All Sicilian bishoprics were under royal patronage as they had been founded and endowed by the Norman kings. This enormous influence and authority of the civil over the ecclesiastical power offered considerable advantages and honours to ecclesiastical dignitaries, but hardly contributed to the autonomy or authority of the *braccio* in political and parliamentary activities.

The second estate was the military, feudal or baronial *braccio*, composed of royal vassals who held fiefs *in capite*, directly granted by the sovereign.[26] At the parliament of 1541 the *braccio* consisted of three marquesses, ten counts, two viscounts and sixty-two barons; at that of 1556 of at least one duke, six marquesses, nine counts. Before the end of the century Spanish influence had transformed many of the barons into counts, counts into marquesses, and dukes and marquesses into princes. The lords could send a procurator or be represented by another feudatory. Although these noble families originated from many different countries, by the 16th century they all appeared wholly Sicilian in their spirit, interests and actions. On many occasions, by its clamorous protests or exploitation of parliamentary procedures, this *braccio* personified the close attachment of the Sicilian ruling class to the legal and spiritual traditions of the kingdom.

From 1531, the feudatories sat in their reunions by order of precedence, which distinguished holders of fiefs from simple procurators. They often found the other two *bracci* supporting them in their petitions. In fact they dominated the economy of the island, including that of the major cities, as much as public life. But this predominance and monopoly of the highest public offices was gradually but tenaciously reduced in the latter part of the 16th century by Philip II's ministers.

The last of the *bracci* was the domanial estate, consisting of the *università* or cities and centres of any importance directly subject to the royal demesne. About forty localities were represented. According to the committee of twelve, which had been elected in 1398 to reclaim lands previously alienated from the demesne or enfeoffed, there were forty-five of these localities. The number varied, as did that of the fiefs, following the somewhat limited movements of population and wealth. The cities or *terre* were represented in parliament by ambassadors (*syndici*, procurators), normally chosen by

[26] In 1627 Philip IV declared that the military *braccio* consisted exclusively of nobles who possessed fiefs and vassals. The declaration confirmed a traditional criterion of eligibility.

councillors or jurors more or less according to procedures used to nominate municipal representatives for other events. The cities and minor centres generally sent only one representative; the major cities sent two or four, and Palermo sent six. But whatever their number, each city had only one vote.

All procurators, whether ecclesiastics (representing individuals or religious communities), feudatories or cities, were requested in the summons and again when they appeared in parliament to present full and adequate mandates to approve decisions beneficial to the kingdom. Considerable attention was paid to this rule, as could be seen in the writs of 1541 and 1555, and also in the mandate of the commune of Corleone to its ambassadors in 1439. The election had been made by the captain, *baiulus* and jurors as legal representatives of the city, and "for greater prudence" by some thirty "honest men". The ambassadors were given the duty and powers to attend and to be entirely free to reply according to their judgement (*sub quacumque forma, voluntate et opinione melius visa et placita eisdem ambasciatoribus*), and to vote in the name and on behalf of the city, to discuss and conclude any matter, whether known or unknown to those who had elected them, with full (*omnimodo*) powers, as if the city itself had been present. Palermo, however, gave its representatives to the parliament of 1478 powers limited by "instructions and memorials" to listen, refer back and await further instructions.

The *bracci,* once in session, were called the "three *bracci* of the kingdom": their official title was that of representatives of the entire, "most faithful" kingdom of Sicily, in whose name and on whose behalf they acted. On the other hand each *braccio* represented an identifiable sector of the population of the country. The ecclesiastical *braccio* was the defender of the general interests of the clergy; the military *braccio* was formed of the higher nobility but also represented the non-feudal nobles; the domanial *braccio* acted in the interests, and pledged the inhabitants of all the royal demesne, even of centres not directly represented.

After a solemn religious ceremony, the three *bracci* listened to a speech from the sovereign or viceroy, delivered from a special tribunal. The members were grouped according to their *braccio*, but did not sit in order of precedence. This was the only way to avoid ceremonial problems. The speech (*proposta*, *proposición, propositio*) tended increasingly to be read by the Protonotary, the viceroy's *alter ego* in parliamentary affairs. The leading prelate of the ecclesiastical order replied with a shorter, more formal but careful speech on behalf of the three *bracci*, and hence of the kingdom. Then each of the *bracci* met for discussions, deliberating separately, but maintaining contact with the other *bracci* and the viceregal court through ambassadors. No minutes of these separate meetings appear to have been kept; so we know little about the discussions, procedure or negotiations with the viceroy. Scipione di Castro, in his well-known *Avvertimenti al Sig. Marc'Antonio Colonna quando andò Vice Re di Sicilia* (1577), described the meetings as limited to a discussion and deliberation of the reasons for and timing of the concession of a *donativo*. Each *braccio*, according to di Castro, had to decide seven things: whether to concede the *donativo;* to refuse it; its size; the source from which to pay it; the length of its duration; the conditions on which it was to be granted; the proposals to submit for the king's approval.[27] As di Castro noted, decisions were taken by majority vote within the *bracci* and all votes were equal, but the moral authority of the "first voice" or leader of the *braccio* was of great influence. Much depended on his tact and energy, just as the success and speed of the negotiations depended on agreements between the government and the three leaders. The greater or lesser esteem accorded to parliament, the *bracci* and its members depended on the energy of the leaders.

Voting in the *bracci* could be open or secret. The parliament of 1562 decided that the voting of the *donativo* should always be open, on the grounds that this was both customary and for the general good, and because everyone should be prepared to acknowledge his own responsibility. A *capitolo* of Philip II also confirmed the practice of open voting as it was based on ancient custom and it would be absurd (*incongruum*) to abandon it.[28] A vote of parliament presupposed favourable votes by all three *bracci*. However, this was not axiomatic.

[27] Besides these seven points, di Castro listed six reasons why a viceroy might feel defeated: because his proposal was refused; because he was offered less than he had demanded; because the conditions tied to the offer were excessive; because the demands of the *bracci* were against the viceroy's own interests; because they nominated a parliamentary representative to go to Madrid, whom the viceroy did not approve of; because the "deputies" were his enemies, or extremely stubborn and rigid.

[28] A document of 1464 quotes the viceroy as stating that "in matters of the kingdom it is not necessary for all the *terre* to be in agreement, but the major part is enough; and what the major part agrees to, the minor part – even if reluctant and in opposition –

More than once, one of the *bracci*, without openly refusing its vote in favour of the *donativo*, held back by submitting some petition. On these occasions the viceroy's councillors, or the viceroy himself, affirmed that the majority principle was valid not only for the deliberations of the single *braccio* but for those of parliament: if two of the *bracci* voted in favour they outvoted the opposition of the third. Such an affirmation, however, would appear to be a tactical manoeuvre to oblige the hostile *braccio* to withdraw, rather than a declaration of principle.[29]

There can be little doubt that the most frequent and important object of parliamentary discussions was the vote over the *donativi*. As time went on, exceptional temporary *donativi* acquired the characteristics of ordinary ones, so that the discussions related to more than one. The vote constituted the most serious and notable act of collaboration between subjects and sovereign. It met the requests of the administration and provided finances for general needs. The *bracci* decided the method of payment and sources of income, in order to ensure that the funds were used only for the stated purpose and that the burden was fairly distributed. A normal condition of the *donativi* was that during the period of their exaction king and government could not ask the kingdom for other taxes.

Not unnaturally the Sicilian parliament tried more than once in the 16th century to reintroduce the practice of bilateral contractual grants established by Alfonso the Magnanimous in 1446, which made subsidies dependent on royal acceptance of the *bracci*'s requests. Ferdinand the Catholic had abrogated this practice and the attempts to revive it could only have appeared to the Spaniard rulers as arbitrary and little less than seditious – unless of course the sum offered was so large as to justify an exception.

Apart from technical conditions relating to the exaction of the *donativo*, all parliamentary proposals were regarded as requests of

---

is obliged and held to follow; and this has been the constitutional and continual practice observed in this kingdom".

[29] The episode took place in the 1591 parliament, when the military *braccio* formally opposed the grant of a *donativo*. Unfortunately, too little is still known of the details and significance of the clash, as the Spanish archives have not yet been sufficiently explored. Cf. H. G. Koenigsberger, *The government of Sicily under Philip II of Spain. A study in the practice of empire,* London, 1951.

"favours" (*grazie*). It was up to the king to grant or refuse his approval, or impose various reservations and limitations. This superiority of the sovereign in legislative matters might have taken the form of a simple right of veto. But political considerations usually led to some form of agreement. The sovereign remained supreme legislator; according to the official doctrine of absolute monarchy, his will was law. But the doctrine reflected prestige rather than fact. The ancient laws and customs of the kingdom could not be changed without the consent of the *bracci*. The viceroy had the power to issue new laws, and frequently did so, sometimes following the suggestion of one or more of the *bracci*. But these decrees could not interfere with the ancient laws, especially the *Capitoli del regno*, which previous sovereigns had granted in response to proposals or petitions of the *bracci*. The fact that these rights were published – like the privileges of the individual cities – made them better known and easier to defend. More than once the chief magistrates of Palermo and Messina endured persecution and even imprisonment by the viceroy rather than give up any of their local rights.

Just as they used lawyers to draw up their proposals, the *bracci* employed the most persuasive ambassadors to present these proposals to the king. But the increasing inflexibility of the Spanish monarchy tended to discourage, without ever formally forbidding, the despatch of such embassies. Under Alfonso the Magnanimous embassies had formed part of the normal procedure; in the 16th century they became rare. On the other hand, the viceroys did not feel their dignity offended by taking over these duties. They were, in any case, obliged to express their opinion on parliamentary proposals, even though the really important opinion would come from the Supreme Council of Italy at Madrid.

But if the Sicilian parliament's defence of its individuality and interest lost an important weapon because of these difficulties over its embassies, it acquired another weapon in the form of the Deputation of the kingdom of Sicily. Before the Deputation there had been "deputies", but their duties were not continuous and were limited to fulfilling specified functions. These deputies, however, developed into an autonomous legally recognised institution. In 1446 parliament had nominated deputies to control the distribution, exaction and correct employment of its *donativo*. They formed a delegation of parliament with executive duties to carry out the will of the three *bracci* once parliament was dissolved. The same would seem to apply to the deputies whose nomination was requested by the parliament of 1474. On that occasion, however, John II imposed severe limitations: he refused to grant deputies the power to enforce the observance of the *capitoli* of the kingdom, and only granted to a limited number of deputies the right to supplicate the king or viceroy against transgressions of the *capitoli*, should it prove necessary.

From the last quarter of the 15th century, there were frequent examples of deputies and parliamentary deputations appointed to control the exaction of taxes and watch over the observance of the *capitoli* and privileges of the kingdom. A deputation was appointed for each new *donativo*. They were clearly becoming important, authoritative, active and jealous of their independence and position in their relations with the royal administration. The parliament of 1514 wanted the sovereign to recognise and confirm that "the deputies of the kingdom have power equal to that of the said three *bracci*". The parliament of 1518 repeated the request.

Under Philip II, with his passion for bureaucratic tidiness, the Deputation acquired its final form. It was legally recognised and organised as the sole body concerned with *donativi* (*una tantum omnium donativorum constitui visa est deputatio*), according to the decision of the three *bracci* in 1567. When a new parliament met in 1570 the Deputation was renewed. According to the act nominating its members, the duties of the deputies were to control the exaction and utilisation of the *donativi* and draft supplications to the king and his viceroy on any matter necessary for the king's service. According to other decrees of 1571, 1575, 1581, 1582, 1583 and 1588 the Deputation was formed of twelve members, four for each *braccio*, and normally included the leaders of each. It lasted from one parliament to the next. The presidency changed each month. It had its own staff and by the end of the 16th century held regular meetings with full formality every Thursday in a special room of the royal palace.

The particular concern of the deputies was, in the words of the parliamentary votes of 1585 and 1588, to guard over the "*capitoli*, constitutions, *grazie* and privileges conceded both in general and in particular to this most faithful kingdom", especially those granted by the reigning sovereigns in return for payment. For this purpose the deputies were not only to supplicate but, according to the 1588 vote, "to do everything that the Kingdom would do when meeting collegiately [i.e. as a parliament], as it has been given these powers".

This Deputation of the kingdom of Sicily, which survived into the following centuries, was similar not only in name but also (at least partly) in its functions to analogous institutions and organs of the Catalan, Aragonese and Valencian *cortes*, especially the *Deputació del General de Catalunya* and of Valencia. Its existence and activities undoubtedly gave parliamentary votes greater authority and efficacy. But its decisions only became obligatory if approved by the viceroy.

4

The States of the Church

Although documents frequently mention "general parliaments", general assemblies of the entire States of the Church, or even of a group of provinces, were extremely rare. The only well-documented meeting was that held at Fano in April–May 1357 by Cardinal Egidio d'Albornoz when he promulgated his constitutions. Other inter-provincial assemblies were held in 1371, 1372, 1373, 1374 or 1375 and probably in 1388. They were exceptional, wholly outside the constitutional organisation of the state, with none of the real attributes of a parliament.

Assemblies of individual provinces were more frequent, not only because they were easier to convoke, but probably also because they were more useful to the administration. They were held at differing intervals, with no regularity, in the Romagna, Patrimony, Campania, Duchy and more limited areas, such as Montefeltro, San Leo, Farfa, etc. But far more numerous than any of these were the provincial assemblies of the March of Ancona. After a brief resistance to the revocation of communal franchises at the beginning of the 14th century, the parliament of the March accepted a role of unconditional subordination to the legates or rectors of the province. This was the only parliament of any significance in the States of the Church, and hence alone worthy of detailed examination.

One effect of the Albornoz constitutions of 1357 had been to make the Ancona assembly an auxiliary organ of the provincial administration. A direct result was that the frequency of its sessions increased. The most solemn meetings were those called by each new rector of the province to read aloud the documents of his nomination, exact the customary oath of fealty and obedience, promulgate new laws, and swear to carry out his duty and respect the rights and privileges of all concerned. But numerous other sessions were held, both "ordinary" meetings to decide the total amount and distribution of military or other dues, and "extraordinary" meetings summoned to adopt whatever measures were judged necessary in the face of new or unexpected dangers. Sometimes meetings were called to listen to the rector's decision about feuds, would-be rebels, political, military or other measures.

The general or "state" assemblies were summoned by the pope or his legate, provincial assemblies by the legate or rector of the province. In the latter case, when the offices were not combined, the rector *in spiritualibus* convoked the ecclesiastics, while the rector *in temporalibus* (who only had jurisdiction over clergy if he was himself a priest) convoked the secular members, both feudatories and communes. The writs of summons were virtual citations to appear before judgement. They were precise and peremptory, naming the place and time of the meeting, ordering those convoked to appear, and specifying the details of the mandates to be brought by representatives. A good example is the summons sent out by the papal vicar Cardinal Albornoz on 27 December 1366: "We have decided to hold a general parliament at Ancona on 14 January. Therefore with the present summons we request and urge your loyalty. Under threat of a fine of a thousand silver marks, other spiritual and temporal penalties of our choice, confiscation of your possessions and loss of all office, we order you expressly not to fail to send an ambassador, with full and adequate mandate drawn up in the prescribed manner, to give counsel, and accept and promise to carry out what will be decided upon in parliament. If you do not obey and are contumacious, negligent or disobedient – which we do not believe – we shall proceed to judgement against you in the aforesaid manner."

Obligatory attendance was also decreed in the Constitutions of Albornoz. The seriousness of the duty was even underlined by a decree increasing penalties threefold for offences against delegates attending or returning from parliament in obedience to the order of the legate or rector.

These writs of summons (*mandata, licterae pro parlamento, licterae parlamenti*) were more or less the same for all provinces in all periods. They were notified by special couriers and acknowledged by receipts. They almost always stated the reason for the convocation, although in summary manner, in order to allow the participants to prepare their replies. Until the late 14th century summons were sent to all bishops, prelates, abbots, priors, parish priests, cathedral chapters, cities, communes, castles and *terre*, probably according to lists occasionally brought up to date. But sometime before the beginning of the 15th century the clergy and feudal lords ceased to be summoned.[30]

Throughout the Papal States obligation to attend the assemblies could be dispensed by the pope: thus Velletri was exempted by Boniface VIII, while Terni unsuccessfully claimed dispensation from Gregory X. But no such concessions appear to have been granted to the communes of the March of Ancona. As was made clear – particularly to ecclesiastics – attendance was not only a legal but a moral obligation. Failure to attend could not be tolerated since it implied disloyalty and disobedience. Nor, according to the administration, were such obligations fulfilled if representatives did not possess truly adequate mandates, with powers "to listen, treat, conclude and obey".[31] For at the end of the meeting, one by one

[30] The last time the clergy participated in a parliament of the March of Ancona was in 1367. By the beginning of the 15th century the feudatories were no longer to be found, and the assembly was frequently called the "council of orators and syndics".

[31] The mandates of the communal representatives at the assembly of 1305 were good examples of these requirements, granting necessary and sufficient powers to obey the orders of the papal legates; representatives at the provincial parliaments of Recanati were given full powers, without reservations. Sometimes, however, the order was not obeyed to the letter and the mandate, instead of giving unlimited powers, contained more or less explicit reservations: at the Macerata parliament of 1337 several of the

the participants promised and swore to observe the decisions of the president. The representatives of the major cities, in fact, had to provide suitable witnesses as guarantors.

The pre-eminent and authoritarian position of the papal representative, who sat *pro tribunali* as if presiding over a trial, was in keeping with this procedure. Correspondingly, the participants came forward as if they were debtors, promising to meet their obligations. In fact, unless they were requested to offer counsel or deliberate or state their opinions, the declarations of those present were little more than expressions of their respective obligations.

On the other hand, those who felt themselves unjustly taxed could appeal directly to the pope. In 1357 the commune of San Ginesio protested to the pope that at the end of a parliament held at Macerata the provincial rector had imposed higher taxes on the commune than the maximum laid down in the papal *capitoli* and privileges, and asked for a corresponding reduction. A similar protest occurred over the subsidy imposed on the communes in the parliament of Bologna of 1375. Once again, the first to appeal was San Ginesio, this time backed up by Tolentino, on the grounds that they had been taxed excessively and more heavily than the other communes; they were successful in obtaining a reduction.

On some occasions the delegates agreed – without any formal procedure – to submit some recommendation or request to the papal curia. Accordingly, orators or ambassadors of the province or parliament were sent to Rome. In 1367, Innocent VI ordered the legate of the March to accept the request sent him by the city of Recanati.[32] In 1419, after a parliament held at Recanati, envoys petitioned Martin V to hold the provincial curia permanently at Macerata, as it was the most central city and the easiest to reach from all parts of the province.

As has been stated, at a certain moment the composition of the assembly of the March of Ancona became more restricted and

representatives with inadequate mandates of this sort were sent back to obtain full powers. The representative was called an "orator" or "syndic" or "ambassador"; but the terms were not always synonymous, as sometimes a syndic was accompanied by one or more orators.

[32] The mandate of Recanati to its representatives to the parliament of 25 March 1425 would seem to allude to concerted action by the communes, for although it was a full mandate, it was accompanied by instructions to reach agreement with the deputies of the other communes.

homogeneous. The ecclesiastics, who had appeared in the assembly of 1367, were no longer to be found in those of 1375 or 1389. The feudatories also no longer appeared (though it is impossible to state from what date) and parliament consisted solely of the ambassadors or *sindaci* (usually called orators by the early 16th century) of the *civitates, universitates et loca*. Instead of a parliament or "council of orators and ambassadors", the assembly tended to be described as a "congregation". By the second half of the 16th century the municipal orators were described as deputies, to be distinguished from those of the parliamentary Deputation (*Deputati provinciae Marchiae*). But both groups were called "noble men".

Meetings were summoned by the legate, rector or governor-general of the March on his own initiative, for instance in response to requests for finances from the papal curia, or – as in 1528 and 1535 – on the advice of his council. At a later stage the proposal came from the "ambassador of the province" (*sindicus provinciae*), who in title and function would seem to be a representative of the provincial congregation in its relations with the papal delegate. But from 1585 the *sindicus* was substituted by a new permanent collegiate organ, the *deputacio ad negocia*, responsible for proposing the convocation of the provincial assembly.

Because of the frequency of convocations, by the last quarter of the 16th century the activities of the congregation developed rapidly, its sphere of competence grew more extensive and its rules of procedure became more explicit. The writs of summons, although sometimes still presented as "intimations" and expressed as commands, were no longer backed by threat of sanctions. The order to send representatives with adequate powers was observed, but not to the letter. On more than one occasion, in fact, parliamentary decisions were blocked by the presence of an indefinite number of deputies with mandates only to "listen and refer back". A summons of 1578 deplored the fact – which it explained optimistically as the result of inexperience – observing that "if any of the deputies wants to make known some other need of the province, he will be listened to". The explanation was obviously euphemistic. In 1572 the city of Macerata had given its two representatives a mandate and power to agree to everything they judged consistent with the interests of the province, but not to agree to any matter on which they opposed the government. In 1581 Macerata's mandate to its representatives allowed them to agree "to all and every matter which proves necessary and opportune and for the benefit, honour and utility of the said province and our said community". But it added that the representatives were to oppose *in forma iuris* whatever harmed or threatened the rights or privileges of the city. They were not to vote against but subsequently accept the will of the majority (as would be the practice of a true parliamentary assembly), but to make a formal administrative appeal against what was regarded as an unjust decision.

By tradition representatives were convoked to this singular assembly primarily to listen to what was decided, so that active consent was regarded as less important than lack of opposition. What gave force to the proposals was basically the decision of the government authorities. In consequence, consent was of value only in so far as it facilitated a rapid execution either of decisions relating to the internal organisation of parliament or of other measures announced to the participants. But by the later 16th century the position was clearly changing and representatives began to possess powers and take decisions.

The matters to be placed before the orators or deputies of the March, which were usually stated or indicated in the writs, related to nominations, public works, extraordinary contributions, examination of revenue and expenditure, etc. It was important to state the reasons for the convocation in the writs of summons so that the local administrations would feel sufficiently persuaded by the general utility of the measures to instruct their envoys to accept the government's proposals or requests. Certainly no agenda was prepared, at least until the last quarter of the 16th century. Sometimes the cities even took the initiative and asked that an assembly be called only after certain questions had been resolved, threatening an appeal to the pope if they were not listened to.

The assemblies were usually held at Macerata, but sometimes at Fermo, Recanati, Ancona and other cities, even at Rome. In 1566, perhaps for the first time, a meeting was held at Loreto, next to the sanctuary. It was significant that a new session in May 1585 proposed that Loreto became the permanent seat of all future provincial assemblies, because it had the advantage of being exempt from the jurisdiction of the rector of the March. But this proposal was accepted only in 1613.

Meetings though not held regularly were clearly frequent, but a request of 1528 for annual meetings was not accepted. In 1730 biennial congregations were decreed. The sessions were extremely short, usually only lasting one day.

Our knowledge of the activities of the provincial assembly of the March of Ancona in the period following the 16th century confirms our impression of its development. The congregation became a permanent body, organised coherently and achieved considerable importance in its relations with the legate or governor. It was the expression of the autonomy of the province. At the same time, it signified the participation of the population in the administration and government through the representation of the communes in both the congregation and its deputations and organs. The assembly's vote acquired progressively greater authority: although never in a position to challenge papal authority, it was superior to that of the local representatives of the papal curia.

Before these belated and still limited developments, this parliament of the States of the Church was of little importance. It is hard to believe that it took part in the exercise of legislative, political or administrative functions.[33] At moments when peace or the Church's sovereignty was threatened, it was undoubtedly useful to convoke some of the most responsible and authoritative subjects in the area, especially as the assembly was the most suitable place to study what measures should be taken. But this was quite different from a political function. It was no more than a casual, exceptional activity, outside and additional to the true functions of a parliament. The assembly

[33] It is true that the Albornoz constitutions asserted that they had been read and approved in the parliament of Fano of 1357. There can be no doubt that they were promulgated there – hence their publication – and it seems probable that they were read aloud, although the text is so long that it would have taken the major part of the three days of the session. But it is impossible to believe that those present at the Fano parliament were in a position to discuss the content of the constitutions, and even less likely that they were able to express consent or dissent. Not only was this neither the practice nor in the spirit of the assemblies of the States of the Church; but the constitutions themselves, which were promulgated in a parliament held to celebrate the arrival of a new rector, spoke of publication – and not of approval – of these regulations. In fact, the same constitutions had already been "read and published" in the "public parliament" of Montefiascone of 1354, as were other, similar legislative measures in a parliament of 1420.

had no political competence, nor did it become a deliberative organ with powers of its own or authority to decide any measures of a general character. At most, its meetings were purely consultative, with no power to bind the leaders of the province; otherwise, they were simply reunions with no collegiate sense, where individual participants offered counsel in their own name or on behalf of the community they represented.

The parliament of the March of Ancona was thus a provincial parliament in a very literal sense: it represented a restricted territorial area and possessed extremely limited powers. Nevertheless, even before its definitive reorganisation by Sixtus V in 1585, it served a purpose. It represented a check on arbitrary actions by provincial rectors and to some extent controlled their activities through its capacity to appeal to the pope. Even more, it signified a limit to the power of the popes themselves, as it forced the curia to recognise that financial demands could only be imposed with the consent of the assemblies, and that large-scale legal changes (such as those of Albornoz) required at least the convocation of parliament. The very number of sessions held by the assembly was symptomatic of these functions: thirty-seven in the 14th century, at least nineteen in the 15th and over sixty in the 16th century. In fact, as the congregation developed, it was able to act as a defence and brake against the progressive centralisation of the States of the Church.

5

Friuli

Before the end of the 14th century already the authority of the parliament of Friuli as a representative and deliberative body was so great that frequently – and particularly during periods when the see was vacant – it rivalled the leading court officials in importance. Its efficacy in helping to settle the difficult problems of the succession naturally increased its prestige. As early as the patriarchate of

Bertoldo of Andechs (1218–50) ecclesiastical dignitaries, "free" and "ministerial" feudatories and communal representatives were consulted about the most important decisions. The three orders normally acted together in parliament. This "colloquy" had a separate personality from its directive and executive organ, the Council. Parliament assumed a stable position in the government of the country during the patriarchates of Pietro (d. 1301) and Ottobono dei Razzi (d. 1315). From then on, the "colloquy" controlled the patriarchal government, and in particular its finances.

The basic reason for this progressive extension of the authority of parliament and its executive organ was probably the ecclesiastical character of the principate. The inalienability and indivisibility of the territory – which derived from the fact that it was not hereditary – acted as an effective defence against the claims of neighbouring powers. It may also have tended to soften the rigidity of feudal ties, and create a greater reciprocal respect and desire to collaborate. In fact, the most notable characteristic of the Friuli parliament in the patriarchal period was its unity, its quality of a collegiate body so closely and intimately bound together as to give the impression of a single "estate" rather than of an assembly of estates. Yet this did not happen because the assembly was the expression of a single social class. It was the unity and autonomy of a purely artificial body – parliament – which as a corporation expressed political interests differing from those of both the sovereign and the individual groups from which it drew its members.

The assemblies were convoked by the patriarch or his delegate (by special mandate) or, during vacancies in the patriarchal see, by the administrators responsible for the state – the *vicedomino*, the vicar *in temporalibus*, and others. Thus, the "general colloquium" of 1333 was convoked by the two "guardians and conservators" of the rights and jurisdictions of the Church of Aquileia. The sole exception to this rule was the summons issued by the commune of Udine in 1385, as a sign of its refusal to recognise the patriarch Philippe d'Alençon. But this very fact rendered the convocation corrupt and illegal in the eyes of its enemies.

The assembly was summoned at the discretion of the patriarch, who was under no obligation to convoke it regularly. In the entire period before the patriarchate's annexation by Venice (1420), the occasion and location of the parliament of Friuli depended on the patriarch. Sometimes the need to summon parliament was self-evident; at other moments the patriarch's councillors or, later, the "general council of the colloquy" – the parliamentary councillors or deputies – may have suggested that a convocation was opportune. But in principle the patriarch's right of convocation represented one of his highest prerogatives "as lord of the land". On the other hand, his freedom to invite whoever he wished became restricted. At least from the end of the 14th century, there was a fixed list which he could not change. This certainly contributed towards the growth of a sense of unity, an *esprit de corps*, as nobles and communal representatives were bound together in *vicinitas et confraternitas* like a corporation. This sense of unity could be seen in the voting procedure – not by estates but all together – and in the efficiency and vitality of the assembly's representative organ, the Council.

Only two documents seem to indicate obligatory attendance: a writ of summons of 1384, referring to the "pressing mandate" (*mandatum et instantia*) of the patriarch; and a writ sent to the commune of Cividale by the *vicedominus* Odorico di Strassoldo in 1359, containing the phrase "by the debt of fealty by which you are bound to the Church of Aquileia". Nevertheless, the obligation seems to be confirmed by the need felt by the inhabitants of Cividale to excuse their absence in 1389 on the grounds of inadequate notice, and by the frequent appearance in the writs of such formulas as "without adducing excuses or pretexts".

On the other hand, at least twice – in 1352 and 1353 – the patriarch in his opening speech to parliament "excused himself for not convoking the colloquy earlier because so many matters had intervened". It was clear that parliament was regarded as a useful instrument of government. It recognised the virtual right, or at least interest, of the members to be convoked.

There was thus both an obligation and a right to attend meetings. Attendance was compulsory, but must have been regarded as a privilege and an excellent occasion to discuss matters of general and specific interest. It was a public duty, but in the personal interest of each participant. To facilitate attendance, the writs were sent out well in advance, usually eight or nine days before the meeting, together with safe conducts (*affidationes*).

Once the assembly met, a list of those present was drawn up, perhaps to check if the quorum was adequate. Lists of the subjects to be discussed existed, at least from the mid-14th century, and were probably prepared by the patriarch and parliamentary council together. But the participants were not informed before the opening session.

The *propositiones*, or solemn opening speeches, were only made by the patriarch or one of his vicars. But already before the mid-14th century, similar speeches – in practice, petitions – may also have been made by the members, so the patriarch and members could collaborate in determining the subjects for discussion. The terminology echoed the ritual of meetings of the general chapters of religious orders, for all *propositiones* were answered by *definitiones*, adopted by the participants without fixed order, following on direct discussions with the patriarch. The discussions, in dialect, were peaceful for the most part. Decisions were taken by a majority vote of those present. But for matters relating to taxes, the choice of councillors, or special parliamentary commissions, the four orders (the nobles were divided into "free" or "ministerial" groups) met and decided separately.

A Council was elected by parliament to carry out duties of a more permanent character, which exceeded the competence of the brief sessions. The councillors were first mentioned in a document of 1269, where they were described as *consiliarii terre Forijulii*. This was the Council of the patriarch, who added persons of his own choice to those of parliamentary nomination. There is no evidence to show why the patriarch accepted this Council in the first place. But if it maintained the point of view of parliament against the prince, on more than one occasion it exercised a moderating and conciliatory influence on the assemblies. Thus the Council acquired the character of a propitiatory organ, an intermediary between prince and assembly. By 1329 the Patriarch Pagano della Torre requested the nomination of the Council, as it would enable him "to provide better for both small and great matters". By 1352 even the authoritarian Nicholas of Luxembourg admitted that the strength of the regime was to be found in the ability and loyalty of the members of the Council. In this original manner parliament and patriarch resolved the problem of all similar assemblies: how to create an organ which could assist the prince in executive matters, while retaining the confidence of parliament.

By the time the Council had fully developed – in the second half of the 14th century – it possessed dual functions as a parliamentary organ and a government council. It acted as a parliamentary organ because it had received a general or specific mandate. On the one hand, its duty was to carry out whatever parliament had been unable to complete through lack of time. On the other, it had certain specified tasks, which ranged from deciding lawsuits to the elaboration of legislation, from working out the criteria to be followed in exacting a tax to the examination of accounts presented by members of the assembly. In exceptional circumstances the Council was given full powers by parliament.

As a government council, it assisted the patriarch in studying and decreeing all necessary political, military or administrative measures. It was responsible for the replies to be given to foreign powers, the despatch of ambassadors, the convocation of parliament and preparation of its agenda, the levy of troops, the adoption of necessary measures in emergencies requiring ratification by the following session of parliament. It attended the patriarch daily, looked after the maintenance of public order and the execution of sentences, delegated specific tasks to certain of its members, chose commissioners to control the military levy, which in turn formed the basis for the distribution of financial impositions, nominated commissions "to settle disputes", or "to examine property". But like parliament, it apparently lacked any chancery or personnel of its own.

The dominance which the Friuli parliament rapidly developed over the public administration and in its relations with the patriarch brought out clearly its representative function as the *universitas patriae Forijulii*. It is enough to point out that the patriarch himself, like all the other lords, accepted the taxes or distribution of military or financial dues imposed by the commission nominated by parliament. In this, as in all its activities, parliament represented the country: indeed these various parliamentary attributes should not be considered as separate activities, but as a single general function of the representative body. This emerged more clearly perhaps in the Friuli parliament than in any similar institution we have discussed.

But we should remember that besides its representative function, parliament also possessed a separate judicial function.

The almost unlimited competence of its executive organ, the Council, bore witness to what the Friuli parliament could do. Unfortunately we are not in a position to describe its range of powers with any precision. What would have been a valuable source – the *deliberationum generalis colloquii patrie Forijulii eiusdem consilii*, mentioned in a document of 1382 – has since disappeared. Nevertheless there is adequate documentation for a general description.

The judicial functions of the Friuli parliament were as old as the assembly itself. The genesis of these functions has been traced back to provincial reunions held by local leaders in Istria (and probably elsewhere in Italy, as in other countries) as early as the 11th century. They met in order to settle disputes, lay down rules for the maintenance of peace, and carry out judicial activities. It has also been related to the creation of an intermediate grade of jursidiction between baronial and royal jurisdiction, corresponding to the ducal powers of the patriarchs recognised by the Emperor Henry IV and his successors. It is quite clear that from the earliest times the parliament of Friuli exercised its jurisdiction over all matters relating to the keeping of the public peace: from cases of rebellion, conspiracy or treason to thefts on public highways. When the patriarch's marshal judged such crimes, he acted as parliament's deputy. By the beginning of the 13th century parliament also acted as a court of appeal against judgements of the patriarch (particularly in feudal cases of vassals *in capite*), and even of ecclesiastical tribunals. This power can only be explained in terms of the ecclesiastical personality of the prince who presided over parliament. Finally, parliament sometimes acted as a supreme court of appeal for civil cases of a certain economic importance which had already been decided by appeal to the patriarchal curia. Many cases were decided by the parliamentary Council, some by members of the assembly, and a few – but the most important – by parliament itself.

Parliament's original right to grant and regulate the size of military levies was transformed into a right to participate in and perhaps even be responsible for the defence of the country. The levy consisted of the *talea*, or knight service, obligatory on parliamentary nobles and the patriarch himself, and the *impositio peditum*, binding on all others. The militia was formed of foot-soldiers and bowmen. Knight service was both ordinary and extraordinary, its length was determined by the Council or parliament but could be prolonged. The *impositio* was either general (a levy in mass) or partial. If partial, it could be levied at a rate of one to ten men subject to arms, or one soldier for every hearth or family (or an equivalent payment in money). Parliament and Council divided the country into zones for purposes of defence, and were responsible for the construction, maintenance and manning of fortifications.

Another original and fundamental aspect of parliament's representative qualities was its right to deliberate over matters of taxation. Here, as everywhere, parliament's right to be summoned to express consent might refer not only to requests for authorisation to exceed the agreed sum, but also to instances where it was within the sovereign's power to exact the tax. The legal basis of taxation lay in the very principles of feudalism. Hence, to explain such obligations simply as customary (*consuetudo antiquissima et diutissime observata*), as did a document of 1313, was inadequate, unless intended as an argument to settle cases where the application of feudal principles was unclear. But in the face of a general and continuous increase of public expenditure (as well as of inflationary tendencies), this taxation proved inadequate. The sources of income had to be increased, and so the consent of the representative body had to be obtained. The granting of taxes became a voluntary act, only partially or indirectly enforceable. By 1336 it was openly stated that the decision to impose old or new taxes had to be taken by parliament. The patriarch had clearly given up all attempts to impose taxes arbitrarily, and on each occasion laid the needs of the state before parliament in order to obtain the necessary aid.

The Friuli parliament did not only deliberate on financial impositions (mainly *colte* and *taglie*) and obligatory labour services for public works. By the end of the 14th century the lords of Porcía could claim that "all new taxes should be deliberated upon by parliament". Thus, in the 15th century the assembly extended its powers to the so-called *charitativum subsidium*, a tax of ecclesiastical character on both clergy and laymen, which hitherto the patriarch had exacted as he wished. According to the customary procedure of medieval finances, every tax corresponded to a given expenditure, so that those responsible for its employment had to account for the full amount. In 1415, to prove his innocence, the Patriarch Ludovico of Teck asked parliament to investigate the truth of accusations that he had employed part of this subsidy for his own use. In this way he subjected himself to parliamentary control over the appropriation of taxes and subsidies.

The legislative functions of parliament can also be discerned in the earliest documents, and may have originated in the powers attributed to the ancient provincial assemblies to keep the peace. In contrast to the uncertainty which characterised these powers in so many provincial estates, they represented a permanent feature of the Friuli parliament until the fall of the patriarchal regime. Parliamentary influence undoubtedly increased. At first the initiative in introducing constitutions belonged exclusively to the patriarch. Later the patriarchs themselves spoke of parliamentary constitutions, as if parliament had not merely sanctioned them with its *auctoritatis interpositio*, but had been involved in their creation. On some occasions at least parliament played the leading role. Laws approved by parliament and the patriarch were sanctioned by a patriarchal decree which ordered public magistrates and feudal judges to enforce their observance. Despite the fragmentary nature of such legislation, it undoubtedly achieved notable results. Parliament also influenced legislation in an indirect manner through its own councillors or commissioners.

Although to begin with parliaments did not intervene in public administration and foreign relations, in time they became increasingly frequent and important. Naturally their influence in both fields became more effective when the patriarchal see was unoccupied; then, as with dynastic crises or regencies in other countries, precedents were created.

In 1331, when an alliance with the Scaligeri was signed, the Patriarch Pagano and the parliamentary Council declared that they were acting "in the name of the whole community of Friuli by virtue of the authority and power previously vested in them by the said community in its general colloquy". The ancient feudal concept of a personal guarantee of the individual members of parliament to carry out the treaty thus gave way and was transformed into a recognition of parliament as the representative organ of the *univer-*

sitas, patria or community of Friuli. Naturally the preliminary negotiations were carried out by special ambassadors or by the Council, while the assembly normally only approved and ratified the treaty.

Parliamentary participation in public administration frequently arose not as a conscious development, but as the indirect consequence of other deliberations, such as discussions relating to the defence of the country, the execution of legislative or economic measures, or the raising of finances. But on certain occasions, although there was no obligation, the patriarch asked the advice of parliament before decreeing some particularly important measure either of his own free will, or following the suggestion of parliamentary counsellors. Gradually the practice of consulting the assembly on financial and economic matters became customary, until finally such consultations were regarded as necessary and obligatory. When the see was vacant, the active participation of parliament in the administration was not only permissible but necessary. It appeared to have no limits, and was applied particularly over nominations to important offices. According to a document of 1380, it was parliament's duty to choose the territorial administrators. The assembly's intervention in matters relating to the patrimonial possessions of the patriarchal see, originally limited to periods when the see was vacant, also tended to continue during the patriarch's life-time, especially when he was abroad.

Parliament also took over the duties of remedying abuses of administrative officials. This was no usurpation, but a duty assigned to the assembly by the patriarch himself, who declared in 1353, perhaps for the first time, that parliament should judge accusations of misappropriation of funds made against some of his most important officials. On other occasions, as for example in 1372 and 1394, parliament itself asked for the same right. In 1389, following a complaint of the representatives of Udine, the Council requested the patriarch himself to respect the "ancient and praiseworthy customs". All who claimed to have suffered injustices could present petitions to parliament. But usually the cases were judged by the Council in its administrative capacity.

It is hardly necessary to state that the institutional development so far outlined referred exclusively to the period before the country lost its independence. The patriarchate's conquest by Venice in 1420 had a profound effect on the whole history of Friuli and naturally on the representative assembly as well, but already before the conquest parliament was losing prestige. After the murder of the Patriarch Bertrando in 1350 a virtual civil war marked the patriarchates. The sense of unity and concord was lost, and the assemblies became increasingly partisan. Parliament lost its role as arbiter and conciliator, and diminished in prestige and authority. With the nomination of Philippe d'Alençon as patriarch in 1380 internal strife grew worse, and even after he renounced the title in 1388 the continual interference of foreign powers prevented the restoration of peace. The most bitter struggle took place in 1419 during the patriarchate of Ludovico of Teck, when the exiles, led by the powerful family of Savorgnan, appealed to Venice. Between 1418 and 1420 all the cities, *terre* and feudatories accepted Venetian dominion in return for pacts guaranteeing respect for their statutes, privileges, customs and franchises. But despite these pacts, the new Venetian officials, led by the lieutenants, attempted to subordinate Friuli totally to the Republic.

The new situation deeply affected the activities of parliament, even before it altered the legal structure of the government of the country. For it diminished the assembly's energies and deprived it of its most treasured attributes. But no radical or rapid formal transformation accompanied this substantial change: otherwise it would be difficult to explain the convocation of a "general parliament" by the lieutenant in 1423 and the following years. On the other hand, when in 1436 an assembly met illegally at Udine to demand the dismissal of the marshal of the *patria*, the lieutenant decreed that all similar meetings were illegal.

The compact unity of parliament, once so strong and closely knit as to make it appear a real, almost a physical person rather than a collegiate body, thus grew weaker and disappeared in the face of internal contrasts, as the importance of the assembly diminished with the country's dependence on Venice. Nevertheless, parliament continued to function and deliberate.

The terms *generale parlamentum, colloquium, concilium seu parlamentum*, or simply *parlamentum* continued to be adopted for the ancient assembly of the *patria*.[34] The feudatories, castellans and representa-

[34] The term *convocatio* was also used, although in the Venetian period it tended to be

tives of noble consortia, or important noble houses, continued to be summoned, although the old distinction between "free" and "ministerial" nobles disappeared in the 15th century. But in contrast to the past, all nobles exercised the right to vote, even if feudally subject to a commune. The leaders of the clergy also continued to attend meetings, but following the example of the bishops of Concordia, who occupied the first seat in the assembly after the Venetian representative, they almost always sent an ecclesiastical representative.

The communes were more numerous than before, as under the new regime the practice of convoking only non-enfeoffed communes was no longer strictly observed. Their representatives ("orators" or "ambassadors") normally came to the assembly with regular and full mandates. Sometimes, despite such a mandate, the representative felt it opportune to ask permission to consult the communal administrators again. Occasionally the mandate was only to listen to the lieutenant's proposals and refer back for a decision, or else to lay before his colleagues (*alli compatrioti*) his commune's point of view and listen to their views. But these limited mandates were exceptional; they were only used in particular circumstances and then apparently solely by the cities of Udine and Cividale, which enjoyed particular legal prerogatives. The commune of Udine formed a separate body from parliament, and possessed far-ranging privileges. Its rival, Cividale, finally followed Udine's example and broke away from parliament in 1569, despite the appeals of the rest of the assembly that it act as leader. Like the city of Udine, the Savorgnan family felt itself superior to parliament, for although its members were entitled to places in the assembly as nobles, they claimed a particularly prominent position as Venetian patricians.

In 1567 parliament was composed of forty-one holders of jurisdictions or lordships, fourteen prelates and ecclesiastical dignitaries, and seventeen representatives of communes: as a group they formed the body of the "prelates, nobles and communes of the *patria*", or the *compatrioti*. Despite the withdrawal of Cividale, the number of members with votes remained more or less the same as a century and more before. Besides the additional "jurisdictions", even the

employed to describe the separate assemblies held for the regions on either side of the Tagliamento river.

city of Venice formed part of the *patria* as a feudatory, and was represented by the lieutenant or one of his agents (*fiscali*). In 1483 the assembly passed a reform to block the number of votes. But subsequently new admissions were allowed. In 1484 a committee of ten members – the so-called *X in parlamento* – was created to take over responsibilities for the convocation and composition of the assemblies. In 1584 it was decided that new admissions had to be approved by a majority of two-thirds of the Council of Ten (*Zonta* like the Spanish *Junta*).

From the beginning of the 15th century parliament was habitually described by the expression *tria membra*, or (exceptionally) *tre stati* or *tres status huius Patrie*.[35] But despite this description, votes continued to be taken by simple majority, without any divisions into separate estates. The question was raised, in fact, in 1486. The castellans wanted a majority of individual votes for decisions, whereas the prelates and communes wanted voting "by orders" (*per membra*). After long consultations the lieutenant came down on the side of the castellans. The question was raised again in 1584, but again the decision was to maintain the established practice. Despite this, on more than one occasion parliamentary committees were formed of six members, two for each estate, so as to balance the representation of the two regions divided by the Tagliamento river.

The power to summon parliament rested exclusively with the Venetian authorities. They took considerable care to impede illegal assemblies, or if necessary to resist proposals from Friulan leaders to convoke parliament.[36] Even when local pressures existed, only the lieutenant, as representative of the *Serenissimo Dominio*, could issue writs. The meetings were held almost invariably at Udine, and were presided over by the lieutenant accompanied by his officials,

[35] This last expression is found, perhaps for the first time, in a Venetian document of 14 May 1474. The account of the assembly of 24 November 1484 spoke of *membra*, and in fact the participants were registered member by member. The same term occurs in other parliaments of the 16th century. The term *stati* is also to be found referring to parliaments of the neighbouring county of Gorizia.

[36] Examples can be found in 1446 and subsequent years when the main cities persistently requested the lieutenant to convoke parliament so that it might examine whether or not a specific measure be continued. The lieutenant, without refusing, stated that "it had not been the custom of his predecessors to summon any convocation in the *patria* without the permission and decree of the Venetian government, and consequently he did not wish to convoke parliament".

who took part without a right of vote. The lieutenant, "after a full deliberation of the said parliament", was responsible for prorogations, and together with the "treasurers of the *patria*", took part in the work of the parliamentary Council. From 1475 parliament possessed a permanent official, the "chancellor of the *patria*", who also acted as secretary of the Deputation.

The matters to be discussed were indicated in the orders sent by the Venetian authorities to the lieutenant and in the writs themselves. But at least in the writs the descriptions were often so vague (e.g. "for various matters to be discussed, decided and decreed") that they created confusion and protests. The summons still possessed a formally obligatory character, but the threat of sanctions was now unusual and superfluous. The communes continued to justify their failure to send a representative, but sometimes (as in the case of Cividale in 1482) the lieutenant advised them in a friendly manner that it was in their own interests to send an ambassador. However, in 1586, apparently following a request of the deputies of the *patria*, the Venetian government decided to impose a fine on all non-justified absentees. As in the past, the representatives of the communes were reimbursed by their respective administrations for their expenses during parliamentary sessions or meetings of the Council or Deputation.

The sessions were usually extremely brief, lasting one or two days. It seems as if sometimes parliament did not meet for several years (as for example from 1464 to 1467),[37] whereas on other occasions several sessions were held in a single year. In the latter case – to judge by the tasks of the assembly and the analogous practice of the Piedmontese estates – the members of parliament may have done no more in the first session than take note of the matters to be decided and examine the requisite measures in general terms. Final decisions were then taken in later sessions. Something similar must have occurred over the difficult questions of a general tax (*trigesima universalis*) and the billeting of troops (*alogiamenta gentium armigerarum*) ordered by Venice.

The meetings began with the speech or proposals of the lieutenant. The members of the assembly replied with long and flowery speeches. A quorum of two-thirds of the members was necessary for lawful

[37] There may, however, only be a gap in our documentation for these years.

deliberations. Decisions were taken "unanimously" or by "majority" vote. But the three groups split up into separate bodies for the election of representatives, "orators", "deputies" or "ambassadors". After each meeting parliament nominated and sent its own "orators" to Venice to gain acceptance of its votes. But permission for this embassy had to be granted by the lieutenant, whose willingness depended on his assessment of the envoy's attitude towards himself. However, as he was only in office for twelve months (sixteen after 1509), he was hardly in a position to prohibit an embassy as his opponents could appeal to his successor.

Parliament's major task remained that of ensuring that the country was governed according to its own constitutions and customs. On this matter at least the desires and aspirations of the members remained unanimous. Parliament continued to decide questions which arose among its own members (except when discontented members appealed to the Venetian government), and to defend its interests against Venetian magistracies. But its main concern was to preserve the legal privileges of Friuli and the Friulans.

The Venetian government not only admitted but appreciated this collaboration in legislative activities. But the legislative procedure was now much longer and more complex. Proposals were fully discussed and then sent to Venice, where they were further discussed and often modified; they finally returned to the lieutenant, who published them. Frequently the members of parliament or their delegates discussed measures of notable importance with the lieutenant's administration. On various occasions a special committee was appointed with full powers to carry out the difficult task of revising the "constitutions of the *patria* of Friuli".

Where the new regime innovated least was in financial matters. Parliament preserved its attributes, prestige and sense of justice almost intact over questions of taxes (*talee, colte,* general taxes and the now important problem of billeting, etc.). However, the Venetian government was in a far stronger position than had been the patriarch to put pressure on members of parliament and force them to accept increasingly heavy demands. Although it displayed a formally scrupulous respect for the terms of the pact into which it had entered when the *patria* had accepted its sovereignty, it did not hesitate to subject Friuli, like all its dependent territories, to the general tax of a thirtieth. But parliament's participation still ensured respect for the traditionally equitable distribution of the taxes in the common interest.

On the other hand, parliamentary control over the actions of administrative officials virtually disappeared. An exceptional and isolated episode occurred in the early years of the Venetian regime in 1436, when an accusation was laid against the marshal, which involved the lieutenant. Even then the Venetian government resisted an illegal assembly of parliament, although it took note of the protest. On other less spectacular occasions it acted in the same way, giving due consideration to parliamentary protests.

The jurisdictional powers of parliament, once so widespread, were overwhelmed by the new order. They were usurped in the first instance by the marshal (no longer "of the *patria*", but "of the lieutenant"), and by the possibility of appeals to the Venetian magistracies. Disputes between nobles were decided by the "curia of peers". Abuses by holders of feudal jurisdictions or local rectors and incidents of brigandage were suppressed or settled by special commissions of "auditors of sentences".

In international relations parliament wholly lost its general representative function. When the commune of Cividale in 1439 expressed its intention of carrying out reprisals against a neighbouring lord, it did so to gain the moral support of the assembly rather than because it recognised any specific competence of the assembly to decide such matters. The conduct of foreign policy belonged exclusively to the Venetian government.

In 1483 the members of parliament from the near side of the Tagliamento river obtained permission from Venice to hold separate reunions to settle the distribution of taxes. In the early decades of the 16th century the peasantry began to break away and organise themselves as a separate body. During their revolt in 1511 the Friuli peasants were supported against the castellans and even against parliament not only by Udine and the Savorgnan, but by Venice. In this way the peasantry (*comitatinanza*) began to achieve a certain independence and to participate at least indirectly – outside and against parliament – in the decision of matters of general interest. By 1518, although without a seat in parliament, the peasantry were allowed to send a representative to Venice to oppose the requests and votes of the three estates of the *patria* whether submitted to the lieutenant or to the Venetian government. In the second half of the 16th and the early 17th century the *comitatinanza* grew stronger. At a certain point it was no longer a rival, but a parallel body to parliament.

Thus as Friuli changed from an independent sovereign state to a province, so did its structure of government. Its position was perhaps even weaker than that of Sicily and Sardinia within the Spanish empire, as it lay nearer to Venice and was hence easier to control. It became impossible for parliament to exercise any real political activity. The assembly adjusted itself to the new conditions, survived and continued to claim the title and responsibility of representative of the country.

In these new conditions, the position of the executive organ of parliament also changed. It was naturally impossible for the assembly to carry out its tasks during its brief sessions. The greater part of its work was done by the Council, and later by the "deputies of the *patria*". The last recorded election of the Council was in 1437. Like parliament, it had lost its former great authority and most of its powers. But the need for a representative and executive organ of the assembly remained. Already by the second half of the 15th century, a new organ was introduced–the "six deputies of the *patria*", one for each of the estates in the two regions on either side of the Tagliamento river. This creation may well have originated from the experiences of the period after the Council had died. The deputies divided the tasks assigned them by the assembly and assisted the lieutenant in the transaction of business, although he alone possessed executive power for decisions. On more than one occasion the deputies took the initiative in suggesting the convocation of parliament. Their orders (*bandi*) sometimes created discontent, but in the end they were accepted as necessary without discussion. Their prestige had so increased by the later 17th century that a lieutenant issued a decree in 1677 forbidding typographers to continue to print the title "Magnificent Lord Deputies of the *Patria*" in capital leaders: originally they had been described only as *spectabiles*. But if their prestige had grown, their authority had diminished.

6

Monferrat

The first signs of activity of a parliament in Monferrat date from 1305, when a general "parliament of the vassals, men, communes, places and *terre* and of the marquisate of Monferrat" was convoked at Trino by the regents. It was unanimously decided to send representatives to the Empress Iolanda at Constantinople to inform her of her accession to the marquisate following the death of her brother John I. The purpose and method of its convocation make it clear that this was an extraordinary meeting. A real parliament only arose some time later in the 14th century, out of the disorders which accompanied the struggle over the succession.

By the time of the assembly of 1379 there was no doubt that the representatives had a clear idea of their own rights and of the duties of the prince. Parliament made its oath of fealty to the new Marquis John III conditional on his swearing not to commit homicide, violence or injury against his subjects, but to protect their persons, possessions and rights and to carry out "due justice". Even more significant was its refusal to accept the cession of the city of Chivasso to the duke of Savoy on the grounds that "the men of Chivasso did not consent, nor were they present at any agreement".

But this independence did not long survive. In the 15th century the rulers began a policy of centralisation, suppressing local autonomies and liberties. In the early decades of the 15th century parliament still met frequently, but its competence was restricted to deliberating the amount of the subsidy, which was then exacted by the marquis. In the 1430s the wars of Savoy, Venice and Florence against Milan led to the military occupation of the country, and then to the annexation of most of its territories by the neighbouring powers. By then parliament had lost all power of initiative. From 1435 to 1494 it showed no signs of activity. Then parliament met again to nominate the regency council for the young marquis. Its last sign of life was in 1502, when it registered its refusal to billet French soldiers. These final episodes contrasted strongly with the long earlier period of impotence. But it was the assembly's swan song: in 1533, on the death of the Marquis Giangiorgio, the marquisate was annexed by the dukes of Mantua, and parliament disappeared.

The writs of summons to parliament, signed by the marquis or his representative, were identical for feudal families (*consortilia, consortitus*) and communes, and invited the recipients to appear on a given day at a specified place. The only element which distinguished the two types of writ was the specification of the number of "ambassadors" to be sent by communes or consortia. The purpose of the convocation to a "parliament" or "general parliament" (rarely "colloquy") was stated in the most general terms or wholly omitted.

The chancery of the marquisate possessed a list of the members to be summoned. The writs were imperative, although they did not usually contain any threat of sanctions, perhaps because it was obviously in the interest of subjects to take part in deliberations relating to the imposition of taxes and militia obligations. The consortia sent one or two representatives and the communes usually not more than two. The rulers rarely omitted to request that these "ambassadors" be assured full powers. When they did forget, the communes took immediate advantage, sending their representatives with limited mandates. In fact, even in normal circumstances the ambassadors were often sent with mandates merely to listen and refer back, or were given instructions and memorials. But this expedient did not always serve its purpose, and – faced with the duty of assenting to crushing taxes and subsidies – the nominees apparently displayed reluctance to accept their appointment.

The convocations lacked any regularity, sometimes occurring more than once a year, at other times not at all for several years. They were usually held at Moncalvo, where the marquis resided, but there was no fixed rule.

We know nothing about the constitution of the assemblies, about the order or form of their deliberations, or whether a quorum was required. We do not even know what criteria determined whether the consortia and communes voted together or separately. There was so little to discuss that the assemblies usually only lasted one day.

If it proved necessary – as, for instance, to decide the distribution of the subsidy voted by parliament or to continue deliberations on certain questions – the marquis and assembly agreed to nominate councillors. Although there were apparently no fixed rules, some were chosen from among the nobles, others from the ambassadors of the communes. As soon as their task was accomplished, the committees were dissolved. Sometimes their deliberations were submitted for approval or ratification by the assembly.

There can be little doubt that one of the main reasons for the extremely limited attributes of the parliament of Monferrat was its very short life. From the end of the 14th century it underwent a process of regression, which limited its competence to matters of taxation.

The franchises and financial immunities obtained by the communes in the 14th century had deprived the rulers of important sources of revenue. Parliament was the new organ for financial impositions, and by integrating them with what remained of the old taxation system it achieved a compromise between the increased autonomy of the communes and the growing requirements of the marquisate. The subjects safeguarded their franchises and only paid subsidies if they were voted by their representatives; the marquis procured the funds he needed for the country's defence by other means.

In theory there was only one tax, the *subsidium* or *talea*, but its imposition was requested for a variety of needs. The ambassadors' task was to check the legitimacy of the request and agree on the amount to be paid, ensuring that it did not surpass the limits imposed by custom or the financial possibilities of the country. Their consent was requested as a matter of course as a protection of the local franchises and immunities of the consortia, especially in the case of extraordinary requests for "gracious" or "liberal and gracious" subsidies, "not owing, but granted by special grace". But whereas in other states such requests were only granted in return for concessions, in Monferrat the formal wording of the vote did not imply corresponding results.

The obligation of military service had been commuted into payments of money employed to hire mercenaries, apparently following the request of parliament. It was decided upon in the same manner as the subsidies. Hence these military aids or subsidies were also distributed by the assembly or by a committee among the noble consortia and communes and related to their importance, wealth and population.[38]

7

Piedmont and Aosta

The first parliamentary assembly in Piedmont was apparently held in 1328, when the communes were summoned to send ambassadors to Scalenghe to treat of matters of general interest with the prince. Unfortunately our documentation on the assembly is very incomplete. If it is compared to later assemblies, it would appear that convocations of the same type – often for matters not specified beforehand – gradually became customary in Piedmont. After 1342 assemblies appeared to take place more frequently (even more than once a year), and by the end of the 14th century an uninterrupted series had begun.

By the second half of the 14th century not only the frequency but the character of the assemblies appeared to change. In an assembly of 1362 Amadeus VI's captain general in Piedmont, the Conte Verde, complained that the envoys of the commune of Moncalieri had tried to oppose the prince's request for troops, and ordered the communal administrators to nominate two other representatives. This was the first of a long series of episodes in which the communes showed signs of a more independent attitude. By 1375 the description of the assembly of nobles and communal representatives as a *consilium* – an enlargement of the permanent royal council – signified official recognition of the right of the assembly to participate as a consultative body in important decisions. By now, however, prudent signs of opposition to royal demands were becoming more frequent. In

[38] The only example of parliament taking the initiative occurred in 1418, when the assembly asked the marquis to regulate by special decree the monetary exchange rate on the basis of that current in neighbouring countries. It was an analogous request to one made by the parliament of Piedmont.

1372 Moncalieri agreed to royal requests, but insisted on certain technical conditions. In 1376–8 Turin, Moncalieri, Chieri and perhaps some other communes attempted to persuade the sovereign to reduce his claims by delaying tactics. It became regular practice to provide the communal ambassadors with instructions and memorials to subject the vote of the subsidy to certain conditions. In 1410 Turin refused to pay its share of the subsidy as it had not agreed to the vote: its councillors were arrested until payment was made. In 1413 there was general opposition to a new grant: the ambassadors were held as hostages until the communes sent new ones with instructions to accept the request. In 1417 and 1422 the ambassadors were again arrested. The significance of these episodes is that the government did not dare to impose taxes or raise troops by itself, but sought the consent of parliament, if necessary by force.

By the second quarter of the 15th century the communes' *queremonie* became more frequent and detailed, their memorials to their delegates more explicit and open, as if now accepted as customary. At the same time the preambles to the grants of *dona* (*sive subsidia*) underlined the spontaneity and graciousness of the subsidy, offered by the communes without obligation and without creating precedents.

Parliamentary initiative developed. In the legislative field, in practice it already existed in the instructions and memorials given by the communes to their delegates, or by the whole assembly to ambassadors sent to the duke when he was across the Alps in Savoy. But legal recognition of parliamentary competence in legislative matters did not go back earlier than the mid-15th century: its first formal appearance was probably in 1451. In 1459 the grant of a subsidy was expressly tied to ducal approval of eight *capitoli*. In 1468 the estates presented a memorial asking for important reforms in the judicial field, although it is not clear whether this lay behind the statute promulgated soon after by Amadeus IX. In 1473 Duchess Iolanda tried to ignore the reciprocal link between subsidy and legislative measures claimed by the estates, stating that the *capitoli* were the result of deliberations by the "nobles and notable men" authorised and then approved by her. But further initiatives by parliament are to be found in 1476 – when the *capitoli* were accepted in a contractual manner "with the force of a pact and lasting, perpetual privileges" – and again in 1492 and 1496. Not all parliamentary proposals were accepted, and in 1499 there is an example of an attempt to delay some of them. But by this time parliament had gained so much ground that it was difficult to refuse them openly: in 1490 the three estates reacted to a refusal by appointing six "nuncios, legates and solicitors" with full powers to obtain "more fitting and decent" replies.

Parallel to this development, parliament gained increasing influence over the administration and government policy. At first, parliamentary action was of an indirect and negative kind, opposing the grant of subsidies and troops. But gradually it became more open, taking advantage of the weakness of some of the princes or the dynastic ambitions of cadet members of the family. By the time of Philip Lackland, towards the end of the 15th century, parliament became the arbiter of state policy.

Signs of this development were to be seen as early as 1362, when Moncalieri tried to oppose a royal request. By the end of the 14th century parliament was recognised as a council, with the functions of a consultative body. In 1399 it was stated that the representatives of the communes were convoked to give "counsel and advice on the good state of the whole country". In the early 15th century the communes struggled successfully to avoid debasement of the coinage, and gained a compromise over a proposed increase of the tax on salt. By 1437 parliament's prestige was sufficiently great for Duke Ludovico specifically to mention its part in elaborating an edict against usury. In 1444 the three estates took the singular initiative of consulting the law school of Pavia as to the legality of a ducal claim for a *donativo* he wished to offer the Emperor Sigismond. In 1449 Amadeus VIII and his son Ludovico stated that they had summoned the three estates because of complaints against the government and to provide for the war against Milan. In June 1452 there was an almost general boycott of the assembly; in 1456 the estates refused to ratify a treaty with the king of France; in 1458 they refused to state their attitude towards a proposal for an agreement with the duke of Milan; in 1462 they reprimanded Duke Ludovico for accepting French protection and trying to raise troops to serve France. With these successful exploits behind them, it was not surprising that the three estates became even stronger under a weak duke like Amadeus IX (1465–72) and in the following troubled decades. The importance of the three estates was such that international treaties were valid only if ratified by them. The duke of Milan and king of France even sent embassies to, and received them from the Piedmontese parliament. In 1476 Philip Lackland, Amadeus IX and Iolanda appointed the estates as arbiters of their disputes.

Until the early 16th century parliament remained the most important political organ of the state. In 1503, 1505 and 1509 subsidies were only granted as part of an explicit contract approving parliamentary requests. The duke stated in his preliminary instructions for the meeting of 1509 that he was summoning the estates "to see them, deal well with the good men, punish excesses and bad men, and ensure that justice be done and that they all live securely". He then continued that he was convoking them to expound, as a father to his children, the difficulties of the moment; and "to hear their complaints and grievances, if they wished to make them, and to receive their good advice on all matters they wished to speak about".

The following sessions displayed the same character of bilateral negotiations. With the wars in Italy at the end of the 15th century the dukes needed increasing sums of money. The estates took advantage to obtain confirmation of their privileges, franchises and liberties, approval of new *capitoli*, accounts of previous grants and restitution of any surplus, assurances about the price of the salt monopoly, abolition of tax exemptions traditionally granted to lawyers and doctors. Above all, they continued their struggle against what they regarded as the excessive influence of Savoyards in the government, forcing the duke in 1530 to promise to appoint an equal number of Piedmontese and Savoyard councillors.

Naturally the negotiations were frequently difficult. Nobles and ecclesiastics often raised objections to paying the subsidy. The duke and his councillors sometimes opposed the requests of the estates. But they were in a weak position. The communes insisted on respect of their privileges and continually recalled their parliamentary envoys, thus impeding any rapid agreement. Until the French occupation of 1536, the three estates were in a dominating position. Before passing to this last period of their life, it will be as well to look at their structure and organisation.

The Piedmontese assembly was normally convoked directly by the sovereign, or by his lieutenant in the ducal council. Besides the place and time of the convocation, the writs of summons stated the motivation for the meeting, but usually in a vague and summary manner "for matters of some importance for the good state of the country", "to listen to what we shall state". The type of mandate requested of the communal ambassadors varied. Sometimes – usually at the beginning of a new cycle of sessions – the writs stated that the ambassadors were to attend the *congregatio* (or *dieta* or *iornata*) with a mandate to listen and refer back; at other times – usually when the assembly had to reply to previous requests – the writs required the ambassadors to bring a full and sufficient mandate to decide and conclude. On rare occasions they also stated the *intencio* of the duke (usually a request for a subsidy), and the hour of the meeting; or else they stated "in the evening" or "to stay overnight", to indicate that the reunion would be held in the evening and the following morning. The writs were sent to the ducal officials in the communes, the communal councillors, or to the commune as an *universitas*.

Oral summons were far less frequent and related almost exclusively to prorogations of sessions, when the communal ambassadors were to return home for instructions. On these occasions they all knew when the next session would be held, and in fact called it an *assignatio*, and not a convocation.

The writs were usually worded partly in the form of a request, partly as a command with a more or less explicit threat in the case of failure to appear. Sometimes the threats were carried out in order to force the hand of communes which were trying to delay proceedings by failure to send a representative. Although it would hardly be true to say that the communes always received the writs with diffidence and had difficulty in electing deputies, not infrequent examples of such difficulties are to be found. Although there are only few instances of sanctions and coercion, they probably had a psychological effect. But in practice the communes almost always responded promptly to the summons. They had no need to refuse. They took care to safeguard their own interests by providing their ambassadors with detailed instructions on each occasion, and by a careful choice of the most expert, capable and trustworthy men. Many of the deputies were descendants or near relatives of previous ambassadors, or had represented their communes in numerous assemblies. They were nominated either directly by the communal council or by citizens appointed for this purpose. They formed a virtual political élite.

The sessions almost always consisted of several meetings. There was a continual movement of ambassadors of the single cities or of the whole assembly (when the prince was in his Savoyard possessions on the other side of the Alps), while regular consultations took place between the cities on the attitude to adopt towards ducal requests.

The ambassadors of the communes were thus summoned in the first instance to listen to the statements and requests of the prince. After the sovereign or his representative had spoken, the assembly was prorogued until a later date in order to give the ambassadors time to refer back to their communal council or special committee and obtain full powers to accept the duke's request. The new meeting of all the ambassadors then offered either what was requested or a smaller sum, subject to various conditions. The negotiations were usually lengthy, however, and the sessions could last for several months.

The terminology used for the assemblies was for a long time uncertain, and indeed in some cases non-existent. There was probably no need for a specific denomination, as this was no legally recognised institution, but was considered as a practical creation for the prince's convenience. At a later stage the various descriptions – *colloquium, consilium, parlamentum, iornata* – were replaced by the term "three estates" (*Tres Status, Trois Estatz*). The new term was undoubtedly a French importation and appeared for the first time in Piedmontese documents towards the end of the 1430s, a few years later than in the duke's Savoyard possessions.

The change in terminology was hardly accompanied by any substantial modification of the organisation. In fact, even after the new term was in common use, the division of the assembly into its three parts remained infrequent and casual. It was by no means abnormal for the ecclesiastical order not to attend the meetings; nevertheless, the assembly continued to be described as the "three estates". But after the French occupation of Piedmont in the early 16th century the clergy began to take part.

In contrast to other parliaments, the Piedmontese assembly had no official list of members. In consequence, we know very little about the participation of nobles and ecclesiastics. The nobles attended not as members of one of the privileged orders, but rather as representatives of their consortium or family. They also attended as holders of fiefs. When the assembly met to give counsel, they acted as individuals; when it was a question of granting subsidies (increasingly the most important reason for holding assemblies), they acted as holders of fiefs, although their fiefs were small and unimportant.

Only ecclesiastics who held fiefs were subject to subsidies. Hence they were the only members of the clergy to take a regular part in the assemblies. Otherwise the clergy as a body attended assemblies only if called upon to give counsel on a matter of particular importance. We know nothing about the composition of the ecclesiastical estate in parliament.

Our knowledge of the third estate ("those of the communities", "deputies of the said communities", *comunitates*), although considerably greater, is still inadequate on a series of important points. It would appear from indirect evidence that – in contrast to the general pattern elsewhere – meetings were attended not only by the "domanial" communes directly dependent on the prince, but also by other communes. These other communes even included those subject to both feudatories and larger communes. In analogous manner, it would appear that not only the feudatories *in capite* participated, but also their noble vassals: they were described as "nobles and vassals". Thus the Piedmontese parliament was characterised by a more complete representation than in many other states.

The choice of ambassadors, legates or deputies to the assemblies was regulated by each commune according to its normal practice of nomination to office. There are no examples of popular elections. Normally the municipal councillors (*decuriones, generali credentia*), the "electors of officials", or specially nominated "wise men" elected the representatives. Once elected it was impossible to resign without valid reasons. Expenses were reimbursed and salaries paid by the communal administrations at the end of the assembly (or even before, in the form of an advance).

But these ambassadors can hardly be regarded as representatives, not so much because they were not elected, but because usually they were sent with limited powers or specific instructions. However, it is necessary to point out that these limited mandates applied primarily to the initial stage of the session.

The meeting place was decided upon on each occasion. Parliaments were held in the open in 1286 and in 1462, when Philip Lackland was pardoned by his father Ludovico. But these were both extraordinary assemblies, parliaments in a purely formal sense, where dynastic events, declarations of war or peace and sovereign laws were formally announced, but where no parliamentary deliberations took place.

Various types of assemblies were held, which are often difficult to distinguish from one another. For example, assemblies – analogous in composition to ordinary parliaments – were called when a certain number of communes failed to pay their share of the subsidy. Other meetings worked out technical projects, usually in the economic field, with the collaboration of experts chosen by the communes. Yet others had a local character and varied content. Others were parliaments in a purely formal sense, summoned to swear oaths of fealty. Even more untypical were those assemblies convoked spontaneously, or at any rate without the presence of government officials, to agree for example on their reply or the choice of ambassadors. Some of these meetings aroused the prince's anger, and were accused of being seditious (*conventicula*) or against the common interest. For the most part they were certainly preparatory reunions, unofficial and, strictly speaking, illegal. Nevertheless, in a purely material sense they were, *de facto*, parliamentary assemblies.

We have no precise information about procedure, whether, for instance, a quorum was necessary, or how discussions and decisions took place. The prince or his representative (often the governor of Piedmont) spoke to the participants and asked for counsel or a specific military contingent or money. The envoys of the communes asked for permission to refer back, and on their return offered a subsidy, sometimes directly to the general treasurer. Thus the general treasurer also participated in the parliament's work, supervising the distribution of the subsidy, calling meetings for technical measures such as the drawing up of accounts, sometimes paying the tax officials their expenses and wages.[39]

[39] These wages were usually then paid over to the communes which the tax officials

By the late 15th century certain developments had taken place. More than once the three estates asked to meet and deliberate collegiately. In 1473 requests for subsidies made separately to the communes were opposed on the grounds that following ancient custom such decisions were made collegiately, and that all separate grants were invalid. In 1478 some of the bishops complained that they had not been invited to deliberate on the decision to send ambassadors to Philip Lackland and maintained that "neither the three estates nor the congregation can be held without the ecclesiastical leaders". By this period parliament had undoubtedly acquired considerable powers of initiative and knew how to protect its rights. Indeed, in 1490 Gian Galeazzo Sforza, duke of Milan, instructed his ambassador to warn the regent – the duchess of Savoy – not to oppose the decisions of the three estates openly.[40]

As the Franco–Spanish wars in Italy continued in the early 16th century, the position of the duchy of Savoy became increasingly precarious. As shown, the power of parliament increased through the needs of the duke. But the hostility of this Piedmontese assembly to Savoy hindered the duke in his attempts to protect his territories. In 1518 war was averted. In 1530 Savoy was lost through the insistence of parliament that its *dona* or *subsidia* be used exclusively for the defence of Piedmont. In 1536 the end came with the occupation of most of Piedmont by the French.

The assemblies continued to be summoned not only by the French lieutenant-generals, but also by the duke in the small area he still possessed. It was an unconscious irony that the duke's assemblies were still called "congregation of the *patria*". But their protests against the duke's weakness towards the Emperor Charles V served no purpose. They now only existed to raise sums of money for the war.

In the French part of Piedmont the estates were also summoned to raise money, but at the same time they were required to swear oaths

represented in order to compensate the communes for what they had paid to their parliamentary "ambassadors".

[40] Another example is to be found in a letter to Galeazzo Maria Sforza from the Milanese ambassador, Giovanni Bianco, in 1479. Bianco stated that he had been informed by the representative of Ivrea, Luigi Tagliandi, that "in all serious matters, it is the three estates which conclude, deliberate and govern this country, nor is the lord powerful enough to undertake any enterprise by himself without the aid of the three estates".

of fealty to the king of France. When the estates attempted to protest against the demand for money by sending an envoy to the king, the envoy was imprisoned. The communes continued to protest and assert their privileges. But by 1550 Henry II felt strong enough to instruct his lieutenant-general, de Brissac, to confirm or replace members of the assembly at his will. Parliament became a regular but subordinate part of the administration. It met annually, but its dependence on the local French authorities was underlined by its limited power to appeal over the head of the lieutenant-general to the king.

With the restoration of Emanuel Philibert in 1559, the end of the estates was in sight. A meeting was held in 1560, when the three estates accepted an increase in the price of salt, but insisted on keeping their own franchises and privileges. No further meeting was called. The duke's justification was that he had conquered and not inherited his duchy, and so was not obliged to swear to observe the traditional customs; nor did he owe gratitude to subjects who had collaborated with the French. Castilian in education and experience, with a personal knowledge of the dangers of estates through his experiences in Flanders, it was not surprising that Emanuel Philibert should have resisted sharing his sovereignty with his subjects.

At first sight it seems curious that the suppression of the Piedmontese estates was not followed by that of the assembly of the valley of Aosta. The valley, which lay in the heart of the Alps, had never been effectively governed by the dukes of Savoy. During their long absences local customs had grown up, limiting ducal power. These *consuetudines et libertates*, which probably originated in the last decade of the 12th century, formed the nucleus of widespread feudal and communal autonomies. The valley sent representatives to the assemblies of the estates of Savoy, and occasionally to those of Piedmont. At a certain point the valley began to call its own assemblies and council: before the first documented account in the early 16th century, meetings must already have been held to choose envoys to the estates of Savoy and Piedmont and then to ratify and carry out the deliberations of the three estates. In 1531 the general council of the valley discussed the duke's requests that it nominate a certain number of experts and representatives to revise some of the customary laws, and that it make a contribution to pay for a military contingent. In 1532 the general council met again to discuss another request for a military contingent, and the measures to be adopted to suppress heresy in the valley. In 1536 this assembly of estates nominated an executive organ, the *Conseil des Commis*, to ensure a greater continuity in its work. The new Council may well have been an imitation, or derivation, of the permanent committees of French provincial estates, such as the *Assemblée des Commis* of the Dauphiné. On the other hand, it also resembled the ancient Council of the colloquy of the *patria* of Friuli.

It may well be that the 1531 meeting marked the beginning of a new attempt by the duke – like the kings of France – to obtain finances from the provincial estates rather than from the more dangerous estates general. Once the experiment proved successful, it was continued. Emanuel Philibert had little to lose from a similar practice, especially as the valley of Aosta was too small to assume a really independent attitude.

Appendix to Part IV: Italian parliaments of the 17th and 18th centuries

At the end of the 16th century the overall number of parliaments in Italy hardly differed from that of the preceding two centuries. But the position changed during the course of the 17th century. The Piedmontese parliament was not convoked again after 1560, although two small assemblies remained in the territories of the duke of Savoy: those of the valley of Aosta and the marquisate of Saluzzo. In north-eastern Italy two new "provincial estates" arose at Gorizia and Gradisca. But in the south, the last parliamentary session of the kingdom of Naples was held in 1642, and of the kingdom of Sardinia in 1698. By the opening of the 18th century, in fact, apart from the minor assemblies, only the congregation of the March of Ancona, the colloquy of the ancient but no longer independent *patria* of Friuli, and the still authoritative parliament of Sicily survived.

This decline in the number of assemblies reflected the continuous and persistent policy of monarchs and governments, determined to eliminate all obstacles to the creation of absolutist rule, whether deriving from representative assemblies or from other group or regional privileges and autonomies. Absolutist monarchy, which is usually studied in its French or Spanish context, existed in Italy too: the surviving parliaments were left on the defensive, with little influence. A rapid glance at the various assemblies is sufficient to outline what remained of their previous authority.

Aosta

The survival of the estates of the valley of Aosta was confirmed by Emanuel Philibert in 1561. But their power was negligible. From 1576 the clergy no longer participated. In fact, once the permanent organ of the assembly, the *Conseil des Commis*, had been created in 1536, the estates did not really need to meet frequently: they tended to be convoked every two, three or even four years, and in the 18th century every six years.

There were few institutional innovations in the 17th and 18th centuries. To enable the *Conseil* to function more efficiently, its members were first exempted from the *donativo* (1621), and later paid a salary (1662). But the *Conseil*'s task became increasingly difficult as the government exerted growing pressure. For while Turin wanted obedient subjects, willing to support a rising burden of taxation, the inhabitants of the Valley of Aosta were determined to maintain their rights and pay as little as possible. By tradition the estates submitted requests as a counterpart to the grant of a *donativo*. They demanded above all confirmation and respect of the laws, customs and privileges of the country. Each new sovereign swore to observe these laws. But Charles Emmanuel III, on his accession in 1730, refused to swear an oath, limiting himself to the statement that "His Majesty orders the continued observances of what has hitherto been observed in the Valley of Aosta". Future assemblies no longer requested an oath, but merely the confirmation of the "usages, customs, franchises and immunities". Even this formula was evaded by the sovereigns. The last three assemblies of the estates were held in 1754, 1760 and 1766.

The *Conseil des Commis* continued its precarious existence until a regulation of Victor Amadeus III of 23 March 1773 deprived it of all effective responsibility. With this decree the anomaly of a representative body disappeared.

Saluzzo

The survival of the small parliament of Saluzzo is only really explicable in terms of the peculiar historical development of the state.

The marquisate of Saluzzo emerged as an independent state in the 12th and 13th centuries, asserting its individuality in reaction to the pressures and influence exerted by the neighbouring house of Savoy and the Dauphiné. Its parliament began its life late – in 1444. But in embryo it was already composed exclusively of the cities, villages and *terre*. Its first meeting was occasioned by the demand of the Marquis Ludovico I for financial aid to offer to his feudal lord, the duke of Savoy. The representatives resisted, but finally voluntarily offered a gift on condition that it did not create a precedent. Although there must have been other meetings, the next recorded one was held in 1548, on the death of the last marquis, Gabriel, when the capital, Saluzzo, took the initiative in proposing the submission of the country to France. No other session is documented until 1559. From then on, first under French rule and from 1601 under that of Savoy, the "general congregation" held a position of fundamental importance in the government of the country.

This congregation, composed of the "syndics and consuls" of the main cities and all the other communes, acted as representative of the *patria*. Attempts by the nobility to take part were successfully resisted in 1565 and 1602. Originally only representatives of the free communes attended, but under Savoyard rule the feudal communes also began to be convoked.

Alongside the "syndics and councillors" of the communes, the "elected of the said *patria*" or the "elected commissioners and administrators" first appeared in 1559, when the assembly was under the guidance of the Dauphiné *parlement*. Although only in office for one year, the "elected" acted efficiently as both the instrument and steering committee of the congregation. They treated and decided on its behalf, convoked new meetings, proposed, nominated, acted as judges, and checked financial accounts. They received a salary, and were assisted by a secretary.

Little is known of their relationship with the congregation, or how their composition reflected the struggles for leadership of the different cities and communes. In 1563 a certain number of deputies requested that the "elected" be substituted by two or three procurators. In 1578 the enfeoffed communes were sufficiently numerous to demand that their interests be represented by one of the "elected". Finally, in 1604, the representatives of Dronero, Revello and other minor centres successfully petitioned the duke for the abolition of the "elected" on the grounds of the excessive and wasteful expense. From then on their various tasks were entrusted to separate committees, the secretary, the prefect or the "syndics" of the four main cities (Saluzzo, Carmagnola, Dronero and Revello).

The congregation derived its authority from concessions bought from the sovereigns. It nominated the "elected", the revisors of accounts and secretary of the country, as well as the candidates for the position of prefect of Saluzzo. It discussed all financial contributions, and then distributed them among the communes. It drew up claims and grievances, the *capitoli* to submit to the sovereign. But in the 17th century its effectiveness diminished as the internal cohesion of the country broke down with the enfeoffment of many of the communes and the separation from the assembly of Carmagnola and Dronero. By 1624 the congregation was forced to accept a prefect nominated by the duke. By 1699 both lords and ducal officials took part in the assembly, and various communes decided it was no longer worth while attending. The congregation could not survive in so absolutist a state as Savoy.

The last occasion on which a public discussion of the utility ot an assembly of estates took place in the territories of the dukes of Savoy was during the civil war which followed the death of Victor Amadeus I in 1637. The royal princes Tommaso and Maurizio, opposing the regency of the duke's widow, appeared to favour convoking the old estates in order to nominate a tutor for the young heir. No practical measures resulted, and from that date the estates were doomed.

Friuli

The parliament of the *patria* of Friuli only survived through Venice's immobility and formalistic respect for pre-existing rights. But like the absolute monarchies, the Venetian republic attacked all local or group privileges and rights in order to achieve a uniformity of obedience from its subjects. The most serious blow to the assembly was the feudal law of 13 December 1586, confirming a decree of 1578, which ordered all feudatories to prove the legitimacy of their possessions. The position of the Friuli lords, who still formed the effective ruling class of the country, was severely weakened.

Parliament remained divided into three orders of prelates, castellans and communes, although the term "order" was prohibited in 1672. The main cities, Udine and Cividale, still took no part in the assembly, but from about 1670 Udine began to make its peace: in 1679 the deputies, castellans and representatives agreed that Udine remain the capital city, although it would not constitute a fourth member of the assembly. The deputies of the *patria* tended to act on behalf of parliament. In effect the "three orders" only survived because of their utility as an auxiliary organ of the Venetian administration. Their deliberations were only taken into consideration if they implied no change of the political order. Casanova recounted, for example, how in 1756, when he was in prison, he met the representative of the *comitatinanza* of Friuli, Count Asquin. The count had been imprisoned by the Venetian authorities for creating trouble by requesting the admittance of the peasant group to parliament: *quieta vivere* remained the Venetian motto. The assembly had already lost much of its earlier power. It last met under Austrian rule in 1798.

Gorizia, Gradisca

The Gorizian provincial parliament was created in the 15th century and reformed definitively by Emperor Maximilian in 1500. It probably originated in the old curia of the vassals, but it became a representative institution with legislative, administrative, judicial and fiscal functions. It increasingly resembled the state assemblies or *Stände* of the other German provinces, and in fact used German as the language of its acts. Like the Friuli parliament, it declined in importance when the peasantry (consisting of the rural communes) left to form a separate body. The basis of its efficiency and of the collaboration between the estates lay in the "sworn council of the nobles of the province" (*das geschworene Rat der Landherren*), composed of lords appointed by the sovereign. The acts of its annual meetings were printed until the assembly was suppressed in 1754 by Maria Teresa of Austria.

The imperial county of Gradisca, ceded in 1647 to the Eggenberg family, also possessed its "noble convocation", which assisted the sovereign in the government, especially over matters of taxation. Both the assembly, consisting of noble and ecclesiastical patricians, and their deputies or assessors acted with efficiency. In 1754, when Gradisca was united to Gorizia, the assembly was suppressed.

March of Ancona

The parliament of the March of Ancona not only survived, but increased in activity and autonomy in the 17th and 18th centuries. Its sessions were frequent, although curiously there were occasional interruptions of up to ten years. There was no rule about the frequency of convocations, although votes and requests of 1652, 1699, 1730, 1743 and 1745 indicated two years as the normal period. In 1765 the deputies *ad negocia* were instructed to take care that this regularity of convocation be maintained. By the later 18th century meetings may have become triennial. After 1791 no more congregations were held until 1805. But in 1808 the March passed under French rule.

As in Piedmont, there were tendencies for family dynasties to provide the deputies or orators. The deputies asked for the writs of summons – which included a brief mention of the matter to be discussed – to be sent a month in advance, so that they could decide their attitudes beforehand. By the 18th century, participation in the provincial assembly was so normal that in 1745 the assembly itself asked the governor to order absentees to appear under threat of sanctions. In fact, a quorum was necessary, although its number is not known. The number of represented cities fell during the two centuries from about fifty to forty through the incorporation of minor centres in larger cities, or the granting to certain major cities of independence from the authority of the provincial governor, with their consequent exclusion from the assembly. The decisions of the assembly required a two-thirds majority.

In the earlier period there was freedom of speech for all members. But by the 18th century the right to speak was limited to representatives of the four categories of cities, whose names were then drawn by lot. The same procedure was adopted for the nomination of the provincial deputations.

The functions of the permanent committee of the "deputies *di magistrato*", and their relationship to the "deputies *ad negocia*" of the congregation, are not at all clear. In fact, on more than one occasion the two bodies sat together, forming a *congregatio particolaris*. But probably the prime duty of the former body was to ensure respect for the prerogatives of the congregation and province. Various officials were responsible to the "deputies *di magistrato*". The provincial secretary acted as the liaison between the assembly and the cities; among his duties were keeping the minutes of the meetings and supervising the nomination of deputies. The "principal depositary" exacted the contributions of the communes, and paid the deputies, orators and other officials. There were also various other extraordinary organs, such as the deputations to revise the lists for nominations, to check the depositary's accounts, to collect grievances, particularly against the exaction of the taxes, to look after public health.

In effect, the provincial congregation of the March of Ancona remained an active body; but its functions were exclusively those of an administrative organ.

Naples

Although there was no rule about the regularity of sessions, the Neapolitan assembly met twenty-one times between 1600 and 1642. There were no substantial changes in its procedure, and its sphere of competence remained unaltered. This was particularly true of the "parliament–senate", or mixed commission of barons and representatives of the city of Naples. When government supporters in 1636 attempted to assert the principle that parliamentary decisions in financial and fiscal matters bind the whole kingdom including Naples, the opposition was so strong that the viceroy had to abandon his own supporters.

The struggle between the viceroys and parliament continued throughout the period, culminating in the last two sessions of 1639 and 1642. After the 1639 meeting the assembly sent a message to the king stating that the *donativo* had been granted expressly on condition that viceroys cease to decree impositions which were the responsibility of the general parliament. In 1642 it voted a new grain tax as a substitute for all other ordinary and extraordinary taxes on condition that if any other tax were imposed, even with the consent of parliament, the grain tax was not only to be abolished, but its contributors reimbursed.

These parliaments, like those of the 16th century (for example in 1536 and 1564), showed the surviving strength of the opposition and offer an explanation why no further sessions were convoked after 1642. But parliament was fighting a defensive struggle, marked by compromises. Its members, particularly the barons, protested against the taxes and tricks and the subterfuges of the viceroys, who on more than one occasion demanded that they themselves nominate parliamentary representatives. The barons insisted on their right – which had been prohibited – to send their own envoy to Madrid to protest against abuses. But subsequently they came to terms, either through fear of punishment or because of the difficulties and expense of the journey, or because they were in a minority compared to the viceroy's nominees. In the following session they demanded a penal and fiscal amnesty. Because of these capitulations the barons gained the worst of both worlds: to the government they appeared as rebels, to the population as traitors.

Sicily

The frequent dynastic crises of the 17th and 18th centuries – which left Sicily under the rule of Spain, Savoy, Austria and Naples successively – inevitably affected the Sicilian parliament, both in the regularity of its sessions and in its activities. But in general terms it would be true to state that the Sicilian parliament remained a symbol for the population of the autonomy and individuality of the island.

There were no significant innovations in this period in the assembly's structure or functions. In the mid-18th century, the marquis of Villabianca could confirm Scipione di Castro's diagnosis.

But by then some of the barons had lost interest and ceased to attend the meetings. Perhaps for this reason, as much as because of the government's unofficial but effective seizure of control of the communal administrations, parliament was no longer able to act as effectively as before. In fact, under Philip III and Philip IV the parliamentary *capitoli* (1668, 1680, 1690, 1698) limited themselves almost exclusively to local or even personal interests. On the other hand, the concern of the governments – particularly after the risings of Naples and Palermo in 1647 and Messina in 1674 – seemed to be to maintain the *status quo* and avoid creating unnecessary trouble. It was a policy of letting sleeping dogs lie which resulted in an almost ruinous respect for local privileges and autonomies. Indeed the viceroys almost always supported the Sicilians when they replied to the government in Madrid that the kingdom provided subsidies well beyond its capacities.

Parliament was weakened internally, however, by the great rivalry between Palermo and Messina, which became acute after Messina acquired special privileges in 1591. In 1622 it looked as if the activities of Messina were about to lead to a division of the island into two parts with two separate governments. Thus, at the session of 1612, when parliament voted a huge extraordinary *donativo* of 2,700,000 scudi in order to repurchase the customs and other incomes alienated by the administration, Messina refused to accept its quota as it had not been consulted. The city finally gave way before the viceroy's pressure, but tension remained. Finally, in 1630, when Messina demanded that the island be divided into two separate governments, almost all parliament joined Palermo and the deputation in opposition, on the grounds that it would lead to a division of the assembly. Probably only after the failure of the revolt of Messina of 1674 did the danger resulting from this rivalry diminish.

In general in the 17th century parliament was ready to meet the needs of the sovereign as an act of loyalty, in return for confirmation of the island's privileges: the grant of 1612 was an outstanding instance. But in 1636, for example, parliament opposed the attempt to introduce obligatory military service for certain categories of persons as infringing the island's privileges. In 1642 the assembly proposed financial alternatives to substitute what it regarded as the introduction of a sales tax and stamp duty. In 1650, when the military *braccio* opposed the government's requests, Philip III took the extreme measure of decreeing that the vote of the other two *bracci* was adequate. But this was perhaps a unique case. Even after the revolts of 1647 and 1674 there were apparently no significant developments in relations between crown and parliament during the Spanish period.

Perhaps the most important aspect of the one parliament held under Savoyard rule (1714), as of the parliaments during the Austrian period (1720, 1724, 1725, 1728, 1729, 1732), was the tendency for the viceroy and leaders of the three *bracci* to reach agreement before the assembly met. But by 1732 tension was growing, and the *bracci* would only agree to a huge levy on condition that its exaction be left exclusively to the deputation.

Later, under Neapolitan rule, these tensions built up, as Charles III attempted to impose a new "enlightened" policy. At first, in attacking clerical privileges, he gained some support from the other two *bracci*, especially as he accepted the traditional claim that local bishoprics be reserved to Sicilians. But as he turned towards the abolition of all privileges and exemptions, implying the destruction or subjection of parliamentary institutions, opposition built up, and culminated during the viceroyalty of Marquis Domenico Caracciolo (1781–6). The brusque measures of Caracciolo aroused the reaction not only of the barons, defending their private interests, but of a much wider circle of Sicilians, who were afraid that the unification of the "two Sicilies" would follow and that the island would come under the rule of Naples. With the French invasion, the financial needs of the government forced it to give way. In 1810–11 the *bracci* demanded a complete reform of the taxation system as the price of a *donativo*. The royal attempt to pass over the head of parliament and impose a tax by decree led to an increasing identification of the *bracci* with the people of the island. The following year a successful revolt broke out, and the "general parliament" of 1812 gave the island a new constitutional order, reaffirming the parliament.

Sardinia

The most striking features of the Sardinian parliament in the 17th century were the contrast between the prolonged intervals between meetings and the length of the sessions. Ordinary meetings were held at ten-year intervals, although they were occasionally supplemented by extraordinary meetings. But each session usually lasted several years.

Sardinia alone of the Spanish possessions in Italy remained exempt from the control of the Council of Italy, and subject to the Supreme Council of Aragon. It derived from this a greater element of stability and respect for the traditional parliamentary regime. For the assembly was regarded as similar to the *cortes* of Catalonia. Nevertheless, the *staments* took care to remind the government of their traditions by the publication of parliamentary acts and legal treatises. In 1572 and 1591 F. Bellit and P. G. Arquer published the *Capitols de cort del Stament Militar de Sardenya*, containing all the laws initiated by the military *stament* and adopted by the assembly. In 1645 Johannes Dexart published the *Capitula sive acta curiarum regni Sardiniae*, which included not only the text of the *capitula* and acts, but an historical and institutional treatise on parliament.

Nevertheless, the history of the Sardinian parliament in the 17th century was by no means tranquil. The attitude of the viceroys, often following royal instructions, and the existence of factions within the military order led to tense relations. During the session of 1612–14, for example, the *staments* made various demands in exchange for the *donativo*, ranging from the abolition of the limitation on powers of attorney and the exclusion of foreigners from parliament to supervisory control over the activities of the governors and assessors. But the most significant measures were those the sovereign decreed restricting the earlier concession of autonomous meetings made by Alfonso the Magnanimous to the military *stament*. The viceroy was ordered to suspend meetings if they took place outside Cagliari or did not conform to specific regulations. The following session of 1624–5 was marked by a prolonged struggle between the viceroy and the leaders of the military *stament* and the city of Cagliari, supported even by part of the viceregal bureaucracy. The determination of the Sardinian leaders to maintain the legal order of the Aragonese period must have seemed both absurd and seditious to the viceroys. The viceroy, Vivas, gained his way, but it was a pyrrhic victory, as the Council of Aragon agreed soon after to carry out an enquiry. Only in the session of 1631–3 was a compromise reached: the military *stament* was allowed to meet in the customary manner at

Sassari as well as at Cagliari, provided that the final decisions were taken in Cagliari at meetings authorised by the viceroy – unless their purpose was to protest against him.

Difficulties continued to emerge in later sessions. In 1641–3 royal representatives claimed that the sovereign "in case of necessity could break all privileges, even if negotiated and agreed as pacts". On their side, the *brazos* made a series of demands, including the reservation of lay and ecclesiastical offices for Sardinians, and the creation of a college of six judges to keep watch over the *capitula*. The military leader, the marquis of Laconi, was sent as envoy to Madrid, but obtained nothing. By the time of the next session of 1653–4 relations had worsened and difficulties arose through the rejection of all petitions by the viceregal members of the committee of grievances; the *staments* tried unsuccessfully to condition the ordinary *donativo* to the acceptance of parliamentary demands. A decade later the same problem of initial redress of grievance led to the removal of the military *brazo* from the committee of grievances. Once again the marquis of Laconi was sent to Madrid, but failed to make the grant of a *donativo* conditional on acceptance of parliamentary demands. Relations had so deteriorated that soon after the Spanish government seized the occasion of the murder of the viceroy to execute the leaders of the military *stament*. At the following session of 1677 the parliamentary *capitula* were proposed as petitions and not as demands, enabling the viceroy to declare that the *donativo* had been granted without conditions. Two further sessions were held under Spanish rule in 1688–9 and 1697–9, after which no further writs were issued.

After Sardinia passed to Savoy in 1720 the customary *donativi* continued to be exacted without summoning the *bracci*, but merely by consultation with the leaders of the *staments* and the members of the military *braccio* resident at Cagliari. Preparation for regular convocations took place in 1728, 1731, 1734 and 1750–1, but were never completed. The Savoyard government had little sympathy for such assemblies, as it explained in its instructions to the new viceroy, Marquis Falletti di Castagnole, in 1735: although the king had thought of convoking parliament to gain an increased *donativo*, he had not done so as the *staments* would probably have claimed a remission of what was still owed, if not indeed a reduction of the taxes because of the bad harvest.

The Sardinian parliament, in fact, only emerged again in 1793 when the French attempted to invade the island. The military order in Cagliari convoked first itself and then the entire military *stament*, demanding renewed convocations of parliament, confirmation of the laws and privileges of the kingdom, a monopoly of offices for Sardinians, the creation of a Ministry for Sardinian affairs at Turin, and of a Council of State at Cagliari. For two years, from 1795 to 1797, representatives of the *bracci* then collaborated in a provisional government of the island. It looked as if parliament was about to achieve its demands when the death of Victor Amadeus III led to a return to the old methods.

It can hardly be denied that these Italian parliaments of the 17th and 18th centuries, in their structure, procedure and concepts, were – as Marquis Domenico Caracciolo described them – little more than survivals from the Middle Ages. They represented a phase of parliamentarism destined to die or be replaced.

Nevertheless, there were signs of developments in the 18th century. In Lombardy, Maria Teresa warned her son Ferdinand, as governor, of the pretensions of the state congregation which claimed to "represent the nation, like the estates of our provinces of Germany". In Tuscany Pietro Leopoldo projected a new constitutional order, which went distinctly beyond the existing parliaments, although it was by no means so developed as the assemblies which were to emerge after the French Revolution: representatives of the communes were to form provincial assemblies which were to elect a general assembly with widespread powers.

But besides these projects or claims, something new could be seen in some of the existing parliaments. In Sardinia the military order resident in Cagliari had not only summoned its colleagues from Sassari, but had begun negotiations with the leaders of the other two *staments* for the creation of a true parliamentary assembly. Displaying a clear attitude of independence and attachment to the interests of the country, these leaders refused to dissolve themselves, and for a period of two years directed the public administration through a deputation renewed every two months. The *staments* had created a new style of parliament: meetings were held in public; new members were admitted to strengthen the representative quality of the assembly; a start was made to suppress the feudal order; parliament claimed that it represented "the entire Sardinian nation", and was responsible to it. Although the experiment ended abruptly with the death of the king, this parliament displayed not just technical innovations, but a new spirit, a new and greater sense of responsibility.

The Sicilian parliament of 1810 showed the same spirit when it refused to vote new subsidies until the entire system of taxation had been revised on a more egalitarian basis. But different results emerged in Sicily because of the English occupation of the island: the constitution of 1812 created a new type of assembly, resembling the English parliament.

PART V

The characteristics of parliamentary assemblies

I

Representation

The close ties of fealty and administrative responsibility which bound sovereign and feudatories together help explain the origins of the early assemblies. The king asked for counsel, and in matters of particular significance turned not only to his court officials, but to a wider group of leading personalities who would be affected by the decision. The request and offer of "counsel" was legally and logically linked to that of "aid": for the king's loyal and responsible subjects could not advise the king about what policy he should follow without also offering him the means to carry it out. For ordinary administrative matters the king possessed the income of domanial possessions, customs duties and the profits of the mint. But these sources of income could not be increased arbitrarily. For certain events, three or four cases sanctioned by feudal custom, he could impose a general tax. But for all other exceptional matters he needed to consult his subjects, either individually or by convoking them to great assemblies, and requesting their aid.

Undoubtedly such consultations could and did occur without the creation of a parliamentary assembly. But the offering of advice and assistance by parliament represented a technical progress: it was simpler for the sovereign, and offered the subjects a greater defence against unjustified demands. Once the idea of consent within an assembly began to spread, it tended to replace all other methods. The dialogue between sovereign and subjects became a dialogue between the king and his government and parliament. The king turned for aid no longer to individuals, but to corporate bodies – estates, *bracci*, *colloquia*, congregations – which had the power to grant his request because they personified the community, the "kingdom", the country, the *patria*, the *Land*. Indeed, the *Landstände*, assemblies of estates, were not representatives of the country, but were the country itself.

To convoke parliament meant to convoke the kingdom, or all the population. In Spain the consent and will of the *cortes* of Aragon meant the consent and will of all the Aragonese. It was on these grounds that James II decreed at the *cortes* of Lerida of 1301 that the *cortes'* decisions were binding on those both present and absent. In like manner Peter II of Valenza, in convoking the *cortes* of 1343, stated that he was holding a "parliament with all the inhabitants of the kingdom". The convocation of a new session of the Castilian *cortes* was called "another kingdom" (*otro Reino*). Even Charles V at the *cortes* of Toledo of 1525 declared that it was necessary to reply to the proposals and requests presented by the kingdom (*por parte del reino*) – that is, by the *cortes*. This identification was traditional and unquestioned. Already in the mid-13th century Alfonso the Wise stated in his *Partidas* that the court was the place where the vassals, officials and men of the kingdom appeared before the king. The same concept was to be found again in the Castilian *cortes* of 1629 and later. Nor was it a purely formal question of terminology. It was a functional concept, embracing a whole series of actions. It applied to the oath of fealty sworn to a new sovereign by the assembly in the name of the country, and given by him in the same manner. But it also applied to all decisions of the assembly – especially in financial matters – which both king and subjects considered as binding on the whole community.

It was on the basis of this identification that the *cortes* derived their varied but far-reaching constitutional powers. To realise how extensive such powers could be, it is enough to look at the famous pact of the *cortes* of León of 1188, or the agreement between Charles III of Navarre and John II of Castile of 1414, by which Charles promised friendship and alliance until such time as the *cortes* of Navarre decided a war to be just.

These examples from the Spanish parliaments are not only of general, but of specific value, as they provided the models for the Sicilian, Sardinian and Neapolitan parliaments. In Sardinia, for instance, the parliamentary envoy charged with carrying the votes of the *brazos* to the court was called the representative of Sardinia (*sindico de Cerdeña*). Analogous examples could be cited for all the Italian parliaments. In Friuli, where, even under Venetian rule, the "colloquium" was synonymous with the "united inhabitants of Friuli", parliament was "of all the *patria*", and the Council of parliament was the Council of the *patria*. On occasions the writs of summons in Friuli were justified by reasons very similar to the principle *quod omnes tangit*. Deputies elected by parliament were considered as *electi pro patria*.

The same concept was to be found in other countries. In England parliament was stated to represent "the body of all the realm". In France in 1484 the Chancellor spoke of the estates as representing all the subjects, while in 1579 the *Vindiciae contra tyrannos* spoke of "all the people or the estates which represent them". In Poland the diet was considered as a "general convention . . . the body of the kingdom with full power to represent absentees".

Representation was thus the premise and foundation of parliamentary institutions, and hence of all their attributes and actions. They had been created or recognised by sovereigns, who engaged in politico-legal negotiations with them as organs representative of the country. The assemblies met, deliberated and acted in the name and on behalf not only of those present, but of the whole community.

This concept of representation would logically presuppose either an investiture from above or election from below. But the concept of investiture was little more than a legal fiction. On the other hand, although there were no elections in the modern sense, by requesting and accepting grants from the assemblies in the name of the community, the sovereigns effectively recognised and attributed to the assemblies their character of representative bodies.

But this representative character was only one aspect of the activities of parliamentary institutions. Although created as an instrument to facilitate discussions between the head of the state and his subjects, parliament sometimes acquired an independent character, a personality legally recognised even internationally: some parliaments sent and received embassies, approved and ratified treaties. Within the state, parliament exercised constitutional powers: it recognised new sovereigns and, even more, new dynasties; it examined the legality of royal writs summoning parliamentary sessions; it scrutinised and then accepted or refused government requests for financial aid; it sometimes took part in government activities by the nomination of its own members; it participated in legislative activities and in the administration through the choice of officials, the submission of *querelae*, control over the exaction of finances, among other duties. Parliament thus shared in the exercise of sovereignty.

These attributes and powers are so varied that they can be brought forward to justify a whole series of differing definitions of parliamentary institutions. But the basic definition would seem to be the following one: parliament – or the estates or *bracci* of parliament – formed a politically representative body, representing the subjects in the structure of the state. Where it existed and was able to carry out its functions, the political regime was neither absolutist nor wholly monarchical, but to some extent mixed or dualist. However, this dualism between king and estates naturally did not imply equality between the two constitutional organs; it was unbalanced and parliament played the weaker part.

But what was the specific nature of this form of representation? Was parliamentary representation merely a legal fiction, or an historical reality creating a representative regime?

The first point to note is that for the most part parliaments spoke and acted not in the name of or on behalf of the people or the country, but for themselves, as the "three estates" or *bracci* of parliament. They substituted themselves, as a tangible body, for a hypothetical entity – the people. Hence the representative quality was indirect and improper, effected through placing this parliamentary body between king and people. Although the community was conceived of as an ideal unity in medieval society, in practice it added up to the sum of the various estates of society, each of which was regarded as a separate entity. Thus the representative nature of these tripartite parliaments was composite: it resulted from the representative character with which each of the estates was invested in relation to the subjects belonging (or considered as belonging) to its own estate. Obviously, its representative character was imposed from above, and not below – a passive, not an active quality.

In some of the sessions of the French estates general – for example, at Tours in 1484 – the clergy were represented by ecclesiastics elected by the assemblies of the *bailliages*. But in general, in the Italian parliaments as in the English, only the upper ecclesiastical hierarchy or the holders of major benefices were summoned, qualifying as great landowners or feudatories rather than as clergy. For the same reason royal officials entered parliament, sometimes as representatives of vacant benefices (for example, in the Sicilian parliament), while the minor clergy had no direct representation.

Ecclesiastical members of parliament thus attended the assemblies through their personal status. But the ecclesiastical order in parliament, as a whole, was considered as possessing the power and function of representing the entire clergy. This very function often limited the interest or suitability of ecclesiastics to participate in parliamentary sessions: the "three" estates in all the Italian parliaments (with the exception of Sicily and Sardinia) in practice became only two, as the ecclesiastical order withdrew, on the grounds that it was not directly involved in the decisions adopted by parliament.

The composition of the noble estate varied from parliament to parliament. In some – the Piedmontese or Friuli parliaments – only holders of fiefs or representatives of noble consortia took part. In others – as in Sardinia – besides the feudatories, all the nobles participated, so that at least in theory the former might have been in a minority. For although the documents spoke of a qualified, and not a simple numerical majority (*maior et sanior pars*), no norm, regulation or clear precedent existed to indicate the procedure to be followed. Finally, it should be remembered that the feudatory represented his vassals and the entire population of his fief. Thus the composition of this estate could vary to a large degree, and was clearly distinct from that of the other estates.

The third estate in the Italian parliaments nearly always consisted of the representatives of domanial communes, not subject to a feudal lord. Sometimes enfeoffed urban communes or villages were also admitted. But it was assumed that this restricted group of municipal administrators or delegates represented all people who were not already represented in or by the other two estates. In this manner the three estates constituted parliament, and parliament represented the country, acting as the *patria* or *Land*.

In their daily activities it is extremely probable that these tripartite assemblies found great difficulty in harmonising their particular interests. But the need and practice of unanimity forced them to do so. Philip II's attempt to declare the decisions of only two of the three *bracci* valid was opposed by the Sicilian parliament as a deliberate distortion of an adequate and reasonable system. In Aragon he only succeeded in introducing such an innovation after crushing a revolt of the whole country: the Aragonese *cortes* had four, not three, estates.

Thus, although there was no element of popular choice or election, parliaments represented the community and expressed if not the will, at least the interests of subjects. In one sense these parliaments were representative, for the social structure of the assemblies resembled that of the communities. There was an identity of interest between the estates and their corresponding social categories and the community: all were concerned to limit the weight of taxation and arbitrary administration, to maintain the autonomy of their country and ensure respect for their rights. This was often only one side of the coin. But in this respect parliamentary assemblies were representative.

2

Mandatory powers

Although nobles and ecclesiastics attended by personal title, all other participants in parliamentary assemblies presented a formal mandate authorising their presence as representatives of communes, ecclesiastical corporations, etc. The use of parliamentary mandates spread because of the difficulty of communications: they served to prove the legitimacy of the representatives' claim to sit in parliament and fulfil parliamentary functions. But they were also important documents for the government as they provided the necessary proof of the fitness of the assembly to act on behalf of the entire community.

Unfortunately, virtually nothing is known about how such representatives were chosen, with the exception of Piedmont, where the assembly was strongly influenced by the example and procedures of the French estates general, and which was consequently in no way typical of the other Italian parliaments. In Piedmont the methods of choice varied widely. In many cases there was either a popular election by the general council of the city, or a more restricted choice by deputies appointed specifically for this purpose by the council or by municipal officials. These deputies, or *sapientes*, were usually experts in financial matters or communal accountants or treasurers (*rationatores*, *clavarii*). Both the parliamentary delegates or ambassadors and the *sapientes* had long experience of parliamentary matters. The *sapientes* frequently included former parliamentary ambassadors, and not surprisingly dynasties of parliamentarians tended to emerge. The suffrage was thus restricted, particularly as the ambassadors could be chosen from among the members of the general council.

There can be little doubt that this method of choice exercised a direct influence on the behaviour of the ambassadors in parliament. Had they been chosen by a heterogeneous electoral body, which ceased to function until the following election, they would have been far less tied. As representatives of a homogeneous and permanent group, such as the municipal council, they could not ignore their duty.

The degree to which a parliamentary representative could exercise freedom of choice depended on whether he was given full powers or a limited mandate. Perhaps the most extreme case was the permanent control exercised over the representatives of Cagliari by the *tretzena de cort*. But in general the difficulty about restricted, clearly delimited mandates was that they presupposed a precise knowledge of what was to be discussed and decided upon in the assembly. As the writs of summons were frequently phrased in general and vague terms, it was impossible to instruct the ambassador. Moreover, if all the participants had been too closely bound by their mandates, it would have been impossible to reach any decision at all. The writs, therefore, demanded that delegates should not only be experienced in public business and have power to act according to their own judgement, but that they should also have adequate power to pledge the commune to their decisions.

Unless a delegate was sent to listen and refer back, he possessed a notable power of discretion even when a limited mandate existed: he could judge what was or was not opportune in all matters except those explicitly laid down in his mandate. Precisely because he was a representative he had to have considerable freedom of action. He could not ignore the fact that he was a member of a representative assembly with more general and higher powers and duties, responsible not only to his own city, but to the country, *patria* or kingdom.

One of the normal purposes of parliamentary assemblies was to submit requests or protests against administrative abuses. Attendance implied that petitions and complaints, given to the ambassador at the local or even individual level – would be discussed and included in the document submitted by the assembly to the sovereign. Quite often the limit to the representative's mandate consisted only of this obligation to put forward requests or protests and insist on their acceptance. Sometimes this duty was regarded as so important as to condition the representative's vote on royal demands. But once these petitions had been taken into consideration, the parliamentary delegate resumed his freedom of action.

According to Roman law and medieval common law, the delegates were required to come to the assembly with full powers, adequate to pledge the people they represented. In the mid-13th century Philippe de Beaumanoir wrote that, according to *droit coutumier*, "no power of attorney is worth anything, unless he who grants this power does pledge himself to uphold firmly and stably whatever shall be decided or said by his attorney". In practice, the degree of limitation or powers of attorney may well have been crucial to the strength of the parliamentary institutions. In England the Commons under Elizabeth could never have acted in so unprovincial a manner without full powers. In France the failure of the estates general may well have resulted from the limited mandates of the representatives.

In the early great assemblies, the participants were summoned authoritatively, as if to appear before judgement. The lay and ecclesiastical lords were to appear personally, the others were to send "ambassadors", "procurators" or "honest men" capable and "sufficiently instructed", with full powers to listen and decide. The writs for the great assemblies in France in the early 14th century instructed the ecclesiastical chapters and the *bonnes villes* to provide their representatives with full and adequate powers. The close analogy with judicial practice was underlined by the custom of making three calls at the beginning of each parliamentary session before declaring absentees contumacious.

The writs of summons not only insisted upon full and adequate powers, but sometimes threatened those who came with limited or irregular mandates that they would not only be refused admittance, but also declared absent and contumacious. Nevertheless, when faced with unexpected situations, even representatives provided with full powers might feel the need to request permission to confer with their electors. The occasion might be a real one or simply a pretext to delay a decision. Hence these requests to refer back did not necessarily imply a limited mandate. Indeed, the initiative for a prorogation was occasionally taken by the government itself for political and not legal reasons, in order to ensure a favourable vote. Charles V acted in this manner at the Valladolid *cortes* of 1523, and more than one example can be found in the Piedmontese and Friuli parliaments. Even a limited mandate could be acceptable to the government, if it favoured royal requests.

Full powers were not the absolute rule in either the Italian or the Spanish (at least Castilian) parliaments. In the Castilian *cortes* of Medina in 1318 and Madrid in 1329 a considerable number of the communal representatives had limited mandates which they had sworn to obey. The writs of summons for the Toledo *cortes* of 1525, the Valladolid *cortes* of 1542, the Toledo *cortes* of 1559 tried to avoid these limited mandates by sending out an exemplar of the required form of mandate. When almost all the procurators arrived at the *cortes* of Madrid of 1562 with limited mandates, they were sent back to obtain fuller powers. At Madrid in 1566, Cordova in 1570 and Madrid in 1573, they were made to swear that they possessed full powers. But in 1579, 1582, 1588 and as late as 1623, limited mandates were still predominant.

Numerous examples could also be pointed to in the Italian parliaments, although the use of limited mandates was never predominant. The one exception was the Piedmontese parliament, as usual similar to the French estates general, and in this respect to the estates of the Low Countries as well. In Piedmont (as in Savoy), each parliamentary session consisted of two phases. In the first instance the ambassadors listened to the government's requests, discussed them among themselves and then referred back. After local consultations, the ambassadors were elected anew, this time with specific mandates and instructions on the matter to be decided. Many of these mandates varied in the conditions they insisted upon. But in general full powers were given. Nevertheless, even these full powers could be accompanied by specific instructions. Vercelli in 1465 gave its representatives "a full, free and general mandate, with full, free and general powers of decision", but added that the ambassadors were not to pledge themselves to anything important without first gaining the agreement of the two municipal councils.

Thus no typical pattern, but a wide variation of mandates existed in Italy. The ambassadors, as representatives of individual cities, were in a position of dependence. But at the same time, because of their legal status as members of parliament, they were able to make positive decisions of general value. Because parliament was representative, the position and function of its individual members was representative. For parliament was recognised as speaking and acting in the name and on behalf, not of restricted and more or less qualified groups, but of the entire community.

One final point needs to be made. It has often been stated that the participation of the cities in parliament originated virtually as a gift, or as a new privilege granted by the sovereign. But there can be little doubt that formerly it was an obligation rather than a right, an order rather than a concession to the communes. Even when the great assemblies were purely feudal, the sovereign could ask for advice and aid throughout the country: the enlargement of the assemblies was of advantage not so much to the new participants as to the public administration.

Thus at a certain point, the cities, boroughs, *comunità* in Italy, Spain, France and elsewhere were summoned to parliament as a measure of general utility, with no intention of granting them any privileges. This collective summons was based on a single but adequate criterion: the status of the communes, their independence of the feudatories, and hence their autonomy, as shown in their franchise and statutes. Only at a later stage did the question of individual admissions arise. But in these instances the convocation of new communes resulted from an assessment of their demographic and economic importance. It did not imply the grant of a new franchise, but the recognition of the development of a previously small centre to the level of the communes already summoned to parliament. Whether the summons constituted a privilege or a duty depended upon an evaluation of the possibilities offered by participation in parliament.

3

The contractual nature of parliamentary agreements

We have seen how in their origins parliamentary institutions were strengthened by the diffusion of the democratic concept implicit in the formula *quod omnes tangit.* Similarly, in the age of absolutism the assemblies found the strength to survive through the deep-rooted belief in the contractual nature of agreements between sovereigns and their peoples or estates.

Medieval history is marked by solemn pacts or constitutions accepted by sovereigns in response to demands that their rights be recognised. These demands were made by subjects who claimed special recognition because of their legal status or political actions. A well-known series of such agreements can be pointed to in the 12th, 13th and 14th centuries: the peace of Constance of 1183, Alfonso IX's constitution for León of 1188, the Magna Carta of 1215, the Golden Bull of Hungary of 1215, the Provisions of Oxford of 1257–8, the *privilegio general* of Aragon and the Catalan constitution *Una vegada lo any* of 1282, the Castilian constitution of Valladolid of 1307, the *Joyeuse entrée* of Brabant of 1356. But there is also an even longer series of agreements whose contractual nature is masked by their formal description as unilateral "gracious" concessions: for example, the oath of Jean de Valenrode of Liége of 1418, the agreement of 1472 between the marquis and estates of Brandenburg, the pact of Tübingen of 1514. The purpose of each of these constitutional agreements was to settle ideological or political conflicts, and to establish or register a new equilibrium of forces. Each intended to delimit the extent of the sovereign's powers in relation to the rights he recognised as belonging to the people. The agreements were often broken by the ruler, but even this did not imply a repudiation of the principle and practice of collaboration, of agreements and pacts between sovereign and people.

The importance of these pacts was underlined by their insistence upon the perpetuity and irrevocability of the concession, and by their acceptance by the sovereigns as contracts between two parties. They reflected the limited nature of sovereignty in the Middle Ages.

The sovereign needed the collaboration of his subjects, and hence had to reach agreement with them through reciprocal concessions. He took the initiative by summoning his subjects to an assembly to ask for their advice and aid. The agreements reached in these assemblies marked the boundary between his power and the original rights or acquired privileges of the people – or rather of the estates or communities – who thus gained acknowledged powers within the state.

Nor were these pacts purely theoretical. A regular and continuous series of agreements were made in parliament which required application. The parliaments, estates or *bracci* discussed and decided upon the demands of the government, just as sovereigns and governments examined, modified and accepted parliamentary requests. All these agreements were bilateral contracts, but they applied to the administrative system. Thus, on both the political and administrative level, relations between sovereign and country were based on a contractual belief.

With the development of absolutism from the 15th century, not only parliamentary institutions and all surviving forms of corporative or territorial autonomies were attacked, but so were contractualist concepts. Ferdinand the Catholic denied all affirmations of bilateral obligations in Sicily; Charles V and Emanuel Philibert of Savoy refused to swear the traditional oaths to observe the concessions of their predecessors; the Spanish court no longer wanted to hear of "donatives", with their implication of a voluntary act, but insisted upon "services".

As the polemic between the surviving assemblies and the supporters of absolutism developed, the question whether or not sovereigns were held to observe inviolably the contracts they had signed with their subjects acquired a special interest. Could the king impose taxation and lay down laws without the consent of his subjects? If the king had signed a pact, was it perpetually valid, even if the sovereign maintained that it was prejudicial to his prerogatives and the good of the country? It is in 16th-century France that the discussion can be followed most easily, in the writings of Hotman,

Matharel, Bodin and Grégoire.[1] For where sovereigns attempted to assert their absolute power, the polemic became most lively. But not only in France but in Catalonia, Aragon, Sicily and Sardinia, the parliamentarian doctrine was asserted both in publicists' writings and in parliamentary discussions and declarations. In 15th-century Catalonia, Tomas Mieres asserted that it was clear that royal constitutions, once sworn by the sovereign, were of perpetual validity and could not be derogated or revoked by the sovereign, while contrary acts could have no validity, even if reinforced by further oaths. In the 1660s the advocate of the military *stament* of Sardinia, D. Joseph Martinez Figueras Alarcon, sent a memorial to Queen Maria Teresa of Spain asserting the perpetual validity of old pacts. On the opposing side, the chanceries claimed unconditional obedience, and were supported by other publicists.

The survival of parliamentary doctrines in this rising tide of absolutism was assisted, at least in part, by the widespread publication of the old texts: for these laws underlined the reciprocal nature of the concessions and so justified the defence of ancient privileges granted "with the force of contracts", or "as perpetual privileges" or as "laws agreed by pact".

But in the 17th and 18th centuries, as the tradition grew weaker, it became more difficult to assert the contractualist concept with confidence. As policies of enlightened despotism were imposed, the position of the parliaments was further weakened by the claim of the sovereigns to work directly for the public interest, without the representative bodies acting as intermediaries.

4

Limitations of post-medieval parliamentary practice

There can be little doubt that from the mid-16th century parliaments were on the defensive. Outwardly they may still have appeared to

[1] See below, Part 5, Chapter 5, pp. 245 ff.

be important institutions, sometimes even formally acknowledged as possessing constitutional authority. But apart from England, they were no longer of prime importance in the history of their countries, and – except for specific moments – no longer took the initiative. It is enough to look at Germany and the Empire, where the *Landstände* still enjoyed extensive powers: their behaviour was conservative; there was no development.

Nevertheless, to gain the correct perspective it is necessary to remember that this absence of dynamism was characteristic not only of parliamentary institutions, but of all constitutional thought of the time. The political and legal theorists of the 16th century assumed a perfectly static order laid down by God, which was to be regarded by men as inviolable and eternal. Parliaments worked within this structure, within the assumptions of the age. Moreover, they were concerned not with distant ideals, but with immediate, practical problems.

In fact, even in the Middle Ages parliaments were in no position to take significant initiatives and put them into practice. To do this they would have had to transform themselves into organs of government. But this would have been possible only through revolutionary action. The very mechanics of parliament worked against it. For parliament not only worked slowly, but was of short duration, with irregular, often hasty meetings. The position, almost the duty of the assemblies, was to make sure that the sovereign and his collaborators carried out their task of governing the country with the utmost parsimony. They never questioned the sovereign's right to govern, and indeed were willing to give advice and help. But the size of public expenditure and new financial requests alarmed them and aroused their opposition. This double duty of controlling governmental requests for finances, but providing necessary and adequate funds on each occasion, was carried out scrupulously, even with mistrust and hostility. But it did not imply that the assemblies were in a position to carry out a policy of their own. Their resistance, which frequently resulted not from any hope of a tactical advantage, but from a deep-felt need, ran the risk of being considered obstructionist, almost seditious. It must have been difficult to reach agreement each time, particularly as the demands for taxation increased continually. As absolutism developed, it not only increased its financial demands, but threatened the tradition of pacts, concessions and privileges which the estates had obtained and conserved with difficulty in the 13th, 14th and 15th centuries.

But parliamentary action was not purely defensive: resistance was accompanied by demands. At the end of the 16th century, the Italian parliaments were anything but willing to accept without discussion. The concept of reciprocal concessions was still expressed unequivocally. Subsidies were bargained over and made conditional on the acceptance of parliamentary votes, framed to impede the king and government from acting arbitrarily in matters touching the commonweal. In all periods the assemblies submitted their grievances, and demanded preliminary redress. It may well be that the number of parliamentary requests to be accepted declined in the later 16th and 17th centuries in Italy as in the Castilian *cortes*. But it remains of importance to examine the nature of these requests.

The first and most important demand was almost always the confirmation of previous pacts and privileges, if possible by oath. It was a request for a solemn and formal reaffirmation of parliament's right to exact respect for what it regarded as legitimately acquired privileges, to be defended against abusive and illegitimate aggressions. Another commonplace demand in Spanish Italy was that the offices and dignities of the various states be reserved for local inhabitants. It was a measure of defence against the increasing subordination of the provinces, and resembled similar demands made by other countries. At the same time, it signified a protest against past and present sovereigns who disregarded their promises to take full account of the qualities of their most worthy subjects.

These and all the other requests need to be judged in the context of the discussions, claims and offers made at different levels by the various groupings of each individual parliament, according to its structure and regulations. The Sardinian parliament of 1624 provides an example.

On this occasion the military *brazo* seized the opportunity offered by the submission of its *capitula* for royal approval to denounce the subversion of the ancient and respected principles of government. "In earlier sessions this *stament* of the kingdom of Sardinia proposed numerous *capitula* for the service of his Majesty and the common good of the country: some were immediately accepted and decreed by the viceroy, others were sent to Court to be submitted to the sovereign for definitive approval and royal sanction. Relying on their approval, the *stament* agreed to the closure of the sessions. But not only were the *capitula* which had been submitted to the Supreme Council of Aragon not accepted, but some of those approved by the viceroy were modified or even revoked without the *stament* being able to act in support of its votes because of the closure of the session. Now the *stament* is presenting these votes again because of their utility, and requests their acceptance: it is essential that they be submitted to His Majesty once more, but this time before, and not after, the end of the session."

This first attempt failed, as the viceroy replied that it was customary to transmit the *capitula* to the king only after the closure of parliament. The military *brazo* responded by sending a special message with the *capitula* to Philip IV and the Council of Aragon: "The purpose of the *cortes* is to uphold justice, redress grievances, change and correct laws, revive laws fallen into disuse or violated by administrators, grant compensation to subjects who merit it, and acknowledge the debt of faithful subjects for favours received from sovereigns by the concession of existing and new *donativi*. This has always been the case, and has been seen to be the case in Sardinia from the time of the most noble ancestors of His Majesty, following the practice of the *cortes* of the kingdoms of the Crown of Aragon and in general of his other kingdoms. Unfortunately, His Majesty is not present in person, and so the *stament* has decided to send him its 'syndic', ambassador and procurator in order to avoid the difficulties which have emerged in the past through failure to approve various *capitula* useful to the service of his Majesty and the common good of the kingdom, and through the revocation of many of the *capitula* previously decreed by the viceroy in the name of His Majesty, without parliament being able to remedy the situation because of the closure of the session. Now the *stament* supplicates His Majesty to accept and decree these *capitula* before the closure of the present parliament."

That the *stament* should "supplicate" implied perhaps a lowering of the dignity of parliament. But it did not diminish the efficacy of the parliamentary votes as a protest against more or less intentional violations of a legal order, whose observance had been won as a counterpart to the granting of subsidies. The protests might be unsuccessful, but they were not lacking in courage. At Palermo and Messina the parliamentary leaders were forced to escape or risk arrest. At Cagliari, after the last three sessions of the Sardinian parliament, almost all the leaders of the military *stament* were executed, on the pretext of the murder of the viceroy, the marquis of Camarasa.

Was this attitude merely one of anachronistic conservatism, of a backward mentality, insisting on anti-historical positions in the face of a transformed royal authority, as the comte de Boulainvilliers wrote in the 18th century? It seems implausible that for decades these ruling classes should have continued to act without any constructive sense or hope.

The *raison d'être* of the static conservatism of the estates is to be found in their calculations of what could be obtained as compensation for what they were called upon to offer. Their reaction to a rapacious and in large part arbitrary central administration was to accentuate their supervisory functions and increase their demands. Without any apparent awareness that these actions might appear dangerous or anachronistic, they stood firm on their old positions, particularly in their relations with the administration, as if nothing had changed, as if the modifications which had occurred were something extraneous to the traditional relationship between the sovereign and the community of his subjects. In the Italian case, one needs to remember that the parliaments lived in a sort of limbo, as representatives of restricted, provincial communities, with no way of influencing or even participating in the new political world of monarchical power. They acted only at a viceregal level. What might have seemed a matter of constitutional importance elsewhere diminished in Italy into a mere act of administration. The sudden changes of state policy of Richelieu's *arcana imperii* reverberated on the provinces as facts which could not be explained in any rational, methodical manner. Thus in effect the estates were involved in purely administrative activities. Their limited efficacy in Italy resulted from both the relationship of these parliaments to the whole structure of government, and the limited, inferior position of their states, subordinated as they were to greater powers.

This inferiority applied as much to Friuli under Venetian domination as to Sardinia or Sicily. They were all provincial assemblies or estates. The parliaments did their best to ignore and exclude the consequences of this relationship and dependence, to regard the institutional changes and events in these other countries as extraneous. Each country looked only to itself. Sicily and Sardinia consistently ignored John II's oath, binding himself and his successors, to keep the two islands perpetually joined to the Crown of Aragon;[2] their parliaments continued to act on the level of local interests, even though they were forced to note that, because of the size of the empire, the sovereign lived far away and could not rule directly. Hence in practice they acted at a viceregal level, although Sardinia tenaciously maintained its right (denied at Naples and blocked in Sicily) to send its "syndic" to court after each session to treat, discuss and conclude affairs directly with the sovereign or with the Council of Aragon as his representative.

The administrative sector was thus the only one open to parliamentary initiative. Here the parliaments spoke up against the most arbitrary actions, despite threats and intimidations, and proposed long series of measures to put in order or improve various aspects of the administration; to carry out this task, they were even prepared to overcome their reluctance to increase the burden of taxation or diminish the fiscal exemptions of certain groups. But however courageous or useful these initiatives might seem, they represented little more than public denunciations. For within the structure of government, real authority lay with the executive, which possessed extremely wide discretional powers as the representative of royal authority. Probably the major limitation to these powers was to be found not in the parliamentary assemblies, but in the venality of office.

The major check on the executive which the parliaments could impose was the size of grant they were prepared to offer. They could not displace the executive, nor in fact did they wish to do so, for they formed part of the same political class and held judicial and administrative offices. Indeed members of parliament with royal offices frequently boasted of their success in gaining parliamentary

[2] However, once the Habsburg family acquired the Spanish monarchy it also preferred to ignore this ruling: Sicily was placed under the Supreme Council of Italy, while Sardinia was left under the Council of Aragon.

approval for government requests and openly asked for fitting rewards. After the *cortes* of Madrid of 1617 the municipal procurators put forward a series of requests, stating what each had done for His Majesty's service: the president of the assembly replied on the king's behalf, stating the *mercedi* granted to each, but warning them not to publicise the sale of their vote. A similar practice existed in the Sardinian parliament, and for Sicily it is enough to read Scipione di Castro's description.

But even apart from these temptations, the instruments the Italian assemblies possessed were inadequate for more than a simulacrum of the *ius resistendi* possessed by parliaments of certain other countries as a result of pacts with their sovereigns. It is enough to contrast the Italian parliaments with the extreme case of the Polish assembly, with its pact *De non praestanda oboedentia*. The Sardinian parliament had never managed to obtain anything similar to the Aragonese *justicia*, or even the nomination of judges of the *contrafueros* to guard against violations of the rights of the country, as existed in so many other parliaments (Catalonia, Württemberg, etc.). But it appeared to possess a fairly important instrument of control in its *greuges* or grievances. Their importance was morally and legally notable: parliament refused to discuss grants until its grievances had been redressed. But this was purely a formality because of the long delays between sessions, and even more because of the procedural regulations of the assembly. For if all the judges nominated by the viceroy declared an appeal invalid, no further action could be taken. But each grievance was at least examined critically, and even if rejected, indirectly had some effect.

The real power of these parliaments, in fact, lay in their ability to discuss and delay, condition or even refuse the government's requests for financial aid. But experience showed that a refusal led not only to the abrupt closure of the parliamentary session, but to royal reprisals and to a serious questioning of the contractual basis of relations between government and representatives. In practice, the parliaments lost whether they gave in to the government or slammed the door in its face. Hence a refusal was regarded as an extreme, almost a revolutionary solution: it was enough to threaten a refusal, and not risk any more. Behind this complicated game of threats and counter-threats, both sides fundamentally wanted to reach agreement, whether based on the preceding or a new balance of power. For parliamentary compromises were always expressions of a balance of power within the state.

Thus however limited or static, the presence and activity of these parliaments of the post-medieval period were useful, if nothing else as a brake and obstacle to royal absolutism.[3]

5

Parliament and political writers

To conclude a comparative study of parliamentary institutions an examination of their repercussions on public opinion is of considerable importance. Unfortunately, the difficulties of research in this field are almost insuperable for Italy. In the first place, the major parliaments – those of the South – developed in regions with the least advanced literary and cultural traditions, offering infinitely less in the form of written evidence than such areas as Lombardy or Tuscany. In the second place, these southern parliaments were not legal institutions, at least in the 14th and 15th centuries, but were similar to earlier politico–feudal assemblies of an extraordinary character, without autonomy or particular value. In consequence, none of the great political or juridical theorists, such as Aquinas, Marino da Caramanico, Andrea da Isernia or Luca da Penne, judged them worthy of note. It is necessary to turn to political theorists and publicists, both in Italy and throughout Western Europe for assessments of the character and position of parliaments. But even in these writers references were neither frequent nor explicit before the 15th and 16th centuries. Before this period

[3] Contemporaries were aware of this function of parliaments in an absolutist age. The comte de Boulainvilliers emigrated to England to publish his history of the French parliaments in 1782, because of the danger French historians and publishers believed to exist if one spoke freely of such matters. H. de Boulainvilliers, *État de la France contenant XIV lettres sur les anciens parlements de ce royaume jusqu'à Charles VIII*, London, 1782.

politicians and theorists remained concerned – in a typically medieval manner – with metaphysical or abstract questions. They tried to justify the politico–legal organisation of human society, the relations between this and the next world, or the *respublica christiana*. They did not on the whole deal with the concrete daily problems which formed the substance of parliamentary discussions.

Little is to be found in the early 14th-century writers. Marsiglio of Padua, with no direct knowledge of parliaments, turned to the example of the Church Council as representing the community of the faithful in order to formulate his well-known constitutional proposals in which the more able part (*valentior pars*) of the citizenry represented the entire community. Both William of Ockham and Nicholas of Cusa had a more direct experience of representative institutions in England and the Empire, and showed a certain appreciation of their utility. For William of Ockham, parliament was to be considered basically as an instrument to limit the powers of the sovereign, defend the rights of subjects, and enact reforms. Ockham's state was both representative and administrative. Nicholas of Cusa's theory revolved around the triple concept of church–council–empire: as papal power corresponded to imperial power, so an analogous representative assembly was to correspond to the Church's council. As the pope personified the community of the faithful, so the emperor personified his people. Hence it was up to his initiative to convoke a "universal council", to be attended by the princes, rectors of the provinces, clergy and envoys of the cities and major *universitates,* which would consequently represent the whole empire and exercise the powers of the community and enact legislation.

There can be little doubt that for both these writers parliamentary assemblies represented institutions which seemed to them to correspond to the needs of the time, as well as to their own personal political concepts. In Nicholas of Cusa's case, the insistence on popular will and the sovereign's obligation to convoke the assembly and then accept the *communis sententia* shows how far he had moved away from the customary theoretical schemes of the medieval monarchy towards proposing an almost "constitutional" regime.

But by the time of Nicholas of Cusa a direct interest in parliament was by no means unusual. In Spain it was especially important in the

Crown of Aragon. In his *Extragravatorium curiarum*, written in 1413,[4] Jaime Callis offered the first systematic study of a parliamentary institution, bringing to bear on the subject not only his personal experience, but the doctrines and concepts of a series of jurists concerned with wholly different problems (glossators, post-glossators, canonists). The central argument for Callis was that of the prerogatives of the sovereign and his constitutional position in relation to the *cortes* and country. He not only assumed that the king's power was limited by the agreements he had sworn to observe, but asserted courageously that the king only had the right to dissolve parliament after the assembly had completed such duties as had been laid down in the writs of summons. Thus, for Callis, the king voluntarily limited his own power, in order to collaborate with the *cortes* not only in constitutional, political and financial matters, but also in administrative affairs, such as the control of officials or redress of grievances.

Callis's work is important both in its own right and because of its influence on two other Aragonese writers, Tomas Mieres and P. G. Belluga. Mieres, in his *Apparatus super constitutiones Cathaluniae* (1439),[5] insisted that sovereign, officials and subjects all owed respect and obedience not only to divine and natural law, but to man-made, "positive" law: thus decrees of the sovereign which went against the laws he had sworn in parliament were without legal validity. According to Belluga in his *Speculum principum* (1449),[6] parliament's authority derived not from legal decrees, but from custom. However, if the sovereign received a sum of money from the people to accept laws made by parliament, these laws assumed the nature of a contract and could not be revoked by the sovereign or his successor. Nevertheless, Belluga – a royal councillor – felt obliged to show the difficulties created by cases where the sovereign had a just and necessary cause to act differently. Belluga, although less forthright than his predecessors in upholding parliamentary prerogatives, asserted the prince's need to take advantage of

[4] J. Callis, *Curiarum Extragravatorium per dominum Jacobum de Calicio,* Barcelona, 1518, Lyon, 1556.

[5] T. Mieres, *Apparatus super constitutiones curiarum generalium Cathaluniae*, Barcelona, 1621.

[6] P. G. Belluga, *Speculum principum ac iustitiae,* Paris, 1530.

parliamentary collaboration in the interest of the commonweal. His work had repercussions not only in Spain, but in Italy (particularly in Sardinia) and even in France where, a century later, Bodin polemicised with him.

But it should be noted that none of these three writers suggested that the king of Aragon was subject to parliament. This was to be asserted by the French Protestant François Hotman in 1573 in his famous *Franco-Gallia*,[7] where he used the examples of Aragon and England to maintain that the king of France's power was limited by the law and that he had an obligation to uphold the inviolability of the authority of the representative assembly. According to Hotman, the king of Aragon was elected by parliament with specific limits to his power and warned by the *justicia* of his dependence on the assembly.

Hotman's curious and untrue assertion had echoes across the Channel: in 1574 the *Réveille-matin des François et des leurs voisins*, published at Edinburgh and dedicated to Elizabeth, repeated and developed this concept of the sovereignty of parliament and its superiority over the monarch. This extremist idea was refuted by Antoine Matharel in his *Ad Hotomani Franco-Galliam responsio* (1575),[8] where he questioned the veracity of Hotman's assertions about Aragon. For Matharel, the mythical *lex regia* proved his argument that the people no longer possessed its ancient and original power, having transferred it to the sovereign.

But it was Jean Bodin, in his *Six livres de la République* (1576),[9] who destroyed these pro-parliamentarian theses to assert the greatness of sovereign majesty and the limits of parliamentarian authority and prerogatives. For Bodin, every body or state was governed by command and obedience. Public power belonged to the sovereign, who exercised it by laws or through his magistrates. Because of his sovereignty, the king had no need of the consent of his subjects to lay down laws. But this did not imply that he was not bound to respect the laws of God and nature and even the *lex gentium*. The sovereign swore to obey the laws and could not break his word. But if there were just reasons he could, by special and not by a

[7] F. Hotman, *Franco-Gallia, libellus statum veteris Reipublicae Galliae, tum deinde a Francis occupatae describens*, Geneva, 1573.

[8] A. Matharel, *Ad F. Hotomani Franco-Galliam responsio*, Paris, 1575.

[9] J. Bodin, *Les six liures de la République*, Paris, 1576.

general derogation, apply the law in a different manner. But he could do this only in so far as he did not prejudice the rights of individual subjects. For a sovereign could not unilaterally break a pact he had freely entered into. Parliament's true function was to supplicate the sovereign, "without any power to order, or to decree, nor with any deliberate voice". It possessed greater authority only if the sovereign was captured in war, mentally ill or a minor.

Pierre Grégoire faced these same problems in his *De Republica libri sex et viginti* (1586).[10] After a carefully balanced account of both sides of the argument, Grégoire insisted on the obligation to observe a contract. By agreeing to a pact, the sovereign became a contracting party, and contracts were passed on to heirs. Although it was true that the prince was "free of the laws" (*legibus solutus*), once he had agreed to bind himself, and had bound himself, he had become similar to a private citizen and was bound as much as the other contracting party. To repudiate a pact could not but appear iniquitous. Monarchs did act arbitrarily and break their contracts. But practical examples of tyranny did not affect the principle of what was required of good and legitimate princes. The only case in which it was permissible to break a contract was if the effects of such a pact would be substantially to diminish the inalienable rights of the kingdom. But even then the king was obliged to consult his leading councillors before deciding. For if the prince was "father", "guide", and "steward" of the commonweal (*res publica*), the true sovereign was the commonweal itself and not the prince.

This is hardly the place to enter into a discussion of English political writers of the 16th and 17th centuries, whose theories and disputes were so closely related to the striking political developments and upheavals of the period. It is enough to remember the names of Thomas Smith, Hooker, Hobbes, Harrington, Filmer, Algernon Sidney, Halifax, Locke and so many others. A crucial argument in this continuous discussion about sovereignty was whether the prince's superiority was proven by his power to convoke and dissolve parliament. The argument was finally settled in 1694 in parliament's favour by the passing of the Triennial Act.

By the 18th century the convocation of the estates general in France was little more than a distant memory, but this memory

[10] P. Grégoire, *De republica libri sex et viginti,* 1586, Lyon, 1609.

was nostalgically idealised. At the opening of the century, Fénélon outlined a scheme for the transformation of absolute monarchy into a monarchy tempered by the three estates. They were to be convoked every three years with the right to deliberate for so long as they wished on all matters, from the law to international relations. They were also to act as a court of appeal for the deliberations and accounts of the provincial estates, which were to be formed throughout the country. It was a complex and imaginative plan, aiming at innovating all sectors of public life from below as well as from above, in part by reviving past traditions. This nostalgia for the estates general reflected not only a widespread desire to emerge from the despotic absolutism of a decadent monarchy, but a protest against the provincial *parlements*, which claimed to represent the community.

These idealised national traditions, as much as the concrete examples of parliaments in England, the Low Countries and certain German states, offered comfort and support to the diffusion of radical ideas, and led to a desire to renew the experience of state assemblies. Even the abbé Mably, refuting the physiocratic belief in natural causes and hence in an objective justification of absolutism, proposed that power be entrusted to a sovereign assembly. In 1750 Mirabeau proposed the general institution of estates, such as still existed in Brittany, Burgundy, Languedoc and Provence, on the grounds that they administered better than the intendants. In 1760 the *parlement* of Rouen asserted that so long as the estates existed, the government and country flourished; "but once the sessions of the estates were no longer called, private interests took charge, and under the pretext of expediting decisions, the will of the country was no longer listened to or understood".[11] With Montesquieu the belief in a representative regime took a decisive step forward[12]. The time was drawing near for a new type of parliamentary institution, which was to emerge from the shock of the French Revolution.

[11] Quoted in E. Carcassonne, *Montesquieu et le problème de la constitution française au XVIIIe siècle*, Paris, 1927, pp. 292–3.

[12] It would be difficult to trace so important a tradition in Italy as in France. But the strong influence of English parliamentary practice on the Veronese Scipione Maffei is worth noting: see L. Rossi, "Un precursore di Montesquieu: Scipione Maffei", *Scritti vari di diritto pubblico*, vol. VI, Milan, 1941, ch. 6, "La costituzione inglese secondo il Maffei".

Appendices

APPENDIX I

Glossary

affidationes	(Friuli) special passes to guarantee safe journey of delegates to assemblies
ambasciatores	(States of the Church) envoys to parliament
assemblées d'états	(France) orders or estates meeting together in assembly
assisae regis	(England) in 13th century reunion of king with ecclesiastics, barons and occasionally knights of the shires
aulici	king's courtiers
baiulus	(Sicily) local administrator who chose representatives of towns for assemblies
bonnes villes	(France) post-Carolingian, communes with status of feudal vassals
braccio, bracci, brachium, brachia	(Sicily and Sardinia) orders or estates
bras, brazos	(Sardinia) orders or estates represented in assembly
capitoli, capitula, capitulos	(Piedmont, Saluzzo, Sardinia, Sicily) petitions from estates granted by the king
colletta	(Sicily) general levy
colloquium	(England) later title for court or great council of 13th and 14th century
colloquium	(Empire, Germany) assembly with obligatory attendance by princes, important subjects, envoys of the cities. In 13th century more similar to earlier *curia* or courts than to contemporary *colloquia* in England, Spain, etc.
colte	(Friuli) tax see: *colletta*

comitatinanza	(Friuli) order of peasantry
concilium	(England) special solemn session of the royal court (see also *curia*)
concio	(Empire) plenary session of imperial diet
congregatio	(States of the Church) usual late name for parliament also term used for Piedmontese assembly
coniurationes	(Aragon) leagues
Conseil des Commis	(Aosta) executive assembly after 1536
consiliarii	king's ministers or counsellors
consortilia, *consortitus*	(Monferrat, Piedmont, Friuli) feudal consortia who sent representatives to parliament
conventus	(England, Germany and elsewhere) restricted assembly of local lords, ecclesiastics, royal officials including thegns and ealdormen held when king wanted their advice, usually at great religious festivals
cort	(Catalonia) court, assembly
cortes, *corts*	(Spain) assemblies summoned by the king to deal with affairs of state (like *curiae*, *colloquia* elsewhere), which gradually developed into representative institutions
curia	court, meeting to discuss affairs of state with varying composition from country to country and from century to century
curia	(Empire, Germany) remained for much longer than rest of Europe a feudal assembly but ultimately did not include third estate
curia generalis	(England and Empire, Germany) attended by chief barons, ecclesiastics and counsellors
curia plena	*curia* attended by all eligible representatives
curia reducida	(Spain) *curia* attended by certain representatives only

curia solemnis	see: *curia generalis*
decuriones	(Piedmont) municipal councillors
Deputies di Magistrato	(March of Ancona) committee with general executive functions
Deputies de negocio	(March of Ancona) committee with specific functions but sometimes acting like the above
diet	(Empire) assembly attended by ecclesiastics, chief subjects, counsellors and also by communes' representatives
diets	(Piedmont) parliament
donativo, donativi	(Aosta, Naples, Piedmont, Sardinia and Sicily) voluntary parliamentary grant of money to king
dret general	(Sardinia) customs duty
estates	(France, Germany, Navarre, Netherlands, Piedmont, Savoy, Sardinia, Scandinavia) more usual title for representative institutions, although strictly speaking later meaning is an order or division of a representative institution
fiscali	agents of lieutenant of Venice
fueros	(Aragon) local customs
fogatge	(Sardinia) general hearth-tax
furs	(Valencia) customs, see: *fueros*
generalitat	(Catalonia) permanent parliamentary commission after 1301
generalis credentia	(Piedmont) municipal council
giustizieri	(Sicily) official who administered large districts
grazie	(Sicily) favours demanded of king by parliament – petitions
greuge	(Sardinia) Catalan word used for grievances aired by parliament
habilitators	(Catalonia, Sardinia) members of committee in control of titles

Hoftage — (Empire) national assembly or court *diet* attended by major dignitaries of Empire and its kingdoms (bishops, princes, town administrators, etc.)

impositio peditum — (Friuli) general or partial levy of infantry

infanzones — (Aragon) nobles without jurisdictional rights

iornata — (Piedmont) parliament

iutges de greuges — (Catalonia, Sardinia) members or examiners of committees dealing with grievances

iutges esgravadors — (Sardinia) see: *iutges de greuges*

justicia — (Aragon) early 14th century creation, a constitutional magistrate who personified parliament

letrados — (Castile, Sardinia) lawyers

magnum concilium — (England) later title for *curia*, see: *concilia*

maiores — (Spain) chief administrators of cities

membri — (Friuli) estates of parliament

Notabelversammlungen — (Germany) meetings of notables in 13th and 14th century

oratores — (States of the Church) early 16th century term for *syndici* or *ambasciatores*

parlamentum — in usage as term for assembly in papal documents from late 11th century

parlamentum — (England) final title of courts

parlement — (France) assembly, title used first by end of 11th century but from c. early 14th century becomes a judicial organ

Parliament — (England) in 13th and 14th centuries assembly dealing especially with judicial problems of any size with representatives of all social groups, convoked on fixed dates often in session longer than other assemblies. By end of 14th century only procedure differentiated it from *colloquium* or *curia*, it thus dealt with national political issues

patria — (Piedmont, Friuli) the nation

piazze — (Naples) see: *sedili*

placita — (France) judicial assemblies

proceres — magnates, greater nobles, ecclesiastical dignitaries

propositiones — (Friuli) solemn opening speeches at assemblies

provisores gravaminum — (Sardinia) see: *iutges de greuges*

Reichstag — (Empire, Germany) title of *curia* from 1495

ricos hombres — (Aragon) members of highest nobility who were representatives in assemblies

sapientes — (Piedmont) "city elders" sometimes appointed as deputies in parliament

savi — see: *sapientes*

sedili, seggi — (Naples) seats in assemblies assigned to barons and various classes of citizens

sindaci, syndaci — (Piedmont, Sardinia, States of the Church) representatives to royal *stament*

sindicus provinciae — (States of the Church) ambassador of the province, representatives of provincial congregation in its relations with papal delegate

stament — (Catalonia, Sardinia) synonym of *brazo* or estate, there were military, ecclesiastical, royal or domanial *staments* representing their respective social orders

Stände — (Empire, Germany) equivalent of *staments*

stati — equivalent of *staments*, see: *estates*

subsidium — tax granted by assembly

syndici — (Sicily) at end of 13th century special envoys at general assembly

taglie — (Friuli) compulsory financial contributions of military service

talea — (Friuli, Monferrat) see: *taglie*, English tallage

tractadors	(Sardinia) members of committee dealing with financial, fiscal and legislative matters
tractatus	(England) uncommon title for great council in 13th and 14th century
trois estas or trois états	(France) from early 14th century title of provincial assemblies where financial and administrative matters were discussed by representatives of the clergy, nobility and professional, merchant, urban class (the third estate)
università	(Naples, Sicily) communes
Usatges or Usatici	(Barcelona) local customs
vicedomino	(Friuli) patriarch's representative at first sometimes responsible for convoking assembly
ville	(Catalonia) small towns
witenagemot	(England) see *conventus*, assembly of the *witan* or wise men

R

APPENDIX 2

Rulers in Europe

FRANCE *Carolingians*	ENGLAND *Anglo-Saxons*	EMPIRE (Germany and Italy)
879–84 Carloman	871–901 Alfred	881–7 Charles the Fat
		891–4 Guy of Spoleto (Italy)
		894–8 Lambert of Spoleto (Italy)
		896–9 Arnulf of Carinthia
		Medieval Empire
898–922 Charles the Simple	901–25 Edward the Elder	
936–54 Louis IV d'Outremer	925–40 Aethelstan	
954–86 Lothaire	959–75 Edgar	962–73 Otto I the Great (Germany from 936)
986–7 Louis V		973–83 Otto II
Capetians		
987–96 Hugh Capet		
996–1031 Robert II the Pious	978–1016 Ethelred the Unready	1002–24 Henry II
1031–60 Henry I	1016 Edmund Ironside	
	1016–35 Canute	1024–39 Conrad II
	1035–40 Harold I	1039–56 Henry III
	1041–2 Hardicanute	
	1042–66 Edward the Confessor	
	1066 Harold II	
	Normans	
	1066–87 William the Conqueror	
1060–1108 Philip I	1087–1100 William Rufus	1056–1106 Henry IV (3 rivals)
1108–37 Louis VI	1100–35 Henry I	1106–25 Henry V
1137–80 Louis VII	1135–54 Stephen	1125–37 Lothar III
	Plantagenets	
	1154–89 Henry II	1138–52 Conrad III
		1152–90 Frederick I Barbarossa

887-1492

turias and León	Castile (Counts dependent on kings of León until 1027)	Aragon	Navarre
·910 Alfonso III			
·14 Garcia			905–26 Sancho I
·24 Ordono II			
·5 Fruela II			
·30 Alfonso IV			
·50 Ramiro II			926–66 Garcia II
·5 Ordono III			
·67 Sancho II			
·82 Ramiro III	970–95 Garcia Fernandez		966–93 Sancho II
·99 Bermudo II			
·1027 Alfonso V	995–1021 Sancho Garces		993–1000 Garcia III
–37 Bermudo II	1021–4 Garcia Sanches		
	1029–35 Sancho I		
1037–65 FERDINAND I		1035–63 Ramiro I	1035–54 Garcia IV
	1065–72 Sancho II	1063–94 Sancho Ramirez	1054–76 Sancho IV
			1076–94 Sancho V (Sancho Ramirez of Aragon)
–1109 Alfonso VI	1072–1109 Alfonso I (VI of Leon)	1094–1041 Peter I	1094–1104 Peter I
		1104–34 ALFONSO I	
1109–26 URRACA		1134–7 Ramiro II	Navarre separated from Aragon
1126–57 ALFONSO VII (II of Castile)		1137–62 Petronilla	1134–50 Garcia V
–88 Ferdinand II	1157–8 Sancho III	1162–92 Alfonso I	1150–94 Sancho V (I of Aragon)
	1158–1214 Alfonso III or VIII	1196–1213 Peter II	
	1214–17 Enrique I		

France *Carolingians*	England *Anglo-Saxons*	Empire (Germany and Italy)
1180–1223 Philip II Augustus	1189–99 Richard I	1190–7 Henry VI
	1199–1216 John	1198–1208 Philip of Swabia, 1198–1212 Otto IV } rivals
1223–6 Louis VIII		1212–50 Frederick II
		1246–7 Henry Raspe anti-king
		1247–56 William of Holland anti-king
		1250–4 Conrad IV
1226–70 Louis IX	1216–72 Henry III	1251–73 Richard of Cornwall, 1257–72 Alfonso X of Castile } rivals
1270–85 Philip III	1272–1307 Edward I	1273–92 Rudolf I of Habsburg
		1292–8 Adolf of Nassau
1285–1314 Philip IV		1298–1308 Albert I of Habsburg
1314–16 Louis X		1308–14 Henry VII of Luxembourg
1316–22 Philip V	1307–27 Edward II	
1322–8 Charles IV		
Valois		
1328–50 Philip VI	1327–77 Edward III	1314–47 Louis IV of Bavaria
		1314–22 Frederick Habsburg anti-king
1350–64 John II		1347–78 Charles IV of Luxembourg
1364–80 Charles V		*1347–9 Gunther of Schwarzburg anti-king*
	1377–99 Richard II	
		1378–1400 Wenceslas of Luxembourg
	Lancastrians	*1400–10 Rupert of the Palatinate (not crowned)*
	1399–1413 Henry IV	
1380–1422 Charles VI	1413–22 Henry V	1410–37 Sigismund of Luxembourg
		1410–11 Jobst of Moravia anti-king (not crowned)
1422–61 Charles VII	1422–61 Henry VI	
		1437–9 Albert of Habsburg
1461–83 Louis XI	1461–83 Edward IV	
	1483 Edward V	
	1483–5 Richard III	
	Tudors	
1483–98 Charles VIII	1485–1509 Henry VII	1440–93 Frederick III of Habsburg

STURIAS AND LEÓN	CASTILE	ARAGON	NAVARRE
8–1230 Alfonso IX			1194–1234 Alfonso
1230–52 FERDINAND III		1213–76 James I	1234–53 Tibaldo I (Thibauld of Champagne)
LEÓN AND CASTILE UNITED			
	1252–84 Alfonso X		1253–70 Tibaldo II (Thibauld of Champagne) 1270–4 1305 Joanna I
	1284–95 Sancho IV 1295–1312 Ferdinand IV	1285–91 Alfonso III 1291–1327 James II	*Under French Rule until 1328*
	1312–50 Alfonso XI	1327–36 Alfonso IV	1328–49 Joanna II
	1350–69 Peter the Cruel 1369–79 Henry II of Trastamara 1379–90 John I 1390–1406 Henry III	1338–87 Peter IV the Ceremonious 1387–95 John I	1349–87 Charles II the Bad
	1406–54 John II	1395–1410 Martin I 1412–16 Ferdinand I 1416–58 Alfonso V the Magnanimous	1387–1425 Charles III the Noble 1425–79 John I
	1454–74 Henry IV	1458–79 John II	
	1474–1504 Isabella	1479–1516 Ferdinand II	1479–83 Francis 1483–1514 Catalina
	CASTILE AND ARAGON UNITED		

APPENDIX 3

Rulers of Southern Italy: Naples and Sicily 1137-1800

NORMANS

1137–54 Roger II (count of Sicily, duke of Apulia, king of Sicily and Naples)
1154–66 William I the Bad
1166–89 William II the Good
1189–94 Tancred
1194 William III (deposed)

HOHENSTAUFEN

1194–7 Henry VIII Emperor m. sister of William III
1197–1250 Frederick II Emperor, I of Sicily
1250–4 Emperor Conrad IV (I of Sicily)
1254–66 Manfred
1266–8 Emperor Conradin (Conrad II; beheaded)

ANGEVINS

1268–82 Charles I of Anjou rules Naples and Sicily

DIVISION OF RULE

ANGEVINS	ARAGON
NAPLES	SICILY
1282–5 Charles I	1282–5 Peter I m. Constance d. of Manfred
1285–1309 Charles II	1285–91 Alfonso
	1291–6 James I
1309–43 Robert	1296–1337 Frederick II of Aragon
1343–81 Joanna I (deposed)	1327 ARAGON TAKES OVER SARDINIA
	1337–42 Peter II
	1342–55 Louis
	1355–77 Frederick III
1381–6 Charles III of Durazzo	1377–92 Maria
1386–1414 Ladislas	1392–1409 Martin I
	1409–10 Martin II (I of Aragon)
	ARAGONESE RULE FROM SPAIN
1414–35 Joan II	1410–16 Ferdinand I
1435–42 René of Lorraine	1416–58 Alfonso V the Magnanimous

NAPLES UNDER DIRECT RULE OF ARAGONESE PRINCES

1443–58 Alfonso V the Magnanimous King of Aragon
1458–94 Ferdinand I
1494–5 Alfonso I (abdicated)
1495–6 Ferdinand II (king of Aragon)
1496–1501 Frederick of Altamira

VICEROYS FROM SPAIN RULE SICILY FROM 1458

SPAIN

NAPLES AND SICILY UNITED UNDER DIRECT SPANISH RULE FROM 1503
1516–56 Charles I
1556–98 Philip II
1598–1621 Philip III
1621–1665 Philip IV
1665–1700 Charles II
1700–13 Philip V

AUSTRIA

1713–34

SAVOY

1713-20

BOURBONS OF NAPLES

KINGDOM OF NAPLES (INCL. SICILY) LATER KINGDOM OF TWO SICILIES UNDER BOURBON RULE FROM 1734
1734–59 Charles III of Bourbon
1759–99 Ferdinand IV of Naples

Bibliography

ABBREVIATIONS

AHDE: Anuario de Historia del derecho español; *AHR:* American Historical Review, *APAE:* Ancien Pays et Assemblées d'États (Standen en Landen); *AS* Cal. Luc.: Archivio storico per la Calabria e Lucania; *AS* Sard.: Archivio storicio sardo; *AS* Sic.: Archivio storico siciliano; *AStD:* Annali di Storia del Diritto; *ASPN:* Archivio storico per le province napoletane; *BIHR:* Bulletin of the Institute of Historical Research; *BRAH:* Boletin de la R. Academia de la Historia; *EHR:* English Historical Review; *BICHS:* Bulletin of the International Commission of Historical Sciences; *ÉTUDES:* Études presentées à la Commission internationale pour l'Histoire des Assemblées d'États; *HZ:* Historische Zeitschrift; *JdS:* Journal des Savants; *MGH:* Monumenta Germaniae Historica; *NS:* Nuova Serie; PL: MIGNE, Patrologia latina; RH: Revue historique; *RHDFE:* Revue historique du droit français et étranger; *RIFD:* Rivista internazionale di filosofia del diritto; *RRIISS:* Rerum italicarum scriptores; *RSI:* Rivista storica italiana; *SBAG:* Schweizer Beiträge für allgemeinen Geschichte; *TRHS:* Transactions of the Royal Historical Society; *ZSSR:* Zeitschrift der Savigny – Stiftung für Rechtsgeschichte.

I. PRIMARY SOURCES

1. *Spain*

Alfonso X, *Las siete Partidas*, Salamanca, 1555

J. Beneyto Perez, *Textos políticos españoles de la baia edad media,* Madrid, 1944

G. de Blancas, *Modo de proceder en Cortes de Aragón*, Saragossa, 1601

P. G. Belluga, *Speculum Principum ac justitiae*, Paris, 1530

D. A. Benavides, *Memorias de D. Fernando IV de Castilla,* Madrid, 1860

P. Bofarull y Mascarò, *Colleccion de documentos inéditos del Archivo general de la Corona de Aragón*, Barcelona, 1847–59

J. Callis, *Extravagatorium curiarum*, Barcelona, 1518

M. Colmeiro, *Cortes de los antiguos reinos de León y de Castilla*. Madrid, 1883–4

B. Desclot, *Cronica del rey en Pere e dels seus antecessors passats*, Barcelona, 1885; trans.: *Chronicle of the reign of King Pedro of Aragon*, ed. F. L. Critchlow, Princeton, 1928–34

H. Finke, *Acta Aragonensia*, Berlin–Leipzig, 1908–22

F. Fita and B. Oliver, *Cortes de los antiguos reinos de Aragón y de Valencia y principado de Cataluña*, Madrid, 1896–1917

Historia de la Corona de Aragon conocida generalmente con el nombre de Crònica de San Juan de la Peña, Saragossa, 1876

T. Mieres, *Apparatus super constitutionibus curiarum generalium Cathaloniae*, Barcelona, 1621

J. de Moret, *Annales del reyno de Navarra*, Pampelona, 1684

T. Muñoz y Romero, *Colecciòn de fueros municipales y cartaspueblas de los reinos de Castilla, León Corona de Aragón y Navarra*, Madrid, 1847

G. Zurita y Castro, *Annales de la Corona de Aragon*, Saragossa, 1578–85

2. *England*

Ancient Laws and Institutes of England, ed. B. Thorpe, London, 1840

The Anglo-Saxon chronicle, ed. B. Thorpe, London, 1861

Annales monastici, IV, ed. H. R. Luard, London, 1864–9

H. Bracton, *De legibus et consuetudinibus Anglie*, ed. G. E. Woodbine, New Haven, 1922

Chronicon, sive Annales prioratus de Dunstaple, ed. T. Hearne, Oxford, 1733

F. W. Maitland (ed.), *Records of the Parliament holden at Westminster . . . 1305*, London, 1893.

Matthew Paris, *Chronica majora*, ed. H. R. Luard, London, 1872–83

T. Rymer, *Foedera, conventiones, literae et cujuscunque generis acta publica*, London, 1704–32

The Statutes of the Realm, ed. A. Luders *et al.*, London, 1810–28

W. Stubbs, *Select Charters and other illustrations of English constitutional history from the earliest times to the reign of Edward I*, Oxford, 1866

D. Wilkins, *Concilia Magna Britanniae ab anno MCCLXVIII ad annum MCCCIL*, London, 1737

3. *France*

P. de Beaumanoir, *Coutumes de Beauvaisis*, ed. A. Salmon, Paris, 1899–1900

A. Bernier, *Journal des Etats généraux de France tenus à Tours en 1484 . . . rédigé en latin par J. Masselin*, Paris, 1835

Capitularia Regum Francorum, ed. A. Boretius and V. Krause, *MGH*, Leg. Sect. II

M. del Laurière, *Ordonnances des Roys de France de la troisième race*, Paris, 1723

Flodoard, *De regis persona et regis ministris, PL,* 125

Les Grandes Chroniques de France, ed. J. Viard, *MGH*, VI

E. Martene and V. Durand, *Thesaurus novus anecdotorum*, II, Paris, 1717

G. Picot, *Documents relatifs aux états-généraux et assemblées réunis sous Philippe le Bel,* Paris, 1901

Recueil des Historiens des Gaules et de la France, vols. X–XI–XIII, Paris, 1767 ff.

4. *Germany, the Empire*

Constitutiones et acta publica imperatorum et regum, MGH, ed. L. Weiland, Hanover, 1833

P. Jaffé, *Biblioteca rerum germanicarum, V, Monumenta bambergensia,* Berlin, 1869

Richeri, *Historiarum libri III,* ed. G. Waitz, Hanover, 1877

5. *Italy*

a. General

E. Alberi, *Relazioni degli Ambasciatori veneti al Senato*, Florence, 1839

Annali Genovesi di Caffaro e de' suoi continuatori dal MCCIX al MCCXCIII, ed. L. T. Belgrano, Rome, 1890

A. Gherardi, *Le consulte della repubblica fiorentina dall' anno 1280 al 1298*, vol. I, Florence, 1898

Landolfo, *Historia mediolanensis ab anno 1095 ad annum 1137*, ed. C. Castiglioni, *RRIISS* V, 3, Milan, 1934

J. C. Lünig, *Codex Italiae diplomaticus,* Frankfurt–Leipzig, 1725–35

O. Morena, *De Rebus laudensibus, MGH, Script,* XVIII

L. A. Muratori, *Antiquitates italicae medii aevi,* Milan, 1738–42

b. Sicily

Annales Siculi, MGH, Script, XIX

Appendicula agli Annales siculi, ed. F. Giunta, in *Cronache siciliane inedite della fine del medioevo*, Palermo, 1955

Bibliotheca scriptorum qui res in Sicila gestas sub Aragonum imperio retulere, ed. R. Gregorio, Palermo, 1791–2

G. B. Caruso, *Bibliotheca historica regni Siciliae,* Palermo, 1719–23

M. De Afflictis, *In utriusque Siciliae Neapolisque sanctiones et constitutiones novissima Praelectio*, Venice, 1606

Diari della città di Palermo dal sec. *XVI al XIX*, ed. G. Di Marzo, Palermo, 1869

C. D. Gallo, *Annali della città di Messina,* Messina, 1756–8

L. Genuardi, *Parlamento siciliano*, Bologna, 1924

Historia diplomatica Friderici secundi imperatoris et Siciliae regis, ed. J. L. A. Huillard-Bréholles, Paris, 1852–61

N. Jamsilla, *Historia de rebus gestis Friderici II* in *RRIISS*, 8 (1723)

G. La Mantia, *Codice diplomatico dei re aragonesi di Sicilia (1282–1355)*, Palermo, 1917

S. Malaspina, *Rerum sicularum libri 6*, in *RRIIS*, 8 (1723)

G. Mastrillus, *De Magistratibus, eorum imperio*, Palermo, 1616

F. Mongitore, *Parlamenti generali del Regno di Sicilia dall' anno 1446 fino al 1748 di D. A. Mongitore*, Palermo, 1749

M. Muta, *In Capitula regni Siciliae, Comentaria,* Palermo, 1605

Ricardus de Sancto Germano, *Chronica,* ed. C. A. Garufi, *RRIISS*, 7 (1937)

N. Speciale, *Historia sicula ab anno 1282 ad annum 1337*, ed. R. Gregorio, Palermo, 1781–92

R. Starrabba, *Lettere e documenti relativi a un periodo del vicariato della regina Bianca in Sicilia, 1411–12*, Palermo, 1876

R. Starrabba, *Il Conte di Prades e la Sicilia (1477–9). Documenti inediti per servire alla storia del Parlamento siciliano*, Palermo, 1872

F. Testa, *Capitula regni Siciliae quae ad hodiernum diem lata sunt,* Palermo, 1741–3

c. Naples

Anonymi monasterii casinensis Chronicon, ed. G. Del Re, Naples, 1845

M. Camera, *Annali delle due Sicilie dall' origine e fondazione della monarchia fino a tutto il regno dell' augusto Sovrano Carlo III di Borbone*, Naples, 1960

F. Capecelatro, *Annali della città di Napoli*, Naples, 1849
J. F. de Ponte, *De potestate proregis, Collateralis Consilii et Regni Regimine,* Naples, 1621
Falco of Benevento, *Chronicon,* ed. G. Del Re, Naples, 1845
M. Freccia, *De subfeudis baronum et investituris feudorum,* Venice, 1579
P. Giannone, *Istoria civile del regno di Napoli,* Palmyra, 1762
Romualdo of Salerno, *Chronicon,* ed. G. Del Re, Naples, 1845
G. A. Summonte, *Dell' istoria della città e regno di Napoli*, Naples, 1675
Testi e documenti di storia napoletana pubblicati dall' Accademia Pontaniana, ser. II, vol. I, *Fonti aragonesi,* Naples, 1957

d. States of the Church
G. Colucci, *Treja oggi Montecchio illustrata,* Macerata, 1770
P. Compagnoni, *La Reggia Picena,* Macerata, 1661
Diario Maceratese Ecclesiastico e Civile, Macerata, 1783
P. Fabre, "Un registre cameral du cardinal Albornoz en 1364. Documents pour servir à l'histoire du patrimonium Beati Petri in Tuscia au XIVe siècle", Ec. franç. Rome-Mél. arch. hist., VII
M. Leopardi, *Annali di Recanati*, ed. R. Vuoli, Varese, 1945
Liber constitutionum Sanctae Matris Ecclesiae (*Constitutiones Marchiae Anconitanae*)
J. Pflugk-Hartung, *Acta pontificum romanorum inedita,* Stuttgart, 1884
G. Ravizza, *Diplomi e documenti di Chieti,* Naples, 1832
A. Theiner, *Codex diplomaticus dominii temporalis Sanctae Sedis,* Rome, 1861
L. Zdekauer, Atti del Parlamento della Contea d'Avignone del 29 maggio 1302, "R. Accad. Linc. – Commiss. Atti Ass. cost. it.", Bologna, 1920
L. Zdekauer, Gli atti del parlamento di Montolmo del 15 gennaio 1306, "R. Accad. Linc. – Commiss. Atti Ass. cost. it.", Bologna, 1916–17

e. Sardinia
P. G. Arquer, *Capitols de cort del stament militar de Sardenya*, Cagliari, 1591
F. Bellit, *Capitols de cort del stament militar de Sardenya*, Cagliari, 1572
A. Boscolo, *I Parlamenti di Alfonso il Magnanimo,* "Acta Curiarum Sardiniae", Milan, 1953

V. F. De Vico, *Leyes y Pragmaticas reales del Reyno de Sardeña*, Sassari, 1781

J. Dexart, *Capitula sive acta curiarum regni Sardiniae*, Cagliari, 1645

A. Era, *Il parlamento sardo del 1481–1485*, "Acta Curiarum Sardiniae", Milan, 1955

F. Loddo Canepa, "Alcune istruzioni inedite del 1481 nel quadro della politica de Ferdinando in Sardegna", *AS Sard.*, XXIV (1954)

Memorial y relaciò de todo lo que ha sucedido en el Parlamento quel celebrò el Virrey Don Juan Vivas, Cagliari, 1624

E. Putzulu, "Cartulari de Arborea", *AS Sard.*, XXV (1957)

E. Putzulu, "Documenti inediti sul conflitto di Eleonora d'Arborea e Giovanni I d'Aragona", *AS Sard.*, XXVII (1959)

A. Solmi, "Le costituzioni del primo parlamento sardo del 1355", *AS Sard.*, VI (1910)

P. Tola, *Codex diplomaticus Sardiniae*, Turin, 1868

f. Piedmont

E. Bollati, *Atti e documenti delle antiche assemblee rappresentative nella monarchie di Savoia*, t. XIV, Turin, 1879

A. Bozzola, *Parlamento del Monferrato*, "R. Acc. Linc. – Commiss. Atti Ass. cost. it.", Bologna, 1926

F. Sclopis, *Documenti ragguardanti alla storia della vita di Tommaso Francesco di Savoia principe di Carignano*, Turin, 1851

Stilus marchionalis seu Leges in Tribunalibus Marchiae Saluciarum, Turin, 1598

A. Tallone, *Parlamento Sabaudo*, "R. Acc. Linc. – Commiss. Atti Ass. cost. it.", Bologna, 1928

g. Friuli

G. Bianchi, *Documenti per la storia del Friuli dal 1317 al 1325*, Udine, 1844

Juliani canonici civitatensis chronica, ed. G. Tambara, *RRIISS*, 24, 14 (1906)

Leggi per la Patria e Contadinanza del Friuli compilate così comandando Pietro Grimani luogotenente generale di essa Patria, Venice, 1687

P. S. Leicht, *Parlamento friulano*, "R. Acc. Linc. – Commiss. Atti. Ass. cost. it.", Bologna, 1917

G. G. Liruti, *Notizie delle cose del Friuli, scritte secondo i tempi*, Udine, 1776–7

M. Sabellico, *Le historie vinitiane*, Venice, 1544

6. *Political theory*

Bernard of Pavia, *Summa de electione*, ed. T. Laspeyres, Ratisbon, 1806

Bernard of Pavia, *Summa Decretalium*, ed. T. Laspeyres, Leipzig, 1860

J. Bodin, *Les six livres de la République*, Paris, 1583

Conrad of Gelnhausen, *De congregando Concilio tempore schismatis*, in E. Martène and U. Durand, *Thesaurus novus anecdotorum*, Paris, 1717

Dino of Mugello, *In regulas iuris pontificii*, Cologne, 1569

G. Filangieri, *La scienza della legislazione*, vol. I, Livorno, 1807

R. Filmer, *Patriarcha, and other political works*, ed. P. Laslett, Oxford, 1949

J. Gerson, *Opera*, Antwerp, 1706

Giovanni of Genoa, *Summa quae vocatur Catholicon*, Venice, 1497

M. Goldast, *Monarchia S. Romani Imperii sive Tractatus de iurisdictione imperiali seu regia et pontificia seu sacerdotali*, Frankfurt, 1614

P. Grégoire, *De republica libri sex et viginti*, Pont-à-Mousson, 1596

J. Harrington, *The Commonwealth of Oceana*, London, 1656

T. Hobbes, *The Leviathan*, ed. M. Oakeshott, Oxford, 1946

F. Hotman, *Franco-Gallia*, Frankfurt, 1665

Isidorus of Seville, *Etymologiarum sive originum libri XX*, ed. W. M. Lindsay, Oxford, 1911

Le Bret, *De la souveraineté du Roy*, Paris 1632

J. Locke, *Two treatises of government*, ed. P. Laslett, Cambridge, 1960

G. Mably, *Réponse aux docteurs modernes . . . ou réfutation du système des philosophes économistes*, Paris 1771

S. Maffei, *Il Consiglio politico inedito presentato al governo veneto nell'anno 1736*, Venice, 1790

Marsilio of Padua, *Defensor pacis*, Basle, 1522

A. Matharel, *Ad Franco Hotomani Franco-gallia responsio*, Frankfurt, 1665

Nicolò of Cusa, *De catholica concordantia*, Basle, 1565

Nicolò of Cusa, *De auctoritate in concilio generali*, ed. G. Kallen, Heidelberg, 1935–6

William Ockham, *Tractatus de Imperatorum et Pontificum potestate*, ed. P. W. Mulder, *Arch. Française. hist.*, XVI, 1923

L. Prosdocimi, *Observantia*, Milan, n.d.

W. Prynne, *The Soveraigne Power of Parliaments and Kingdoms*, London, 1645

A. Sidney, *Discourses concerning Governement*, London, 1698

T. Smith, *De Republica Anglorum. The maner of Government or policie of the Realme of England*, London, 1583

II. SECONDARY SOURCES

1. *Spain, Portugal*

L. F. Arregui Lucea, "La Curia y las Cortes en Aragón", *Argensola*, vol. 13 (1953)

A. Ballesteros y Beretta, *Historia de España y su influencia en la historia universal*, Barcelona, 1918

J. Beneyto Perez, "Jaime Callis y su 'Tratado de las Cortes'", *IXe Congr. internat. sc. hist.*, Paris, 1950, ÉTUDES, XI

S. Bove, *Institutions de Catalunya: Las Cortes, la Diputacio, la Concell de Cent, los Gremis y l' Consolat de Mar*, Barcelona, 1895

M. Caetano, "As Cortes de Leiria, Memoria comemorativa do VII centenario", *Acad. portug. do Hist.*, Lisbon, 1954

M. Caetano, "As Cortes de 1385", in *Homenagem a Gama Barros*, Coimbra, 1951

J. Coroleu and J. Pella, *Las Cortes catalanas, estudio jurídico y comparativo*, Barcelona, 1876

M. Danvilla y Collado, "Nuevos datos para escribir la historia de las Cortes de Castilla en el reinado de Felipe V", *BRAH*, VIII (1886)

M. Danvila y Collado, *El poder civil en España*, Madrid, 1885–7

M. Danvila y Collado, *Estudios críticos acerca de los orígenes y vicisitudes de la legislación escrita del antiguo reino de Valencia*, Madrid, 1905

R. Del Arco y Garay, *Aragón, Geografia, Historia y arte*, Huesca, 1931

B. G. Feyjoo, *Theatro critico universal*, Madrid, 1728–34

J. Gonzales, *Alfonso IX*, Madrid, 1944

L. Kluepfel, *Verwaltungsgeschichte des Königreichs Aragon zu Ende des 13. Jahrhunderts*, Berlin, 1915

V. de La Fuente, *Historia de las Universidades, colegios y demas establecimientos de enseñanza en España*, Madrid, 1884

V. de La Fuente, *Estudios críticos sobre la historia y el derecho de Aragón*, Madrid, 1885

A. de La Torre y Del Cerro, "Orígenes de la 'Deputación General de Catalunya' ", *Disc. R. Acad. B. Letr.*, Barcelona, 1923

A. Lopez-Amo y Marin, "El pensamiento politico de Eximeniç, en su tratado de 'Regiment de Princeps' ", *AHDE*, XVII (1946)

S. de Madariaga, *Spain*, London, 1942

J. de Mariana, *Obras*, Madrid, 1854

A. Marongiu, "Geronimo Zurita e las Cortes d'Aragona", *VII Congr. intern. Hist. Cor. Arag., Cronica, Ponencias*, II, Barcelona, 1962

F. Martinez Marina, *Teoría de las Cortes ô grandes juntas nacionales de los reynos de León y Castilla,* Madrid, 1813

D. Ramos, *Historia de las Cortes tradicionales de España,* Madrid, 1944

J. Rico y Amat, *Historia política y parlamentaria de España*, Madrid, 1860

I. Rubio y Cambronero, *La Deputaciôn del General de Cataluña en los siglos XV y XVI,* Barcelona, 1950

L. Sánchez Agesta, *El concepto del Estado en el pensamiento españôl del siglo XVI*, Madrid, 1959

J. Sempere y Guarinos, *Histoire des Cortès d'Espagne,* Bordeaux, 1815

C. J. M. de Tourtoulon, *Don Jaime Ier, de Aragon le Conquérant,* Montpellier, 1863

P. Valdecantos Garcia, "Los godos en el Poema de Fernán González", *Rev. Univ. Madrid,* VI (1957)

J. Vicens Vives, "La transformació de la Generalitat medieval", *Homen. A. Rubiò i Lluch,* Barcelona, 1936

J. Vicens Vives, *Juan II de Aragón (1398–1479), Monarquía y revolución en la España del siglo XV*, Barcelona, 1953

2. *England*

G. B. Adams, *Constitutional History of England,* London, 1935

M. Ashley, *England in the Seventeenth Century,* London, 1954

E. Barker, *The Dominican Order and Convocation, A study of the Growth of Representation in the Church during the Thirteenth Century*, Oxford, 1913

M. Bigelow, *Placita Anglo-Normannica: Law-cases from William I to Richard I,* London, 1879

H. M. Cam, "Stubbs seventy years after", *Cambridge Hist. Journ.,* IX (1948)

H. M. Cam, "The theory and practice of representation in medieval England", *History*, XXXVIII (1953)
H. M. Cam, "Representation in the City of London in the later Middle Ages", *Album E. Lousse*, III, Louvain-Paris, n.d.
D. Clementi, "That the Statute of York of 1322 is no longer ambiguous", *Album H. M. Cam*, II, Louvain-Paris, 1962
J. G. Edwards, "The *plena potestas* of English Parliamentary Representatives", *Oxford Essays in Med. Hist. Pres. to H. E. Salter*, Oxford, 1934
J. G. Edwards, "*Confirmatio Cartarum* and Baronial Grievances in 1297", *EHR*, LVIII (1943)
J. G. Edwards, *William Stubbs*, London, 1952
L. Ehrlich, *Proceedings against the Crown, 1216–1377*, Oxford, 1921
J. R. Green, *A Short History of the English People*, London, 1874
H. Hallam, *The Constitutional History of England*, London, 1827
G. L. Haskins, "The Statute of York and the Community of the Realm", *American Hist. Rev.*, XLVII (1941)
W. S. Holdsworth, *A History of English Law*, London, 1903
J. C. Holt, "The Making of Magna Carta", *EHR*, 72 (1957)
R. S. Hoyt, "Representation in the Administrative Practice of Anglo-Norman England", *Album H. M. Cam*, II, Louvain-Paris, 1962
E. F. Jacob, "The Complaints of Henry III against the Baronial Council in 1261", *EHR*, XLI (1926)
J. E. A. Jolliffe, "Herrschaftsverträge des Spätmittelalters. Magna Carta", *SBAG*, 10 (1952)
J. E. A. Jolliffe, *The constitutional history of medieval England*, London, 1954
G. T. Lapsley, "The Interpretation of the Statute of York, 1322", *EHR*, 1941
F. Liebermann, *The national assembly in the Anglo-Saxon period*, Halle, 1913
M. Mackisack, *The Fourteenth Century*, Oxford, 1959
F. W. Maitland, *Doomsday Book and Beyond*, Cambridge, 1897
A. R. Myers, *England in the late Middle Ages*, 1307–1536, Harmondsworth, 1952
J. E. Neale, *The Elizabethan House of Commons*, London, 1949
T. J. Oleson, *The Witenagemot in the Reign of Edward the Confessor*, London, 1955

D. Pasquet, *An Essay on the Origins of the House of Commons*, Cambridge, 1925

A. Passerin D'Entrèves, "San Tommaso D'Aquino e la costituzione inglese nell' opera di Sir John Fortescue", *Atti. Acc. Sc. Torino*, LXII (1927)

A. Passerin D'Entrèves, *La teoria del diritto e della politica in Inghilterra all' inizio dell' età moderna*, Turin, 1929

E. Perroy, "Bulletin critique, Histoire d'Angleterre", *RH*, 1940

C. Petit-Dutaillis, "Le roi d'Angleterre et ses parléments au Moyen Age", *RH*, CLIV (1927)

C. Petit-Dutaillis, "Administration monarchique et parlementaire en Angleterre sous les règnes d'Edouard III et de Richard II, *JdS*, 1929

C. Petit-Dutaillis, *Le roi Jean et Shakespeare*, Paris, 1944

A. F. Pollard, *The evolution of Parliament*, London, 1926

G. Post, "The two Laws and the Statute of York", *Speculum*, 1954

F. M. Powicke, "Recent work on the origin of the English Parliament", ÉTUDES, III (1939)

F. M. Powicke, *King Henry III and the Lord Edward. The community of the realm in the thirteenth Century*, Oxford, 1947

C. W. Prosser and M. Sharp, *A Short Constitutional History of England*, London, 1938

D. Rayner, "The Form and Machinery of the 'Commune Petition' in the Fourteenth Century", *EHR*, LVI (1941)

H. G. Richardson, "The origins of Parliament", *TRHS*, 4th ser., XI (1928)

H. G. Richardson and G. O. Sayles, "Early coronation records", *BIHR*, XIII (1928)

H. G. Richardson and G. O. Sayles, "The Provisions of Oxford", *Bull. John Rylands Libr.*, 1933

H. G. Richardson, "The Commons and Medieval Politics", *TRHS*, 4th ser., XXVIII (1946)

H. G. Richardson and G. O. Sayles, "Parliaments and Great Councils in Medieval England", *Law Quart. Rev.*, 1961

L. Riess, *Geschichte des Wahlbrechts zum Englischen Parlement*, Leipzig, 1885

L. Riess, "Der Ursprung des englischen Unterhauses", *HZ*, N.F., XXIX (1888)

G. B. Rizzo, *La responsabilità regia e le deposizioni dei re inglesi,* Milan, 1939

C. Robbins, "Why the English Parliament survived the Age of Absolutism", *Xe Congr: inter. Sc. hist.,* Rome, 1955

J. S. Roskell, *The Commons in the parliament of 1422,* Manchester, 1954

M. M. Rossi, *Storia d'Inghilterra,* Florence, 1948

J. C. Russell, "Early Parliamentary Organisation", *AHR*, XXVI (1941)

G. O. Sayles, "The Changed Course of History: Stubbs and Renan", *Aberdeen Univ. Rev.,* XXXV (1954)

P. E. Schramm, "Ordines-Studien, III, Die Krönung in England", *Arch. f. Urkundenforsch.,* N.F., 1937

G. E. Slocombe, *William the Conqueror,* London, 1959

D. M. Stenton, *English Society in the Early Middle Ages,* Harmondsworth, 1951

C. Stephenson, "Taxation and Representation in the Middle Ages", *Anniversary essays in medieval history by students of Charles Homer Haskins,* Boston–New York, 1929

W. Stubbs, *The Constitutional History of England,* Oxford, 1866

W. Stubbs, *Historical Introductions to the Rolls Series,* London, 1902

T. F. Tout, "The English Parliament and public opinion, 1376–1388", *Mélanges d'histoire offerts à Henri Pirenne,* I, Brussels, 1926

G. M. Trevelyan, *The English Revolution,* 1688–9, London, 1938

G. M. Trevelyan, *A Shortened History of England,* London, 1942

P. Treves, *Politici inglesi del Seicento,* Naples, 1938

H. P. Tunmore, "The Dominican Order and Parliament. An unsolved Problem in the History of Representation", *Cath. hist. Rev.,* XXVI (1941)

R. C. Van Caenegem, *Royal writs in England from the conquest to Glanvill,* London, 1959

D. Whitelock, *The Beginnings of English Society. The Anglo-Saxon Period,* London, 1956

B. Wilkinson, "English Politics and Politicians of the thirteenth and fourteenth centuries", *Speculum,* 30 (1955)

Willard, J. F. and Morris, W. A. (ed.), *The English Government at work,* Cambridge, Mass., 1940

3. *France*

R. von Albertini, *Das politische Denken in Frankreich zur Zeit Richelieus,* Marburg, 1951

A. Artonne, *Le mouvement de 1314 et les chartes provinciales de 1315,* Paris, 1912

J. Bainville, *Histoire de France,* Paris, 1924

G. Bedier, *Les légendes épiques. Recherches sur la formation des chansons de geste,* vols. 3–4, Paris, 1912–13

G. Bedier, *La Chanson de Roland, Commentaires,* Paris, 1927

Comte de Boulainvilliers, *État de la France contenant XIV lettres sur les anciens parlements de France,* London, 1782

E. Boutaric, *La France sous Philippe le Bel. Étude sur les institutions politiques et administratives du Moyen Age,* Paris, 1861

J. Cadart, *Le régime électoral des états généraux de 1789 et ses origines (1302–1614),* Paris, 1952

L. Cadier, *Les états de Béarn depuis leurs origines jusqu'au commencement du XVI siècle,* Paris, 1888

V. de Caprariis, *Propaganda e pensiero politico in Francia durante le guerre di religione, I (1559–1572),* Naples, 1959

W. F. Church, "Cardinal Richelieu and the Social Estates of the Realm", *Album H. M. Cam,* II, Louvain-Paris, 1962

G. Coquille, *Oeuvres,* Paris, 1666

A. Coville, "Les états généraux de 1332 et 1357", *Moy. Age,* 6 (1893)

A. Coville, "Les premiers Valois et la guerre de Cent ans", in E. Lavisse, *Histoire de France,* IV, Paris, 1911

H. Dubled, "Noblesse et féodalité en Alsace du XIe au XIIIe siècle, *Tijdschr. v. Rechtsgesch.,* XXVIII (1960)

F. Dumont, "Recherches sur les Ordres dans l'opinion française sous l'Ancien Régime", *Album H. M. Cam,* I, Louvain-Paris, 1960

G. Dupont-Ferrier, "Histoire et signification du mot 'Aides' dans les institutions financières de la France spécialement aux XIVe et XVe siècles", *Bibl. Ec. Chart.,* LXXXIX (1928)

G. Dupont-Ferrier, "De quelques problèmes historiques relatifs aux 'États provinciaux' ", *JdS,* 1928

G. Dupont-Ferrier, "Ignorances et distractions administratives en France au XIVe et XVe siècles", *Bibl. Ec. Chart.,* C. (1939)

G. Dupont-Ferrier, "Le sens des mots 'patria' et 'patrie' en France au Moyen Age et jusqu'au début du XVIIe siècle", *RH*, 189 (1940)

E. Faral, "Robert le Coq et les États Généraux d'octobre 1356", *RHDFE*, 1945

R. Fawtier, "Parlement d'Angleterre et états-généraux de France au Moyen Age", *C. R. Acad. Inscr. Bell. Lettr.*, 1953

F. Galloudek-Genys, "Fénelon et les États", *Album H. M. Cam*, I, Louvain-Paris, 1960

E. Glasson, *Histoire du droit et des institutions politiques, civiles et judiciaires de l'Angleterre comparées au droit et aux institutions de la France*, Paris, 1882

G. Hervieu, *Recherches sur les premiers états-généraux et les assemblées représentatives pendant la première moitié du quatorzième siècle*, Paris, 1879

C. Hirschauer, *Les états d'Artois de leurs origines à l'occupation française 1340–1640*, Paris-Brussels, 1923

C. V. Langlois, *Histoire de France illustrée* (ed. E. Lavisse), III, Paris, 1911

F. Lot and R. Fawtier, *Histoire des institutions françaises au Moyen Age*, Paris, 1957–8

D. W. Lowis, *The History of the Church in France*, London, 1926

A. Luchaire, *Histoire des institutions monarchiques de la France sous les premiers Capétiens*, Paris, 1905

A. Marongiu, "Les états de Tour de 1484", *APAE*, XVII (1959)

A. Marongiu, "J. Bodin e le assemblee de 'stati' ", *Studi E. Crosa*, II, Milan, 1960

O. Ulph, "The mandate system, a representation to the Estates general under the old regime", *Journ. Mod. Hist.*, XXIII (1951)

E. Perroy, *La guerre de Cent Ans*, Paris, 1945. English ed. *The Hundred Years War*, London, 1959

E. Perroy, *Histoire de France pour tous les Français*, Paris, 1955

G. Picot, *Histoire des États généraux*, Paris, 1888

H. Prentout, *Les états provinciaux de Normandie*, Caen, 1925

A. Rebillon, *Les sources de l'histoire des États de Bretagne depuis la réunion à la France, 1492–1791*, Paris-Rennes, 1932

J. Russell Major, *The Deputies to the Estates General in Renaissance France*, Madison, 1960

J. Russell Major, *Representative Institutions in Renaissance France (1421–1559)*, Madison, 1960

P. Sagnac, *La formation de la société française moderne*, Paris, 1946

C. Seignobos, *Histoire sincère de la nation française*, Paris, 1933

C. Soule, "Les pouvoirs des Députés aux États Généraux de France", *Lib. memor. Sir M. Powicke*, Louvain-Paris, 1965

C. H. Taylor, "Some new texts on the Assembly of 1302", *Speculum*, 1936

C. H. Taylor, "The Composition of Baronial Assemblies in France, 1315–1320", *Speculum*, 1954

P. Viollet, *Histoire des institutions politiques et administratives de la France*, Paris, 1898

K. Wenck, *Philipp der Schöne von Frankreich, seine Persönlichkeit und das Urteil der Zeitgenossen*, Marburg, 1905

4. *Germany*

P. E. Back, *Herzog und Landschaft, Politische Ideen und Verlassungs-programme in Schwedisch–Pommern um die Mitte der 17 Jahrhunderts*, Lund, 1955

J. W. Bandktie, *Jus Polonicum*, Warsaw, 1831

G. Barraclough, *The origins of modern Germany*, Oxford, 1947

G. von Below, *Landständische Verfassung von Jülich und Berg, 1400–1600*, Düsseldorf, 1885

G. von Below, "System und Bedeutung der landständischen Verfassung", in *Territorium und Staat*, Munich, 1923

O. Brunner, "Moderner Verfassungsbegriff und mittelalterliche Verfassungsgeschichte", *Mitteil. Inst. österr. Geschichtesforsch. Eng.*, 14 (1939)

E. Bussi, "La democrazia nel primo Reich", *RIISS*, XXXII (1959)

F. L. Carsten, *Princes and Parliaments in Germany from the Fifteenth to the Eighteenth Century*, Oxford, 1959

A. E. Eugen, *Johan Jakob Moser als württembergischer Landschaftskonsulent, 1751–1771*, Stuttgart, 1887

J. Ficker and P. Puntschart, *Von Reichsfürstenstände*, Graz-Leipzig, 1911–23

O. Gierke, *Das deutsche Genossenschaftstrecht, III, Die Staats und Korporationslehre der Alterthums und des Mittelalters*, Berlin, 1881

P. Guba, *Der deutsche Reichstag in den Jahren 911–1025*, Leipzig, 1884
F. Hartung, Deutsche Verfassungsgeschichte von 15 Jahrhundert bis zum Gegenwart, Stuttgart, 1950
F. Hartung, "Herrschaftsvertrage und ständischen Dualismus in deutschen Territorien", *SBAG*, 10 (1952)
J. L. Klüber, *Oeffentliches Recht des Deutschen Bundes und der Bundestaaten,* Frankfurt a. M., 1840
M. Lintzel, "Die Beschlüsse der deutschen Hoftage von 910 bis 1056", *Histor. Stud.,* 161 (1924)
A. Luschin von Ebengreuth, "Die Anfänge der Landstände", *Hist. Zeitschrift,* 78 (1897)
H. Mitteis, "Politische Verträge im Mittelalter", *ZSSR*, 67 (1950)
J. J. Moser, *Von der deutschen Reichs Stände Landen, deren Landständen, Unterthanen, Landesfreyheiten Beschwerder, Schulden und Zusammenkünften,* Frankfurt–Leipzig, 1769
F. Rachfahl, "Zur österr. Verwaltungsgeschichte", *Schmollers Jahrb.,* 23 (1899)
F. Rachfahl, "Geist und Technik des ständisch-monarchischen Staatsrecht", *Schmollers Jahrb.*, 26 (1902)
F. Rachfahl, "Alte und neue Landesvertretung in Deutschland", *Schmollers Jahrb.,* 33 (1909)
F. Rachfahl, "Das ständisch-monarchische Staatsrecht und die österr. Gesamt. und Landerstaatsidee", *Zeitschr. priv. u. öffentl. Recht.*, 42 (1916)
F. Rachfahl, "Waren die Landstände eine Landesvertretung?", *Schmollers Jahrb.*, 50 (1916)
W. Sickel, "Zur Geschichte des deutschen Reichstags", *Mitteil österr. Inst. Geschichtesforsch.,* 1883
H. Spangenberg, *Vom Lehnstaat zum Ständestaat,* Munich, 1912
H. Spangenberg, "Weltgeschichtliche Bedigungen der Repräsentativverfassung", *Hist. Bibl.,* 141 (1931)
F. Tezner, *Die landesfürstliche Verwaltungsrechtspflege in Oesterreich,* Vienna, 1898–1902
F. W. Unger, *Geschichte der deutschen Landstände,* Hanover, 1844
C. Wacker, *Der Reichstag unter den Hohenstaufen,* Leipzig, 1881

5. *Italy*

a. General

G. Astuti, *La formazione dello stato moderno in Italia,* Turin, n.d.

C. Balbo, *Della Storia d' Italia. Sommario,* Turin, 1846

J. Beneyto Perez, "Il dimotto catalano in Italia", *RSI*, VI (1933)

A. Boscolo, *La politica italiana di Ferdinando I d' Aragona,* Cagliari, 1954

L. Bulferetti, "L'oro, la terra, la società. Un'interpretazione del nostro Seicento", *Arch. stor. Lomb.*, 1953

F. Calasso, *La legislazione statutaria dell' Italia meridionale,* Rome, 1929

G. Candeloro, *Storia dell' Italia Moderna. I, Le Origini del Risorgimento,* Milan, 1956

G. De Vergottini, *Studi sulla legislazione imperiale di Federico II in Italia,* Milan, 1952

N. F. Faraglia, *Il Comune nell' Italia meridionale, 1100–1806,* Naples, 1883

F. Filippini, *Il cardinale Egidio Albornoz,* Bologna, 1933

G. Galasso, *Mezzogiorno medievale e moderno,* Turin, 1965

C. Giardina, *Il Supremo Consiglio d'Italia,* Palermo, 1934

C. Giardina, "Osservazioni sulle leggi spagnole in Italia", *Studi urbinati,* VI (1932)

P. Grossi, *Le abbazie benedettine nell' alto medioevo italiano, struttura giuridica, amministrazione e giurisdizione,* Florence, 1937

P. S. Leicht, "L'introduction des villes dans les assemblées d'états en Italie", *BICHS*, 1937

A. Marongiu, *L'istituto parlamentare in Italia dalle origini al 1500,* Rome, 1949

A. Marongiu, "Autonomia e soggezione degli 'stati' in Italia durante il XVI e XVII secolo", ÉTUDES, XI, 1950

A. Marongiu, "Parlamenti e Governi nella storia costituzionale italiana", *Studi in memoria di L. Rom,* Milan, 1952

A. Marongiu, "La forma religiosa del matrimonio nel diritto bizantino, normanno e svevo", *AS Cal. Luc.*, XXXI (1961)

L. R. Ménager, "L'institution monarchique dans les états normands d'Italie", *Cah. Civilis. mediév-Poitiers,* II (1959)

T. E. Mommsen, *Italienische Analekten zur Reichsgeschichte des 14. Jahrhunderts, 1310–78*, Stuttgart, 1952

C. G. Mor, *L'età feudale,* Milan, 1952–3

C. G. Mor, "Qualche problema circa le assemblee dell' età post-carolingia", *Probl. com. Eur. post-carol.,* Spoleto, 1955
C. G. Mor, "Le assemblee italiane del secolo X", ÉTUDES, XI, 1952
R. Mori, "Aspirazioni Costituzionali nel pensiero politico toscano del settecento", *Arch. Stor. Ital.,* CI (1943)
C. Morossi, "L'assemblea nazionale del Regno longobardo – italico, *Riv. Stor. Dir. It.,* IX (1936)
F. Patetta, Introduction to G. D. Romagnoli, *Della costituzione d'una monarchia nazionale rappresentativa,* Rome, 1938
A. Solmi, "Le Diete imperiali di Roncaglia e la navigazione del Po presso Piacenza", *Arch. stor. Prov. Parm.,* NS, X (1910)
V. Vitale, *Il dominio della parte guelfa in Bologna, 1280–1327,* Bologna, 1898
G. Zanetti, *Il Comune di Milano dalla genesi del Consolato fino all' inizio del periodo podestarile,* Milan, 1935

b. Sicily

C. Avarna di Gualtieri, *Ruggero Settimo nel Risorgimento siciliano,* Bari, 1928
G. Beccaria, *La regina Bianca in Sicilia,* Palermo, 1887
G. Beccaria, "Note critiche sul parlamento di Catania del 1397", *AS Sic. sicil.,* XIII (1888)
G. Beccaria, *Spigolature sulla vita privata di re Martino in Sicilia,* Palermo, 1894
G. Bianco, *La Sicilia durante l'occupazione inglese,* Palermo, 1902
S. V. Bozzo, *Note storiche siciliane del secolo XIV,* Palermo, 1882
F. Brancato, *Il Caracciolo e i suoi tentativi di riforma in Sicilia,* Palermo, 1946
F. Brancato, *L'assemblea siciliana del 1848–49,* Florence, 1946
L. Cadier, "Essai sur l'administration du royaume de Sicile sous Charles Ier et Charles II d'Anjou", *Bibl. Ec. Fr. Ath. Rome,* LIX (1891)
C. Calisse, *Storia del parlamento in Sicilia dalla fondazione alla caduta della monarchia,* Turin, 1887
A. Capograssi, *Gl'Inglesi in Italia durante le compagne napoleoniche, Lord W. Bentinck,* Bari, 1949
M. Caravale, *II regno normanno di Sicilia,* Milan, 1966
C. Caristia, *Teoria e prassi politica nella rivoluzione siciliana del 1848,* Palermo, 1953

B. Caruso, *Memorie istoriche di quanto è accaduto in Sicilia dal tempo dei suoi primieri abitatori sino alla coronazione del re Vittorio Amedeo II,* Palermo, 1745
G. Cassandro, "Lineamenti del diritto pubblico del regno di Sicilia citra Farum sotto gli Aragonesi", *Ann. Sem. giur. econ. Univ. Bari.,* VI (1934)
F. Catalanó, "Il vicerè Caracciolo e la Sicilia alla fine del secolo XVIII", *Belfagor,* 1952
G. Catalanó, *Le ultime vicende della Legazia Apostolica in Sicilia,* Catania, 1950
F. Chalandon, *Histoire de la domination normande en Italie et en Sicile,* Paris, 1907
G. W. Crawley, "England and the Sicilian Constitution of 1812", *EHR,* 1940
R. De Mattei, *Il pensiero politico siciliano fra il Sette e l'Ottocento,* Catania, 1927
R. De Mattei, "Una relazione cinquecentesca sulla 'Forza del Parlamento' in Sicilia", *Liber Memor. A. Era.,* Brussels, 1963
A. De Stefano, *Federico III re di Sicilia (1296–1337),* Palermo, 1937
F. De Stefano, *Storia della Sicilia – Dal secolo XI al XIX,* Bari, 1948
S. Di Castro, *Avvertimenti al Sigo Marc' Antonio Colonna quando andò Vice Re di Sicilia,* ed. A. Saitta, Rome, 1950
G. Di Martino, *Il sistema tributario degli Aragonesi in Sicilia,* Palermo, 1938
G. Fasoli, "L'unione della Sicilia all' Aragona", *RSI,* 65 (1953)
F. M. E. Gaetani Di Villa Bianca, *Della Sicilia nobile,* Palermo, 1756
M. Gaudioso, "Lineamenti di una 'dottrina della consuetudine giuridica buona e approvata per le città del Regnum Sicilae' ", *Riv. Stor. Dir. Ital.,* XXI (1948)
E. Gentile, "La 'curia generale' del regno di Carlo I d' Angiò", *Bollett. Commiss. Acc. Lincei; pubblicaz. atti. ass. cost. it.,* 2 (1917)
L. Genuardi, "La influencia del derecho español en las instituciones públicas y privadas de Sicilia", *AHDE,* IV (1928)
C. Giardina, *Capitoli e privilegi di Messina,* Palermo, 1937
F. Giunta, *Aragonesi e Catalani nel Mediterraneo,* I, *Dal Regno al Viceregno in Sicilia,* Palermo, 1953
R. Gregorio, *Considerazioni sopra la storia di Sicilia,* Palermo, 1805–16

H. G. Koenigsberger, *The Government of Sicily under Philip II of Spain,* London, 1951

H. M. Lackland, "The failure of the constitutional experiment in Sicily 1813–14", *EHR*, 1926

H. M. Lackland, "Lord W. Bentinck in Sicily, 1811–12", *EHR*, 1927.

I. La Lumia, *La Sicilia sotto Vittorio Amedeo II di Savoia*, Livorno, 1877

G. La Mantia, *I Parlamenti del regno di Sicilia e gli atti inediti* (*1541–1594*), Rome – Turin – Florence, 1886

G. Leti, *Vita di don Pietro Giron duca d'Ossuna,* Amsterdam, 1699

A. Marchese, *Parlamenti generali ordinari e straordinari celebrati nel regno di Sicilia del 1494 al 1658,* Palermo, 1717

A. Marongiu, "Le Curie provinciali e generali del regno di Sicilia durante il dominio svevo (1194–1266)", *AS Cal. Luc.*, 1949–50

A. Marongiu, "Note federiciane – Manifestazioni e aspetti poco noti della politica di Federico II", *Studi medievali,* XVIII (1952)

R. Martini, *La Sicilia sotto gli Austriaci* (*1719–1734*), Palermo, 1907

E. Mazzarese Fardella, "Osservazioni sulle leggi pazionate in Sicilia", *Atti. Acc. Sc. Lett. Palermo,* ser. 4, XVI (1955–6)

B. Mazzoleni, *Gli atti perduti della Cancelleria angioina transmitati da Carlo di Lellis,* Parte I, *Il regno di Carlo I,* Roma, 1939

C. G. Mor, "Roger II et les assemblées du royaume normand dans l'Italie méridionale", *RHDFE*, 1958

R. Moscati, *Per una storia della Sicilia nell'età dei Martini. Appunti e documenti 1396–1408,* Messina, 1954

N. Niceforo, "La Sicilia e la Costituzione del 1812", *AS Sic.*, N.S., XXXVIII (1914)

N. Palmeri, *Saggio storico e politico sulla costituzione del regno di Sicilia infino al 1815,* Lausanne, 1847

G. Paolucci, "Il parlamento di Sicilia", *Atti.* R. *Acc. Sc. Lett. Art: Palermo,* IV (1896)

E. Pontieri, *Il riformismo borbonico nella Sicilia del Sette e dell'Ottocento,* Rome, 1944

R. Romeo, *Il Risorgimento in Sicilia,* Bari, 1950

G. Savagnone, "Il sindacato e l'azione popolare contro i pubblici funzionari nel diritto antico siciliano", *AS Sic.*, XXV (1900)

G. Scichilone, "Origine e ordinamento della Deputazione del Regno di Sicilia", *AS Sic. or.,* 1950

R. Starrabba and L. Tirrito, *Assise e consuetudini della terra di Corleone,* Palermo, 1880–82

V. E. Stellardi, *Il regno di Vittorio Amedeo II di Savoia nell' isola di Sicilia dall' anno 1713 al 1719,* Turin, 1862

V. Titone, *La Costituzione del 1812 e l'occupazione inglese della Sicilia,* Bologna, 1936

V. Titone, *La Sicilia Spagnola,* Mazara, 1948

V. Titone, *La Sicilia dalla dominazione spagnola all' unità d'Italia,* Bologna, 1955

R. Trifone, *La legislazione angioina,* Naples, 1921

J. Vicens Vives, *Fernando el Católico príncipe de Aragón, rey de Sicilia,* Madrid, 1952

c. Naples

G. D'Agostino, "Premessa ad una storia del parlamento generale del Regno di Napoli durante la dominazione spagnola", *Atti. Accad. Sc. Mor. Pol. Napoli,* 1966

L. Bianchini, *Storia delle finanze del regno di Napoli,* Naples, 1859

R. Caggese, *Roberto d'Angiò e i suoi tempi,* Florence, 1922

F. Carabellese, *La Puglia nel secolo XV,* Bari, 1901

V. Carignani, "Le rappresentanze e i diritti dei Parlamenti napoletani", *ASPN,* VIII (1883)

V. Carignani, "L'ultimo parlamento generale del Regno di Napoli nel 1642", *ASPN* VIII (1883)

G. Coniglio, *Il regno di Napoli al tempo di Carlo V. Amministrazione e vita economico-sociale,* Naples, 1951

G. Coniglio, "Note sulla società napoletana ai tempi di Don Pietro di Toledo", in *Studi in onore di* R. *Filangieri,* Naples, 1959

B. Croce, *Storia del regno di Napoli,* Bari, 1944

B. Croce, "Il villano di Matera e Ferdinando il Cattolico", in *Varietà di storia letteraria e civile,* 1, Bari, 1949

E. Croce, "I parlamenti napoletani sotto la dominazione spagnola", *ASPN*, LXI (1936)

F. E. de Tejada, *Nápoles hispánico*, I, Madrid, 1958

E. Gentile, "Un documento del novennio di regno di Luigi II d'Angiò", *Misc. A. Luzio,* 11, Florence, 1933

E. Gentile, "Parlamenti generali nel regno di Napoli nel periodo angioino", in *Studi* R. *Filangieri,* 1, Naples, 1959

E. Gentile, "Il parlamento angioino del 1297 per la imposizione di un sussidio di guerra", *Riv. Stor. Dir. Ital.*, XXXIV (1961)

P. Gentile, *La politica interna di Alfonso V,* Montecassino, 1909

P. Gentile, "Finanze e parlamento nel regno di Napoli dal 1150 al 1457", *ASPN*, XXVIII (1913)

P. Gentile, "Lo Stato napoletano sotto Alfonso I d'Aragona", *ASPN*, NS., XXIII (1937)

A. Gimenez Soler, *Itinerario del rey don Alfonso de Aragón el que ganò Nápoles,* Madrid, 1909

E. Jamison, "The Norman administration of Apulia and Capua more especially under Roger II and William I", *Papers Brit. Sch. Rome,* VI (1913)

E. G. Léonard, *Les Angevins de Naples,* Paris, 1954

A. Marongiu, "Il parlamento baronale del regno di Napoli del 1443", *Samnium,* 1950

D. A. Parrino, *Teatro eroico e politico de' Vicerè del Regno di Napoli dal tempo di Ferdinando il Cattolico fino al presente,* Naples, 1770

M. Riccio, *Notizie storiche tratte da 62 registri angioini dell'Archivio di Stato di Napoli,* Naples, 1877

M. Schipa, *Un principe napoletano amico di Dante, Carlo Martello d'Angiò,* Naples, 1926

d. States of the Church

M. Antonelli, "La dominazione pontificia nel Patrimonio negli ultimi venti anni del periodo avignonese", *Arch. Soc. rom. st. patr.*, XXX (1907)

L. Borioni, *La provincia di Macerata, I, Cenni storici e precedenti storici,* Macerata, 1906

D. Cecchi, *Il parlamento nella Marca di Ancona dal 1357 alla fine del secolo XVIII,* unpublished thesis, University of Macerata, 1945

D. Cecchi, *Il Parlamento e la Congregazione provinciale della Marca d'Ancona,* Milan, 1965

T. Codignola, *Ricerche storico-giuridiche sulla Massa Trabaria nel XIII secolo,* Florence, 1940

J. Déer, "Der Weg zur Goldenen Bulle Andreas II von 1222", *SBAG*, 10 (1952)

J. Delumeau, "Le progrès de la centralisation dans l'état pontifical au XVIe siècle", *Résumé des communications du XIe Congrès international des Sciences Historiques,* Stockholm, 1960

G. Ermini, *I parlamenti dello Stato della Chiesa dalle origini al periodo albornoziano,* Bologna, 1930

R. Foglietti, *Notizia intorno al parlamento della Marca di Ancona,* Turin, 1889

P. Fontana, "Il parlamento di Foligno dell' 8 dicembre 1305", *Riv. Stor. Dir. Ital.,* IV (1931)

J. Glénisson, "Les origines de la révolte de l'état pontifical en 1375", *Riv. St. Chiesa It.,* V (1951)

L. Zdekauer, "Per una data sbagliata nell' elenco dei parlamenti della Marca di Ancona (MCCCVII o MCCCXII)", *Atti Mem. R. Dep. St. patr. Marche,* X (1915)

e. Sardinia, Corsica

V. Angius, *Dizionario storico-statistico-commerciale degli Stati di S. M. il re di Sardegna,* s.v. "Sardegna", vol. XVII quater, Turin, 1856

A. Arribas Palau, *La conquista de Cerdeña por Jaime II de Aragón,* Barcelona, 1952

M. A. Benedetto, "Nota sulla mancata convocazione del parlamento sardo nel secolo XVIII", *Lib. memor. A. Era,* Brussels, 1963

M. A. Benedetto, "Nota sulla Deputazione nelle assemblee sabaude", *Lib. memor. Sir M. Powicke,* Louvain-Paris, 1965

A. Boscolo, *La figura di re Enzo,* Cagliari, 1950

A. Boscolo, "Sul Braccio reale nei parlamenti sardi del periodo aragonese", ÉTUDES, XVII (1958)

F. E. De Tejada, *Cerdeña hispánica,* Seville, 1960

R. Di Tucci, *Istituzioni pubbliche in Sardegna nel periodo aragonese,* Cagliari, 1920

A. Era, "Estreme reviviscenza di un secolare istituto", *Annuario Univ. Sassari,* 1946–7

A. Era, "Storia della Sardegna durante il regno di Ferdinando il Cattolico", *V Congr. Hist. Corona Arag.,* Saragosssa, 1952

A. Era, "Contributi alla storia dei Parlamenti sardi", *Studi sassar.,* XXVI (1954)

L. La Rocca, "Istruzioni al marchese Falletti di Castagnole vicerè di Sardegna dal 1731 al 1735", *Studi. F. Ciccaglione,* II, Catania, 1909

L. La Vaccara, *La Reale Udienza. Contributo alla storia delle istituzioni sarde durante il periodo spagnolo e sabaudo,* Cagliari, 1928

S. Lippi, *Inventario del R. Archivio di Stato di Cagliari,* Cagliari, 1902

F. Loddo Canepa, "Ricerche ed osservazioni sul feudalesimo sardo", *Arch. Stor. Sard.,* VI (1910), XI (1915)

F. Loddo Canepa, *Inventario delle R. Segreteria di Stato e di Guerra del Regno di Sardegna (1720–1848),* Rome, 1934

L. Loddo Canepa, "Riformismo e fermenti di rinascita in Sardegna dai primi Sabaudi alla fine del XIX secolo", *Atti V Conv. internat. St. Sardi.,* Cagliari, 1954

F. Loddo Canepa, *La Sardegna attraverso i secoli,* Turin, n.d.

G. Manno, *Storia di Sardegna,* Turin, 1825–7

A. Marongiu, *I parlamenti di Sardegna nella storia e nel diritto pubblico comparato,* Rome, 1932

A. Marongiu, "Il Reggente la Reale Cancelleria primo ministro del governo viceregio in Sardegna", *Riv. Stor. Dir. Ital.,* 1932

A. Marongiu, "Il regno aragonese di Corsica nel suo episodio culminante: la convocazione parlamentare del 1420", *Studi urbanati,* VIII (1934)

A. Marongiu, "La Corona d' Aragona e il regno di Corsica", *Arch. stor. Cors.,* XI (1935)

A. Marongiu, "Parlamento e lotta politica in Sardegna nel 1624–25", *Ann. Univ. Macerata,* 1956

A. Marongiu, "La Sardegna 'spagnola'. Un conto che . . . non s'ha da fare", *Studi stor. giur. A. Era,* Padua, 1963

A. Marongiu, "Sardegna 1624: gravami e voti parlamentari", *Lib. memor. A. Era,* Brussels, 1963

A. Marongiu, "Un documento da aggiungere agli atti del parlamento sardo del 1481–1485", *AS Sard.,* XXVIII, 1962

G. Olla Repetto, "Il primo donativo concesso dagli Stamenti sardi ai Savoia", *Lib. memor. A. Era,* Brussels, 1963

R. Palmarocchi, *Sardegna Sabauda. Il regno di Vittorio Amedeo II,* Cagliari, 1936

I. Pillito, *Memorie tratte dall'Archivio di Stato in Cagliari riguardanti i regi rappresentanti . . . dal tempo della dominazione aragonese fino al 1610,* Cagliari, 1862

B. Pitzorno, *Le leggi spagnole in Sardegna,* Sassari, 1919

E. Putzulu, "La mancata spedizione in Sardegna di Giovanni I d'Aragona", *Atti VI Congr. intern. Studi Sardi,* Cagliari, 1957

V. Salavert Y Roca, *Cerdeña y la expansion mediterranea de la Corona de Aragôn,* Madrid, 1956

D. Scano, *Sigismondo Arner. Notizie storiche e documenti,* Cagliari, 1934

C. Sole, "Gli Stamenti e la crisi rivoluzionario sarda delle fine del XVIII secolo", *La Nuova Sardegna,* 13 (1962)

C. Sole, "Giacobini e realisti in Alghero nel 1796", *Scritti F. Loddo Canepa,* I, Florence, 1959

A. Solmi, "Il sigillo del re Enzo", *Arch. Stor. Sard.,* IV (1908–9)

G. C. Sorgia, *Il parlamento del viceré Fernandez de Heredia (1553–4),* "Acta curiar. regni Sard.", Milan, 1963

F. E. de Tejada, "Doctrinas politicas manejadas en el parlamento sardo de 1481–1485", *Lib. memor. A. Era,* Brussels, 1963

A. Solmi, *Studi storici sulle istituzioni della Sardegna nel Medioevo,* Cagliari, 1918

f. Piedmont

M. A. Benedetto, "Nota sulle assemblee dei domini sabaudi", *Riv. Stor. Dir. Ital.,* XXX (1957)

M. A. Benedetto, "Il 'conseil des Commis' del Ducato d'Aosta", *Xe Congr. intern. Sc. Hist. Roma, 1955,* ÉTUDES, XVIII, Louvain, 1958

E. Bollati, *Le congregazioni dei tre Stati della Valle d'Aosta,* Turin, 1877

E. Bollati, *Le congregazioni dei Comuni nel marchesato di Saluzzo,* Turin, 1880

M. C. Daviso, "Considerazioni intorno ai Tre Stati in Piemonte", *Boll. stor. bibliogr. subalp.,* 1947

J. B. de Tillier, *Histoire de la Vallée d'Aoste,* Aosta, 1888

C. Dionisotti, *Storia della magistratura piemontese,* Turin, 1881

A. Gallenga, *Storia del Piemonte dai primi tempi alla pace di Parigi del 30 marzo 1856,* Turin, 1856

H. G. Koenigsberger, "Parliament of Piedmont during the Renaissance", ÉTUDES, XI (1952)

L. Marini, "La Valle d'Aosta fra Savoia e Piemonte (1601–1730)", *Relaz. e comun. XXXI Congr. st. subalp.,* Aosta, 1956

L. Marini, *Savoiardi e Piemontesi nellò Stato sabaudo,* Rome, 1962
C. G. Mor, "Conte di Savoia, Feudali e Communità in Valle d'Aosta nei secoli XI-XV", *Rel. e. com. XXXI congr. stor. subalp,* Aosta, 1956
A. Tallone, "Di alcuni rapporti fra le assemblee di stati della monarchia di Savoia e gli stati generali e provinciali francesi", *BICHS*, X (1938)
T. Tibaldi, *Storia della Valle d'Aosta,* Turin, 1916
T. Tibaldi, *La regione d'Aosta attraverso i secoli,* Turin, 1900–16
M. Viora, "Su un memoriale del parlamento piemontese al duca Amedo IX di Savoia", *Studi Besta,* II, Milan, 1938

g. Friuli, Gorizia

P. Caldini, "Gli stati provinciali goriziani", *Mem. stor. forogiul.,* XXVI (1939)
G. Cogo, "La sottomissione del Friuli alla signorie di Venezia", *Atti Accad. Udine,* 1896
G. De Vergottini, *La costituzione provinciale dell'Istria nel tardo medio evo,* Parenzo, 1926
C. Fasoli, "Lineamenti di politica e di legislazione feudale veneziana in Terraferma", *Riv. Stor. Dir. It.,* XXV (1952)
G. Grion, *Guida storica di Cividale e del suo distretto,* Cividale, 1899
P. S. Leicht, "Il nome di 'Patria' attribuito al Friuli", *RSI,* XVIII (1901)
P. S. Leicht, "Il parlamento della patria del Friuli – Sua origine, costituzione e legislazione (1231–1420)", *Atti Accad. Udine,* X–XI (1903)
P. S. Leicht, *Studi e frammenti,* Udine, 1903
P. S. Leicht, "Il parlamento friulano nel primo secolo della dominazione veneziana", *Riv. Stor, Dir. Ital.,* XXI (1948)
P. S. Leicht, "Il tramonto dello stato patriarcale e la lotta delle parti in Friuli durante la tregua 1413–1418", in *Miscellenea Pio Paschini,* II, Rome, 1949
A. Lombardo, "Storia e ordinamenti delle magistrature veneziane in un manuscritto inedito del sec. XVI", *Studi R. Filangieri,* I, Naples, 1959
P. Paschini, *Bertoldo di Merania patriarca d'Aquileia, 1218–1251,* Udine, 1920
P. Paschini, *Storia del Friuli,* Udine, 1934–6
G. di Porcía, *Descrizione della patria del Friuli,* Udine, 1897

F. Spessot, "Le Convocazioni di Gorizia e Gradisca", *Studi Goriz.*, 1954

E. Traversa, *Das Friaulische Parlament bis zur Unterdrückung des Patriarchates von Aquileja durch Venedig,* Vienna–Leipzig, 1911

6. *Political Theory*

J. W. Allen, *A History of political thought in the sixteenth century,* London, 1951

H. X. Arquillière, *L'augustinisme politique,* Paris, 1934

F. Battaglia, "Il pensiero giuridico e politico di Nicolò Cusano", *Riv. Stor. Dir. It.,* VIII (1935)

E. Bonnestadt, "Kirche und Reich in Schriftum des Nicolaus von Kues", *Sitzungsber. Heidelb. Akt. Wissensch.-Philos.-hist. Kl.,* 1938–9

E. Carcassonne, *Montesquieu et le problème de la constitution française au XVIIIe siècle,* Paris, 1927

M. D'Addio, *Il pensiero di Gaspare Scioppio e il machiavellismo del Seicento,* Milan, 1962

G. De Lagarde, "L'idée de représentation dans les oeuvres de Guillaume d'Ockam", *BICHS,* IX (1937)

G. De Lagarde, *Marsile de Padoue ou le premier théoricien de l'État laïque,* Paris, 1948

F. Ercole, *Da Bartolo all' Altusio,* Florence, 1932

D. Fiorot, *La filosofia politica dei fisiocrati,* Padua, 1954

O. Gierke, *Johannes Altrusious und die Entwickling der naturrechtlichen Staatheorien,* Breslau, 1880

M. Grignaschi, "La limitazione dei poteri del Princeps in Guglielmo d'Ockam e Marsilio di Padova", *Xe Congr. intern., hist.,* Rome, 1955, ÉTUDES, *XVIII*

G. Kallen, "Die Politische Theorie im philosophischen System des Nikolaus von Cues", *Hist. Zeitschrift.,* 165 (1942)

J. A. Maravall, *Estudias de historia del pensamiento español,* Madrid, 1967

A. Marongiu, *J. Bodin et la polémique sur les états,* lecture given to the "Soc. J. Bodin", Brussels, 4 June 1962

P. Mesnard, *L'essor de la philosophie politique au XVIe siècle,* Paris, 1952

P. Mesnard, *Jean Bodin en la historia del pensamiento,* Madrid, 1962

J. Moreau-Reibel, *Jean Bodin et le droit comparé,* Paris, 1933

A. Posch, *Die "Concordantia catholica" des Nikolaus von Cusa,* Paderborn, 1930
L. Rossi, "Un predecessore di Montesquieu: Scipione Maffei" in *Scritti vari di diritto pubblico,* VI, Milan, 1941
R. Scholz, *Wilhelm von Ockam als politiker Denker und sein Breviloquium 'de principatu tyrannico',* Leipzig, 1944
J. R. Seeley, *Introduction to Political Science,* London, 1896
E. Vidal, *Saggio sul Montesquieu,* Milan, 1950

7. *Legal Histories*

E. Besta, *Storia del diritto italiano – Diritto pubblico,* Milan, 1941
E. Betti, "Le categorie civilistiche dell'interpretazione", *RISG,* 1948
P. Bonfante, *Diritto romano,* Florence, 1900
F. Calasso, *Gli ordinamenti giuridici del rinascimento medievale,* Milan, 1949
C. Calisse, *Storia del diritto italiano,* 1, *Le fonti,* Florence, 1930
F. Carnelutti, *Sistema del diritto processuale,* 1, Padua, 1936
E. M. Chapado Garcia, *Historia general del derecho español,* Valladolid, 1900
E. Chénon, *Histoire générale du droit français public et privé,* Paris, 1926
P. De Tourtoulon, *Les principes philosophiques et l'histoire du droit,* Lausanne-Paris, 1908–10
G. De Vergottini, *Lezioni di storia del diritto italiano – Il diritto pubblico italiano nei secoli XII–XV,* Milan, 1959–60
A. Dumas, *Manuel d'histoire du droit français,* Aix-en-Provence, n.d.
A. Esmein, *Cours élémentaire d'histoire du droit français,* Paris, 1912
A. García Gallo, *Curso de historia del derecho español,* Madrid, 1956
G. Jellinek, *System der subjektiven öffentlichen Rechte,* Freiburg i. B., 1892
S. Kutner, *Repertorium der Kanonistik (1140–1234), Prodromus corpus glossarum,* 1, Rome, 1937
P. S. Leicht, *Storia del diritto italiano, Il diritto pubblico,* Milan, 1950
P. S. Leicht, *Storia del diritto italiano, Le fonti,* Milan, 1956
A. Marichalar and G. Manrique, *Historia de la legislación y recitationes del derecho civil de España,* Madrid, 1861–72
A. Marongiu, *Storia del diritto pubblico – Principi e istituti di governo in Italia dalla metà del IX alla metà del XIX secolo,* Milan, 1956

S. Minguijón, *Historia del derecho español,* Barcelona, 1953
H. Mitteis, *Deutsche Rechtsgeschichte,* Munich–Berlin, 1960
C. Mortati, *Istituzioni di diritto pubblico,* Padua, 1958
F. Olivier-Martin, *Histoire du droit français,* Paris, 1948
F. Olivier-Martin, *Histoire du Droit français des origines à la Révolution,* Paris, 1951
R. Orestand, *Introduzione allo studio storico del diritto romano,* Turin, 1961
A. Pertile, *Storia del diritto pubblico e delle fonti,* Turin, 1897
F. Pollock, *Essays in the Law,* London, 1922
S. Romano, *L'ordinamento giuridico,* Pisa, 1917–18
S. Romano, *Frammenti di un dizionaruo giuridico,* Milan, 1947
R. Schröder, *Lehrbuch der deutschen Rechtsgeschichte,* ed. E. V. Künssberg, Berlin–Leipzig, 1922
C. von Schwerin, *Grundzüge der deutschen Rechtsgeschichte,* Berlin, 1941
A. Tallone, *Storia del diritto pubblico e delle fonti,* Turin, 1897
M. Torres, *Lecciones de historia del derecho español,* Salamanca, 1933–6

8. *General*

F. Bliemetzrieder, *Literarische Polemik zur Beginn des grossen abendlandischen Schismas,* Vienna–Leipzig, 1910
M. Bloch, *La société féodale: II, Les classes et le gouvernement des hommes,* Paris, 1940
L. K. Born, "The perfect prince: a study in thirteenth and fourteenth century ideals", *Speculum,* III (1928)
O. Brunner, "Das Problem einer europäischer Sozialgeschichte", *HZ,* 1954
H. M. Cam, A. Marongiu, G. Stökl, "Recent work and present views on the origins and development of representative assemblies", *Relazioni, Xe Congr. intern. Sc. histor.,* Rome, vol. I, Florence, 1955
A. J. Carlyle, "Some aspects of the relation of Roman law to political principles in the middle ages", *Studi Besta,* Milan, 1937–9
M. V. Clarke, *Medieval Representation and Consent,* London, 1936
P. Congar, "Quod omnes tangit ab omnibus tractari et approbari debet", *RHDFE,* 36 (1958)

M. David, *Le serment du sacre du IXe au XVe siècle. Contribution à l'étude des limites juridiques de la souveraineté,* Strasbourg, 1951

M. David, *La souveraineté et les limites juridiques du pouvoir monarchique du IXe au XVe siècle,* Paris, 1954

G. de Lagarde, "La structure politique et sociale de l'Europe au XIVe siècle", ÉTUDES, III, Louvain, 1939

G. De Lagarde, "Les théories représentatives du XIV au XVe siècle et l'Église", *X Congr. intern. Sc. histor.,* Rome 1955 – ÉTUDES, XVIII, Louvain, 1958

A. Dempf, *Sacrum imperium, Geschichte und Staatsphilosophie des Mittelalters und der politischen Renaissance,* Munich–Berlin, 1929

J. Dhondt, "Ordres ou Puissances? L'exemple des États de Flandre", *APAE,* 1950

K. Eckermann, "Studien zur Geschichte des monarchischen Gedankes im 15. Jahrhundert", *Abhandl. z. Mittel. u. Neu. Gesch.,* 73 (1933)

A. Erens, s.v. "Premontrés", *Dict. Théol. cath.,* XIII, col. 7

R. Fawtier, *L'Europe Occidentale de 1270 à 1380, Ière partie, 1270–1328,* in *Histoire Générale* by G. Glotz, *Moyen Age,* Paris, 1940

H. J. Ford, *Representative Government,* New York, 1924

F. L. Ganshof, "Les relations féodo-vassalliques aux temps post-carolingiens", in *Problemi comuni dell' Europa post-carolingia,* Spoleto, 1955

O. Giacchi, "La regola 'Quod omnes tangit' nel diritto canonico", *Studi in onore di V. Del Giudice,* 1, Milan, 1953

M. S. Giannini, "Parlamento e amministrazione", *Amministrazione civile,* 47–51 (1961)

J. Gilissen, *Le régime représentatif avant 1790 en Belgique,* Brussels, 1952

P. Grossi, "Unanimitas. Alle origini del concetto di persona giuridica nel diritto canonico", *AStD,* 11 (1958)

H. Hallam, *View of the state of Europe during the middle ages,* London, 1818

C. J. Hefele – H. Leclercq, *Histoire des Conciles d'après les documents originaux,* IV, Paris, 1911

J. Hourlier, *Le chapitre général jusqu'au moment du Grand Schisme,* Paris, 1936

R. S. Hoyt, "Recent publications in the United States and Canada on the History of Western Representative Institutions", *Speculum,* 1954

J. Jessmejer, *Das Mitbestimmungsrecht der Untergebenen in den alter Männerordensverbänden,* Münich, 1915

H. F. Jolowicz, "The stone that the builders rejected: adventures of some civil law texts", *Seminar,* XII (1954)

F. Kern, "Gottesgnadentum und Widerstandsrecht im früheren Mittelalter zur Entwicklungsgeschichte der Monarchie", *Mittelalt. St., I* (1915)

H. G. Koenigsberger, "The Powers of Deputies in sixteenth century assemblies", *Album H. M. Cam,* II, Louvain-Paris, 1962

K. Koranyi, "Zum ursprung des Anteils der Städte am den ständischen Versammlung und Parlamenten im Mittelalter", *Album H. M. Cam,* I, Louvain-Paris, 1960

G. Lachapelle, *Les régimes électoraux,* Paris, 1934

G. I. Langmuir, "Politics and Parliaments in the early thirteenth century", ÉTUDES, XXIX (1966)

P. S. Leicht, "Un principio politico medievale", *Rend. Acc. Lincei – Cl. Sc. mor.,* 1920

P. S. Leicht, "L'empereur Frédéric de Souabe et les parlements", *Tijdschr. v. Rechtsgesch.,* 111 (1922)

J. Lejeune, *La principauté de Liège,* Liège, 1949

G. Leone, "De iuribus singulorum jure proprio et non jure Collegii", *Ephem. jur. can.,* II (1955)

R. H. Lord, "The parliaments of the Middle Ages and the Early Modern Period", *Cath. hist. rev.,* XVI (1930)

F. Lot and F. L. Ganshof, *Histoire du moyen âge – Les destinées de l'empire carolingien,* Paris, 1941

E. Lousse, "La formation des états dans la société européenne du moyen âge et l'apparition des assemblées d'états. Questions de faits et de méthodes", *BICHS,* V (1933)

E. Lousse, "Parlamentarisme ou corporatisme? Les origines des assemblées d'états", *RHDFE,* 4e ser., XIV (1935)

E. Lousse, "Les caractères essentiels de l'état corporatif médiéval", *BICHS,* IX (1937)

E. Lousse, *La société d'ancien régime. Organisation et représentation corporatives,* Louvain, 1943

E. Lousse, "La formation des ordres dans la société d'états", *ECIHAE,* VII (1943)

E. Lousse, "La Joyeuse Entrée brabançonne de 3 janvier 1356", *SBAG*, 10 (1952)

G. Mably, *De l'étude de l'histoire,* Paris, 1783

J. B. Mahn, "L'ordre cistercien et son gouvernment des origines au milieu du XIIIe siècle (1098–1265)", *Bibl. Ec. fr. Ath.-Rome,* 161 (1945)

J. A. Maravall, *Ejército y Estado en el Renacimiento,* Madrid, 1961

A. Marongiu, "Il principio fondamentale della democrazia nel XIII secolo", *Paideia,* I (1946)

A. Marongiu, "Valore della storia delle istituzioni politiche", *Scritti in onore di L. Sturzo,* II, Bologna, 1953

A. Marongiu, "Un momento tipico della monarchia medievale: il re giudice", *Jus,* 1954

A. Marongiu, "Monarchia assoluta e istituzioni parlamentari nella politica cinquecentesca", *Rassegna parlamentare,* 1964

A. Marongiu, "Il principio della democrazia e del consenso (Q.o.t.) nel XIV secolo", *Studia gratiana,* VIII (1962)

V. Mazzei, "Le basi filosofiche e giuridiche della nuova Rappresentanza politica", *RIFD*, XXII (1942)

L. Moulin, "Le gouvernment des Communautés religieuses comme type de gouvernement mixte", *Rev. franç. Sc. pol.,* 1952

L. Moulin, "Les origines religieuses des techniques électorales et délibératives modernes", *Studi pol.,* 1953

L. Moulin, "Aux sources des libertés européennes. Reflexions sur quinze siècles de gouvernement des religieux", *Cah. de Bruges,* 11 (1956)

L. Moulin, "The Executive and the Legislative in the Religious Orders", *Intern. Pol. Sc. Ass. – Rome Congress,* 1958

L. Moulin, "*Sanior et maior pars*" – Note sur l'évolution des techniques électorales dans les Ordres religieux du VIe au XIIIe siècle", *RHDFE*, 1958

W. Näf, "Herrschaftsverträge und Lehre von Herrschaftsverträge", *SBAG,* 7 (1949)

G. Nocera, "Res publica?", *Ann. Fac. giur. Perugia,* ser. VIII, 11 (1947–8)

L'organisation corporative du Moyen Age à la fin de l'Ancien Régime, Louvain, 1939

A. Origone, *Note critiche sul concetto di rappresentanza politica,* Rome, 1935

T. Perassi, "Parlamenti medievali e parlamenti moderni", *Riv. dir. pubbl.,* I (1910)

C. Petit-Dutaillis, *L'essor des états d'Occident,* Paris, 1944

G. Post, "*Plena potestas* and Consent in Medieval Assemblies – A Study in Romano – Canonical Procedure and the rise of Representation", *Traditio,* 1 (1943)

G. Post, "Roman Law and early Representation in Spain and Italy", *Speculum,* XVIII (1943)

G. Post, "A Romano – Canonical Maxim 'Quod omnes tangit' in Bracton", *Traditio,* IV (1946)

G. Post, "The theory of public law and the State in the thirteenth century", *Seminar,* IV (1948)

W. Prevenier, "Representatief Karakter van de vlaamse parlementen der XIV eeuw", *Hander. Maatsch. v. Geschied. Oudheidk,* XII (1958)

J. Reviron, *Les idées politico-religieuses d'un evêque du IXe siècle – Jonas d'Orléans et son "De institutione regia"*, Paris, 1930

L. Rossi, *Sulla natura giuridica del diritto elettorale,* Bologna, 1907

A. Sauvy, *L'opinion publique,* Paris, 1958

P. E. Schramm, "Studien zu frühmittelalterlichen Aufzeichnungen über Staat und Verfassung", *ZSSR,* 49 (1929)

E. Sestan, *Stato e nazione nell' alto medioevo – Ricerche sulle origini nazionali in Francia, Italia, Germania,* Naples, 1952

S. Stelling-Michaud, "Le mythe du despotisme oriental", *SBAG,* 18–19 (1960–1)

P. Theeuws, "Jean de Turrecremata. Les relations entre l'Église et le pouvoir civil d'après un théologien du XVe siècle", *Univ. Louvain. Rec. trav. hist.,* 3rd ser., 18 (1943)

P. C. Timbal, *Institutions et faits sociaux,* Paris, 1958

I. Turk, "Charta caritatis prior", *Anal. S. Ord. Cisterc.,* I (1945)

W. Ullmann, *The Growth of Papal Government in the Middle Ages,* London, 1955

W. Ullmann, *Principles of Government and Politics in the Middle Ages,* London, 1961

F. Valsecchi, "Dispotismo illuminato", *Nuove Quest. St. Risorg. e dell'Unità d'Italia,* Milan, n.d.

V. Zangara, *La rappresentanza istituzionale,* Padua, 1952

Index

Entries in bold type indicate important assemblies.